The FIAF Moving Image Cataloguing Manual

Written by Natasha Fairbairn, Maria Assunta Pimpinelli, Thelma Ross

Edited by Linda Tadic

Project Manager: Nancy Goldman
for the FIAF Cataloguing and Documentation Commission

April 2016

fiaf

Fédération internationale des archives du film
International Federation of Film Archives
Federación Internacional de Archivos Fílmicos

Dedication

This manual is dedicated to **Christian Dimitriu** (1945-2016), whose contributions to the field of moving image archiving and FIAF are immeasurable; and to **Ronny Loewy** (1946-2012), whose knowledge of moving image metadata standards was a primary and crucial source of information during the development of this publication.

Acknowledgements

This manual is a result of the combined efforts of many professionals to whom we owe our gratitude.

Contributors to early, formative discussions that informed the basis for our approach include Anna Bohn, Marco Rendina, Rosario López de Prado, Anne-Marie Grapton, Andrea Leigh, and Kelley McGrath.

Many professionals from the FIAF Cataloguing Rules Revision Working Group graciously volunteered their knowledge and experience to the review of this manual. A special thanks to Laurent Bismuth, Georg Eckes, and Detlev Balzer for their thoughtful suggestions for improvement. We also appreciate Detlev for hosting the FIAF Cataloguing and Documentation Commission (CDC) wiki on his filmstandards.org website.

Several of the illuminating charts and examples, and other formatting needs (such as URLs) were kindly handled by Marian Hausner Mats Skärstrand, and Michael Campos-Quinn. Marian Hausner also did a painstaking job constructing the bibliography.

This work could not have been done without the support and guidance of the British Film Institute who contributed institutional policies and documents for our use. In particular, we want to mention Gabriele Popp, who encouraged and supported BFI staff involvement, and Stephen McConnachie, who generously contributed content and freely gave of his time and knowledge.

We thank current and former members of the CDC, the members of the FIAF Executive Committee, and the FIAF Senior Administrator for their support, especially Christophe Dupin, Rachael Stoeltje, and Olga Futemma.

A very special thank you is owed to Nancy Goldman, who managed numerous steps of the project, such as convening and chairing meetings and guiding the project's development. She also contributed to the authoring of the manual and invested many hours in providing valuable insight and constructive criticism.

Lastly, we are indebted to Linda Tadic, who did a superb job of editing the manual and offered us the wisdom of her expertise, especially in the realm of digital media; and also to designer Lara Denil for all her hard work in improving and transforming the final layout of the manual for publication.

Natasha Fairbairn (Co-author)
Maria Assunta Pimpinelli (Co-author ; co-Chair, FIAF Rules Revision)
Thelma Ross (Co-author ; co-Chair, FIAF Rules Revision)

Table of Contents

Introduction

The archival moving image field has changed dramatically in recent years, with technological advances revolutionising cataloguing, preservation, and access practices. To help cataloguers and archivists respond to these changes, FIAF presents the *FIAF Moving Image Cataloguing Manual (FIAF Manual)*, a revision of the 1991 *FIAF Cataloguing Rules for Film Archives (FIAF Rules)*. These new guidelines, created by the FIAF Cataloguing and Documentation Commission and the FIAF Cataloguing Rules Revision Working Group, will help cataloguers create cataloguing or metadata records that will meet requirements of new database technologies and new metadata standards while remaining compatible with older methods and standards.

The Manual offers primarily descriptive cataloguing rules rather than a schema of data elements. However, it is difficult to discuss rules without mentioning data elements where the rules would be applied (e.g., Title, Date, etc.). Thus, the Manual by default provides both a metadata structure (fields or elements) and rules in how to input the values the fields contain. It reflects current and recommended cataloguing practices at international film archives represented on the Commission with the goal of interoperability with related cataloguing and metadata standards.

The cataloguing of moving images encompasses the complex, professional tasks of gathering and arranging data within systems upon which an institution depends. Indeed, accurate, well-organised descriptions of both filmographic and technical information about an institution's collection serve as the basis for informed internal use such as preservation, collections development, and outreach or exhibition. They further constitute the key to accessing collections by external users such as scholars, researchers and the general public – both now and for future generations.[1]

Cataloguing archival moving images combines general archival processing methodologies and traditional library cataloguing. The process of archiving moving images applies practices held in common with archiving other materials such as papers and manuscripts. The materials' origin or provenance is a key element to understanding their significance. Their historical context shows their relationship(s) to other works and, in cases of works with multiple manifestations, the development of individual works. Knowledge of this historical context and development of materials can be useful in their preservation.[2] An attempt has been made throughout the guidelines to address capturing provenance and preservation information.

This manual is intended to address some of the limitations moving image archives face when using guidelines and systems developed primarily for general libraries.

General library catalogues are built to support the discovery of a specific publication and its various editions. This discovery is facilitated by a focus on the creation of access points to author, title and/or subject. Many libraries catalogue through bibliographic utilities to pool effort by sharing records of these single publications. While this shared bibliographic model works well for libraries, since many will have exact copies of the same publication, it does not

1 FIAF, 1991, p. ix.
2 Adapted from AMIM2, p.1.

provide all the functions that moving image archives need. Because moving image archives' collections often include unique or rare holdings, such as pre-print elements, master prints, and unreleased material in addition to viewing copies, they need catalogues that go beyond the functions of a library catalogue to meet many of the collection management needs of archives. The *FIAF Manual* is intended to provide guidance in creating metadata or cataloguing records that fulfill these collection management functions.

This revision of the 1991 guidelines recognises that institutions use a variety of systems and data structures and may find it difficult to implement far-ranging changes in their cataloguing practices. The revisions suggested in this manual will help archives harmonise their practices with related standards, models, and schema, including:

1. The conceptual model *Functional Requirements for Bibliographic Records* (FRBR), published in 1998 by the International Federation of Libraries Association. FRBR is one of the models underlying *RDA: Resource Description and Access*[3], and it provides "a framework that identifies and clearly defines the entities of interest to users of bibliographic records, the attributes of each entity, and the types of relationships that operate between entities."[4]
2. *RDA: Resource Description and Access* (RDA), co-published in 2010 by the American Library Association, the Canadian Library Association, and Chartered Institute of Library and Information Professionals. RDA was developed as a new standard for resource description and access designed for the digital world, and applies FRBR concepts and terminologies. It is intended to eventually supplant Anglo-American Cataloguing Rules (AACR2), which has been the descriptive cataloguing standard in English-speaking communities since the 1960s. Like AACR2, RDA covers all types of content and media.[5]
3. The European Standards Committee (CEN) Cinematographic Works Standard (CWS) (EN 15744 and EN 15907). This two-part standard defines the metadata essential for facilitating data exchange between databases and consistent identification of moving images. The metadata schema (EN 15907), which is based in part upon the FRBR conceptual model, was approved in 2010 and disseminated through four workshops held from October 2010 – June 2011. Brief definitions of key elements in the FRBR-based CEN model are at the end of the Introduction.

For further information about the relationship of this set of guidelines to FRBR, RDA and EN 15907, see Appendix F.3. Although these guidelines are structured to correspond closely with the above standards/models/schema, and use associated terminology, note that neither they nor these guidelines are system-specific. They cover the fundamentals for cataloguers for the construction and management of data and records in whatever system or standards used by an institution.

While these guidelines are intended to be applicable to all forms of moving image materials, archives with extensive broadcasting collections may wish to look to broadcasting-specific metadata schemas such as EBUCore[6] and PBCore[7] for additional guidance.

---

3 The other two conceptual models are FRAD (*Functional Requirements for Authority Data*), http://www.ifla.org/node/7923 and FRSAD Functional Requirements for Subject Authority Data, http://www.ifla.org/node/1297.

4 FRBR Final Reports, p. 3.

5 RDA 0.0 and 0.1, p. 0-1.

6 https://tech.ebu.ch/MetadataEbuCore

7 http://pbcore.org/

FRBR-based CEN Terms in Brief

These guidelines use the terminology of CEN Cinematographic Works Standards for terms reflecting the core structuring of moving image records - namely Work, Variant, Manifestation and Item. It is worthwhile providing brief definitions for preliminary guidance here (whilst FRBR is discussed in more depth in Appendix F.3 Relationship of FIAF Cataloguing Rules to Functional Requirements of Bibliographic Records)

Work

An entity comprising the intellectual or artistic content and the process of realisation in a cinematographic medium, e.g., what the moving image is called, when it was made, who made it, who was in it, what it is about, etc. This core information usually does not change throughout any Variant or Manifestation.

Variant

An entity that may be used to indicate *any change* to content-related characteristics that do not significantly change the overall content of a Work as a whole. This is similar to a Work since it does not yet describe physical or digital embodiments of the content. For example: A film edited for television broadcast will contain most of the content of the original Work, but have some parts edited out.

Manifestation

The embodiment of a moving image Work/Variant. Manifestations include all analogue, digital and online media. Manifestation information can include a description of what the particular Manifestation should ideally contain, regardless of the Items held in the archive. For example: The original release time of a film is 1:30:00, but the Manifestation held at the archive is missing footage so is shorter.

Item

The physical product of a Manifestation of a Work or Variant, i.e. the physical copy of a Work or Variant. An Item may consist of one or more components, i.e. the whole Item may consist of 1 reel or 5 reels, 2 VHS tapes or 1 DVD. An Item record may contain fields or scope for separate barcodes and condition information for each component of the item (each reel for example) if required.

The Item may be whole or incomplete or a fragment. In the case of purely digital media, an Item is defined as the availability of the computer file, irrespective of the number of backup copies that may exist.[8]

8 Taken from EN15907. Item – Definition from the standard. http://filmstandards.org/fsc/index.php/EN_15907_Item

0. Preliminary Notes

0.1 Purpose, scope, and use

0.1.1 Purpose

The primary purposes of the *FIAF Manual* are to suggest recommendations for the description and identification of moving images (with an emphasis on archival moving images), and to define the elements of description to facilitate the exchange of information.

0.1.2 Scope

The manual is designed for use by institutions with moving image collections and cataloguers of moving images as a guide in the preparation of cataloguing records or descriptive metadata. The recommendations apply to generalised film and television collections, and may require elaboration in more specialised institutions whose holdings are exclusively of a single format or type, e.g., commercials, newsfilm, television, unedited footage, etc. For example, those with television collections should additionally consider more specific standards such as EBUcore or PBcore,

Moving images include a range of materials upon which sequences of visual images have been recorded or registered and which create the illusion of movement when projected, broadcast, or played back (by means of a projector, television set, computer, software or equivalent devices). Such images may or may not be accompanied by sound. The definition includes moving images of all types, e.g., features, shorts, news footage, trailers, outtakes, screen tests, educational and training documentaries, experimental or independent productions, study films or video, home movies, unedited materials, television broadcasts, commercials, spot announcements, recorded performances of concerts, ballets, plays, and CCTV footage etc. It encompasses both live action and animation and includes all analogue and digital formats.

While many moving image archives also have audio materials in their collections, this manual does not offer detailed guidance for describing audio media. However, the Manual does provide ways to describe physical and technical characteristics of analogue and digital audio Items to assist with collection and preservation management.

0.1.3 Use

Instead of defining levels of cataloguing, this manual outlines core elements for moving image description. The core elements provide the basis for identification of a resource and for facilitating the exchange of data from one system to another. These are not "core" elements in the sense of a Dublin Core, EBUCore, or PBCore schema, but are rather intended to illustrate common elements that are used in describing moving images and are referenced in the rules outlined in this manual. The elements are largely drawn from EN 15744 and 15907. For a comparison of elements described in this Manual and EN

15907, please see Appendix G, Elements of Description comparison

This manual also provides a list of all the data elements associated with the entities described. Thus, this approach provides a framework for the minimum and maximum amount of descriptive information allowed in a range of moving image cataloguing activities existing in a large variety of environments.

Institutions are encouraged to include as many of the non-core elements as goals and circumstances permit. None are considered mandatory by these guidelines, but an institution may require that some are mandatory for internal purposes.

0.2 Core elements of description[9]

These core points of description are listed with their corresponding terms as presented in the manual. They represent an ideal minimum set of metadata for moving image cataloguing.

CORE CONCEPT	TOP-LEVEL ELEMENT	SUB-ELEMENT
Title	1.3.2 Title [Work]	
Series / Serial[10]	1.3.2 Title [Work]	1.3.2.1 Title Type = Series/ Serial [Work]
Cast	1.4.1 Agents (e.g. Cast, Credits, Person, Organisation, etc.) [Work]	1.4.1.1 Agent Activity = Cast [Work]
Credits (including Production Companies)	1.4.1 Agents [Work]	1.4.1.1 Agent Activity = Credit (use term for actual role) [Work]
Country of Reference	1.3.3 Country of reference [Work]	
***Original Format**	2.3.4 Format of a moving image Manifestation [Manifestation]	2.3.4.1.2 Specific Carrier Type: [Manifestation]
***Original Length**	2.3.5 Extent of a Manifestation [Manifestation]	2.3.5.2 Physical extent of a Manifestation
***Original Duration**	2.3.5 Extent of a Manifestation [Manifestation]	2.3.5.3 Duration of a Manifestation
***Original Language**	1.3.5 Language(s) [Work]	1.3.5.1 Language Term + 1.3.5.2 Usage type [Work]

9 Adapted from CEN TC 372 EN 15744 element set

10 EN15744 definitions "A series is a group of separate items related to one another by the fact that each item bears, in addition to its own title, a collective title applying to the group as a whole. A serial is a type of "short subject" work which is characterized principally by the episodic development of a story". This Core Concept is referencing the name of another Work that a Work may be "part of", where the latter has been conceived within the context/intention of being an element of a Series or Serial. It is not being used here as a Work/Variant Description Type. (See D.1 Work/Variant Description Types)

Year of Reference	1.3.4 Year/Date of reference [Work]	1.3.4.1 Date Type [Work]
Identifier	As appropriate: 1.3.1 Work/Variant Identifier [Work/Variant] &/OR 2.3.1 Identifier [Manifestation] &/OR 3.1.1 Identifier [Item]	As appropriate: 1.3.1.1 Identifier Type [Work/Variant] &/OR 2.3.1.1 Identifier Type [Manifestation] &/OR 3.1.1.1 Identifier Type [Item]
Subject/Genre/Form[11]	1.4.3 Subject/Genre/Form terms [Work]	
Content Description	1.3.6 Content description (synopses, shotlists, etc)	

*The concept of "original" in this manual indicates the first known manifestation of the Work, which is not determined by its release status. The concept of "original" must be flexible enough to be applied to released and unreleased Works. For a released Work, we tend to refer to the "original" Work as the first known release of the first known manifestation. For Works that are not released (e.g., a home movie), the "original" Work is simply the first known manifestation.

See Appendix I.1 Example 1. Feature film in 3-level, 2-level and 1-level hierarchies as an illustration.

Please see Appendix G, Elements of Description comparison for a list of all elements described in this manual.

NOTE: For exchanging data, indicating the origin of the record is important (i.e., name of the institution supplying the record). This data is typically located in a dedicated field at the Work level and automatically generated by electronic systems. This corresponds to CEN EN 15907, 6.2 – Record Source.

0.2.1 Elements of description across Works, Variants, Manifestations, and Items

This section includes sample structures for how the elements can be applied across Works, Variants, Manifestations, and Items. Four models are provided, beginning with the more complete four-level model and ending with a simple one-level model. Models should be applied according to an institution's system and also determined by the amount of information known about an Item.

The full list of elements of description for each entity is set out in the following charts and diagrams, and in Chapters 1-3. See Appendix I, Examples of records containing core elements in the different levels of hierarchy for examples of real records which contain these core elements (as well as others) across the hierarchies.

11 Form = Fiction, Non-fiction, etc. Some institutions may incorporate these as a genre term, whilst others may have them as a separate category to genre.

Extended hierarchy model: 4 levels

Work
abstract entity

- Type - Whole conditions (serial / standalone / component part)
- Identifier (international, in-house unique identifier number)
- Titles (original, alternative, series/serial)
- Country (production country/countries)
- Dates (copyright / production)
- Language(s): original language of conception/presentation
- Notes/History
- Content: Synopsis, Genre, Form, Subject
- Agents: Cast, Credits, Rights holders

Variant
abstract entity
optional

- Type - Whole conditions (serial / standalone / component part)
- Identifier (international, in-house unique identifier number)
- Titles (original, alternative, series/serial)
- Country (production country/countries)
- Dates (copyright / production)
- Language(s)
- Notes/History
- Content: Synopsis, Genre, Form, Subject
- Agents: Cast, Credits, Rights holders

Manifestation
realisation, release, exhibition or distribution entity

- Type: pre-release, theatrical, non-theatrical, transmission, home-viewing, internet, restoration, not-for-release, etc
- Identifier (international, in-house unique identifier number)
- Titles
- Language(s): language of dialogue, subtitles, dubbing, intertitles, etc.
- Format: 35mm film, Digital Cinema Package (DCP), Blu-ray, etc
- Extent: physical, logical, temporal, e.g. duration, running time, length, etc.
- Event: release, transmission, distribution, creation, dates
- Rights context: platforms, territories, dates
- Agents: Creator, Broadcaster, Distributor, Publisher

Item
physical or digital object

- Identifier (inventory numbers)
- Titles (original, alternative)
- Element Type : instantiation type, e.g. original negative, dupe positive, Lavender, sound negative
- Item specifics: carrier, base, gauge, format, digital file type, sound, sound systems, colour standards etc.
- Extent: physical, temporal, e.g. footage, file size, duration
- Access conditions: Condition report - pristine, not for projection, heavy scratches, etc; storage location - home location, current location; Conservation recommendations: urgent transfer required, relocate to sub-zero, etc
- Event(s) (with Dates): creation, acquisition, accession, de-accession, loan, transport
- Acquisition: source, method, funding context, conditions of access, dates
- Agents: donors, archive technicians/conservationists, etc.
- Holding institution: name of the Item holder

Full hierarchy model: 3 levels

Work
abstract entity

- Type - Whole conditions (serial / standalone / component part)
- Titles (original, alternative, series/serial)
- Dates (copyright / production)
- Language(s): original language of conception/presentation
- Content: Synopsis, Genre, Form, Subject
- Agents: Cast, Credits, Rights holders
- Identifier (international, in-house unique identifier number)

Manifestation
realisation, release, exhibition or distribution entity

- Identifier (international, in-house unique identifier number)
- Titles
- Type: pre-release, theatrical, non-theatrical, transmission, home-viewing, internet, restoration, not-for-release, etc
- Language: dialogue language, subtitles, dubbed, intertitles, etc.
- Format: 35mm film, Digital Cinema Package (DCP) , Blu-ray, etc
- Extent: physical, logical, temporal, e.g. duration, running time, length, etc.
- Event: release, transmission, distribution, creation, dates
- Rights context: platforms, territories, dates
- Agents: Creator, Broadcaster, Distributor, Publisher

Item
physical or digital object

- Identifier (inventory numbers)
- Titles ((original, alternative)
- Element Type : instantiation type, e.g. original negative, dupe positive, Lavender, sound negative
- Item specifics: carrier, base, gauge, format, digital file type, sound, sound systems, colour standards etc.
- Extent: physical, temporal, e.g. footage, file size, duration
- Access conditions: Condition report - pristine, not for projection, heavy scratches, etc; storage location - home location, current location; Conservation recommendations: urgent transfer required, relocate to sub-zero, etc
- Event(s) (with Dates): creation, acquisition, accession, de-accession, loan, transport
- Acquisition: source, method, funding context, conditions of access, dates
- Agents: donors, archive technicians/conservationists, etc.
- Holding institution: name of the Item holder

Shallow hierarchy model: 2 levels

Work-like
abstract entity, with some context

- Type - Whole conditions (serial / standalone / component part)
- Titles (original, alternative, series/serial)
- Dates (copyright / production)
- Language(s): original language of conception/presentation
- Content: Synopsis, Genre, Form, Subject
- Agents: Cast, Credits, Rights holders
- Identifier (international, in-house unique identifier number)

Crossover data held in either level or both levels

- Identifier: international, in-house unique identifier number)
- Titles
- Type: pre-release, theatrical, non-theatrical, transmission, home-viewing, internet, restoration, not-for-release, etc
- Language: dialogue language, subtitles, dubbed, intertitles, etc.
- Format: 35mm film, Digital Cinema Package (DCP), Blu-ray, etc
- Extent: physical, logical, temporal, e.g. duration, running time, length, etc.
- Event: release, transmission, distribution, creation, dates
- Rights context: platforms, territories, dates
- Agents: Creator, Broadcaster, Distributor, Publisher

Item-like
physical or digital object, with some context

- Identifier (inventory numbers)
- Titles (original, alternative)
- Element Type : instantiation type, e.g. original negative, dupe positive, Lavender, sound negative
- Item specifics: carrier, base, gauge, format, digital file type, sound, sound systems, colour standards etc.
- Extent: physical, temporal, e.g. footage, file size, duration
- Access conditions: Condition report - pristine, not for projection, heavy scratches, etc; storage location - home location, current location; Conservation recommendations: urgent transfer required, relocate to sub-zero, etc
- Event(s) (with Dates): creation, acquisition, accession, de-accession, loan, transport
- Acquisition: source, method, funding context, conditions of access, dates
- Agents: donors, archive technicians/conservationists, etc.
- Holding institution: name of the Item holder

No hierarchy model: 1 level

Work
Manifestation
Item
properties expressed in one record, with abstract, contextual and object data stored on a single hierarchy level

- Identifier (international, in-house unique identifier number)
- Type - Whole conditions (serial / standalone / component part)
- Titles (original, alternative, series/serial)
- Dates: copyright, production, release, object creation, object acquisition / accession, de-accession, loan, transport
- Content: Synopsis, Genre, Form, Subject
- Agents: Cast, Credits, Rights holders
- Type: pre-release, theatrical, non-theatrical, transmission, home-viewing, internet, restoration, not-for-release,
- Language(s): original language, language of dialogue, subtitles, dubbing, intertitles, etc.
- Instantiation type: e.g. original negative, dupe positive, Lavender, sound negative
- Format/Item Specificss: 35mm film, Digital Cinema Package (DCP), Blu-ray, etc; carrier, base, gauge, format, digital file type, sound, sound systems, colour standards, etc.
- Extent: physical, logical, temporal, e.g. duration, running time, footage, file size
- Event(s): release, transmission, distribution, creation, acquisition, accession, de-accession, loan, transport, dates
- Rights context: platforms, territories, dates, transfer of ownership
- Agents: Creator, Broadcaster, Distributor, Publisher, Donor, Institution technicians/conservationists, etc.
- Access conditions: Condition report - pristine, not for projection, heavy scratches, etc; storage location - home location, current location; Conservation recommendations: urgent transfer required, relocate to sub-zero, etc
- Acquisition: source, method, funding context, conditions of access, dates
- Holding institution: name of the Item holder

Work/Manifestation/Item. Properties expressed in one record, with abstracts, contextual and object data stored in a single level hierarchy **Distribution of the elements of description according to the four entities order**			
Properties	(Work)	(Manifestation)	(Item)
Titles	Uniform, Preferred, Other Title information, Alternative, Supplied/Devised	Title proper	Title proper
Part	Monographic, Analytic, Serial, Collection		
Content	Categories: fiction/non fiction; genre, synopsis, subject, etc.		
Dates/Events	Creation, Production, Censorship, Copyright	Release, manufacture, transmission, distribution, etc.	Object creation, acquisition, accession, de-accession, loan, transport, etc.
Agents	Cast, credits, rights holders, creator, etc.	Distributor, broadcaster, publisher	Donor, Archive/archivist, technician, restorer, etc.
Rights context	Copyright holder and date	Platforms, territories, dates Agents (distributors, license holder)	Transfer of ownership
Event types	Awards Censorship Production IPR registration	Pre-release, theatrical, non-theatrical, transmission, home viewing, internet, not for release, censorship etc.	Acquisition Reproductions Disposal
Format general		35mm film, digital cinema, blu ray, etc.	
Format specific			16mm film pos, 35mm lavender separation, ProRes422 HQ, etc.
Condition report			Pristine, not for projection, heavy scratches, etc.
Storage location			Home location, current location, previous location
Conservation recommendations			Urgent transfer required, relocate sub-zero, etc.

0.3 Sources of Information

Information entered in a record must be derived from a source. Acceptable sources of information for moving image Works, Variants, Manifestations and Items include primary and secondary sources.

Primary sources include information on the actual Item itself. For example, for film materials, titles and main production credits are transcribed from the frames usually in the opening credits. Secondary sources include information written on containers and reference materials.

Although primary sources are generally preferred, this manual allows for the use of secondary sources no matter the entity, attribute or relationship described in recognition that there may be constraints on the amount of research or viewing a cataloguer can do.

Whether information is taken from primary and/or secondary sources as listed in the following, indicate that fact either by means of a note or by some other means (e.g., through coding or the use of square brackets, specific fields, or links to other databases).[12] Add the source of the information in a Note field and include the element name. Cite each individual source of information using an agreed upon, consistently applied citation style, such as *The Chicago Manual of Style*, or other style guide.

Primary source information can be derived from:

a) the title frame(s) or title screen(s)[13]
b) embedded metadata in textual form that contains a title (e.g., metadata embedded in an MPEG video file)[14]
c) an eye-readable label bearing a title that is permanently printed on or affixed to the resource (excluding accompanying textual material or a container)[15]
d) accompanying material or a container issued as part of the resource itself[16]
e) a container that is not issued as part of the resource itself (e.g., a box, case made by the owner)[17]
f) other published descriptions of the resource[18]
g) any other available source (e.g., a reference source)[19]

Examples:

Credit information derived from: AFI Catalog of Feature Films: 1930-1939.

Title derived from film opening credits.

---

12 Based on RDA 2.2.4 Other Sources of Information
13 RDA 2.20.2.3 Title Source
14 Ibid.
15 Adapted from RDA 2.2.2.3 Resources Consisting of Moving Images
16 Based on RDA 2.2.4 Other Sources of Information
17 RDA 2.2.4 Other Sources of Information
18 Ibid.
19 Ibid.

0.4 Display issues

Although these guidelines are primarily focused on content, many users may also welcome some guidance in data presentation. Section 0.4 gathers some of the common display questions with recommendations.

0.4.1 Punctuation

These guidelines do not mandate the use of any particular data presentation standard, such as ISBD punctuation. However, ISBD punctuation is recommended if punctuation guidance is desired. Please consult ISBD[20] for general guidance and examples, or the *FIAF Cataloguing Rules for Film Archives (1991)*[21].

These guidelines do advocate consistent usage where punctuation is needed as a cataloguing construction, for example, to separate Form elements in the creation of Partially or Fully Supplied/Devised Titles e.g.

Jaws. Rushes

For transcribed elements, record punctuation as found. For all other elements, record punctuation as found on the source(s) of information.

0.4.2 Capitalisation and Articles

Some institutions render Work titles in capitals – all upper-case – as a simple typographical method of identifying these key items of information, while others only capitalise the first letter of a title, in accordance with ISBD. Either usage is permitted by these guidelines, although institutions may prefer to retain the conventional practice of capitalising only the first letter of a title and any proper names as dictated by the usage of the language in which the information is given.

Users should recognise that using all capitals may create problems in the future when reformatting to mixed case if preferred in a new system, or when reformatting to mixed caps for display in a web platform where mixed caps is increasingly preferred. Although it is possible to automate the conversion of upper case to mixed caps, that automation cannot easily manage linguistic complexities or semantic rules and exceptions such as proper nouns, or place names. Therefore, it is recommended that an institution transition to ISBD capitalisation when and where possible.

When an "all capitals" practice is followed, institutions have the additional option of reducing to lower case words which are of minor importance to the substantive title (for filing purposes, etc.), such as sub-titles, a definite or indefinite article appearing as the first word of a title, etc. Experience has shown that this practice can make it easier for staff in institutions handling multi-lingual material to recognise, for filing purposes and interpretation, the different significance of words that are articles in one language but not in others.

---

20 http://www.ifla.org/files/assets/cataloguing/isbd/isbd-cons_20110321.pdf
21 http://www.fiafnet.org/~fiafnet/uk/publications/fep_cataloguingRules.html

While the guidelines permit both cases, it is recommended where permitted now or in the future, to use the conventional practice of capitalising only the first letter of a title and other letters as dictated by the usage of the language in which the information is given. Leading articles should ideally be placed in separate fields in keeping with the way systems are being developed for alphabetical sorting. Alternatively some systems (for example, those containing MARC21 records) indicate the number of non-filing characters to skip in alphabetization.

Examples:

Alternative practices | ISBD practice:
Die Hard | Die hard
Die DREIGROSCHENOPER | Die Dreigroschenoper
LES PATTERSON SAVES THE WORLD | Les Patterson saves the world
Les MISERABLES | Les miserables
American in Paris, An | An American in Paris

MARC21 tag example:

245 03 An American in Paris

0.5 Language and script of the description

The language of the original Work can be different from the language of a Manifestation or Item. For example, the original Work title can be in the original creation language, but the item being catalogued is a Variant with the title and key credits in a different language. Where possible, data elements in the catalogue record for the Work are recorded in the language and/or script of the original Work and may be transcribed from the Item of an original manifestation of the Work or taken from other sources.

This will primarily be for data transcribed from the screen, e.g. Title and key agents (director, producer, cast, etc.). Do not confuse this with describing the language of the soundtrack, which is noted in specific language fields.

Data elements for the Variant, Manifestation and Item are recorded in the language that is on the Variant, Manifestation or Item and should be transcribed from the Item or from other sources in the appropriate language. Scripts, symbols or other characters that cannot be transcribed as presented or are other than that used by the cataloguing agency or institution may, if necessary, be transliterated in the script of the institution or replaced with a cataloguer's description. Use a recognised standard for transliteration such as ISO 9 for Cyrillic characters, Pinyin for Chinese characters, or ALA-LC Romanization Tables. Give an explanatory note for the addition, if necessary. Optionally, enclose the cataloguer's description in square brackets.

Example:

Original Chinese Title: 精武英雄
Transliterated Pinyin Title: Jīng wǔ yīngxióng
English Translated Title: Fist of Legend

0.6 Abbreviations

For transcribed data elements, transcribe abbreviations as found. For all other elements, generally do not abbreviate words. Optionally, additional non-preferred title types may also be added to assist in user searching and accessibility (see Appendix A, Titles and Title Types).

0.7 Examples

The examples given throughout the guidelines are illustrative and not prescriptive (unless stated otherwise). They follow *The Chicago manual of style*[22] for the sake of consistency. They are intended to illuminate the provisions of the guidelines to which they are attached, rather than to extend those provisions. Therefore, neither the examples nor the form in which they are presented should be taken as instructions, unless the accompanying text specifically states that they should. Most examples are from actual titles; in the few made-up examples an attempt has been made to formulate realistic data. Examples of complete entries may be found in Appendix I, Examples of records containing core elements in the different levels of hierarchy. Examples of the elements of description in different data structures are shown in Appendix G, Elements of Description comparison. The bibliography follows ISO 690.

0.8 Errors

As these guidelines recognise the importance of researched information in the catalogue entry, unintentional errors or inaccuracies from the Item should not be reproduced at the Work or Variant levels.

Begin with what the source of information says and correct it only when it is known to be ambiguous or erroneous. Correction must be done in such a way that the resource remains recognisable to the users unaware of the error.[23] For example, AACR2 recommends transcribing the error followed by "sic" and sometimes the correct text in square brackets.

Example:

Title (Work): À bout du souffle
Title (Item): À bout du souflee [sic]

OR

Title (Work): À bout du souffle
Title (Item): À bout du souflee [souffle]

In RDA, the title is provided as transcribed without a recognition of the misspelling, with the correct title added in a secondary set of Title and Title Type fields (see A.2.4.1 Alternative title types) and a Note explaining the misspelling.

22 University of Chicago. 2003. *The Chicago manual of style*. Chicago, Ill: University of Chicago Press.
23 YCR, Principle 3, p.4.

Example:

Title (Work): À bout du souffle
Title (Item): À bout du souflee
Title (Item): À bout du souffle
TitleType (Item): Actual title

Note: Title on item is misspelled.

Missing information required to understand and identify a Manifestation, Variant, or Item can be supplied in brackets.

Record <u>intentionally</u> misspelled words as found.

Example:

Title (Work): Inglorious Basterds

0.9 Alternatives and options

Certain of the individual guidelines or parts of guidelines in this manual are introduced by the words, "alternatively" or "optionally." Optional provisions arise from the recognition that different solutions to a problem and differing levels of detail and specificity are appropriate in different contexts. Some alternatives and options should be decided as a matter of cataloguing policy for a particular catalogue or archive and should therefore be exercised either always or never. Other alternatives and options should be exercised case-by-case. It is recommended that all institutions which undertake cataloguing distinguish between these two types of options and keep a record of their policy decisions and of the circumstances in which a particular option may be applied.

The necessity for judgment and interpretation by the cataloguer is recognised in these guidelines. Such judgment and interpretation may be based on the requirements of a particular catalogue or upon the use of the items being catalogued. The need for judgment is indicated in these guidelines by phrases such as "if appropriate," "if important" and "if necessary." These indicate recognition of the fact that uniform regulation of catalogues is neither possible nor desirable, and encourage the application of individual judgment based on specific local knowledge. This statement in no way contradicts the value of standardisation. Such judgments must be applied consistently within a particular context and must be documented by the individual archive.

In addition, adherence to these structures and standards may not be wholly appropriate or possible for some institutions, given the differences in current practice, available cataloguing tools, and other issues. An attempt has been made to design guidelines that can be applied where feasible, but which are not meant to be prescriptive.

1. Moving Image Works and Variants

1.0 Definitions[24]

Brief definitions of the standard CEN terms Work/Variant/Manifestation/Item used in the Manual were provided at the end of the Introduction (see Introduction). This and the following sections provide in-depth definitions of the terms as used in these guidelines, beginning with the highest level in the description hierarchy: Moving Image Works and Variants.

1.0.1 Moving Image Work

A moving image Work comprises both the intellectual or artistic content and the process of realisation in a cinematographic medium, e.g., what it is called, when it was made, who made it, who was in it, what it is about, etc.

A Work as a conceptual entity is the topmost level of description. It may be published or unpublished, complete (whole) or incomplete (unfinished or missing content), edited or unedited. It is intended to function as the "node" that relates all Variants and Manifestations of a Work to a common creation. A Work contains the characteristics that are inherited across any Variant, Manifestation, or Item derived from that Work. It also reflects the original intentions of its realisation, including: circumstances of the creation process such as date(s) and place(s) of production, most contributions by agents such as directors, screenwriters, production companies and cast members, as well as certain statements about the contents.[25]

The concept of moving image Work includes moving image realisations of events or performances – such as edited or unedited recordings of a play or concert performed in a theatre, a sporting event, a street performer, a medical procedure, etc.

In addition, moving images created by use of automatic devices such as surveillance cameras or vehicle-mounted cameras, can also be considered moving image works if they are subject to collecting or publishing activities.

The presence of artistic intent in the creation of a moving image entity is not a prerequisite for considering it a moving image Work. A moving image entity can be considered as a Work on a very broad spectrum of creative intent, from the classic fiction feature film at one extreme (with artistic input from dozens or hundreds of creative contributors), through amateur film (with a modicum of creative intent by one individual), to CCTV footage or other automatic recording outputs at the other extreme.

Works may have one-to-many relationships with instances of Variant and Manifestation/Item and many-to-many relationships with instances of Agent(s,) Event(s), Content(s), Subject(s) and Other Relation(s).[26]

24 For a discussion of other definitions of the "Work" and Variant entities, see F.3 Relationship of FIAF Cataloguing Rules to Functional Requirements of Bibliographic Records

25 Adapted from the definition of a Cinematographic Work in EN 15907, 4.1.1, p.8.

26 Ibid.

Works include:

- moving image realisations based on new scripts or adapted from pre-existing textual works such as novels, plays, etc.

  Examples:

  Hamlet (UK, 1948, Laurence Olivier)
  Hamlet (USA, 1996, Kenneth Branagh)

  Les misérables (France, 1958, Jean-Paul Le Chanois)
  Les misérables (USA, 1998, Bille August)

  Trollflöjten (Sweden, 1975, Ingmar Bergman)
  Il flauto magico (Italy, 1976, Giulio Gianini and Emanuele Luzzati)

  Tosca (Italy, 1939, Karl Koch)
  Tosca (Italy, 1973, Luigi Magni)

- moving image realisations of scheduled performances or events such as concerts, original theatre performances, sports events, etc.[27] These are distinguished from cinematically staged theatrical or musical events for the purpose of creating a unique moving image work such as the Tosca and Hamlet examples provided above.

  Examples:

  Simon and Garfunkel: The Concert in Central Park (USA, 1982, Michael Lindsay-Hogg)

  Olympia 1. Teil – Fest der Völker (Germany, 1938, Leni Riefenstahl)

  Olympia 2. Teil – Fest der Schönheit (Germany, 1938, Leni Riefenstahl)

  Marathon (Spain, 1992, Carlos Saura)

- moving images created by use of automatic devices such as surveillance cameras, scientific or medical instruments, etc.[28]

  Examples[29]:

  Birmingham Town Hall Car Park. Camera 7. (United Kingdom, 2015, NCP)

  University College Hospital. Endoscopy – Colonscope. Patient HX3456. 2010 (United Kingdom, 2010, University College Hospital)

27 Adapted from the definition of a Cinematographic Work in EN 15907, 4.1.1, p.8.
28 Ibid.
29 These are invented examples for illustrative purposes

1.0.2 Moving Image Variant (i.e., Versions)[30]

A moving image Variant is an entity that may be used to indicate *any change* to content-related characteristics that do not significantly change the overall content of a Work as a whole. Such Variants can be produced by minor additions, deletions or substitutions to the content. As a general guideline, changes that would result in a different content description should be treated as a separate Work rather than a Variant.

Changes that could be described as Variants are detailed below, in 1.1.2 Boundaries between Moving Image Works and Variants , and may include the addition of subtitles, dubbing, and editing as a result of censorship or adjustment of duration, e.g. for TV programming. For institutions that have made a policy decision not to use the Variant, these changes may constitute Manifestation differences.

The determination of a Variant requires human analysis, and as such is an interpretative practice. It is not always easy to establish what the Variants may be. For example, an institution may have a television recording of a motion picture broadcast but no way of comparing it with an original theatrical copy as to whether it has been altered in terms of subtle censorship of content or duration

Therefore, this entity is optional. If employed, each instance of a Variant is related to a Work and can have one-to-many relationships with instances of Manifestation(s), Event(s), Agent(s) and Other Relation(s). If no Variant of a Work exists or is known to exist, then this entity can be omitted, connecting an instance of a Work with one or more instances of Manifestation.

1.1 Boundaries between Works and Variants

This section looks at instances of when an entity constitutes a new Work or a Variant of a Work.

Determining boundaries between Works and Variants may sometimes rely upon a cataloguer's judgment, however, in general: If much of the original textual material remains, most of the original footage remains in roughly the same continuity, however abridged, and substantially most of the contributors are the same, the existence of alterations more often than not constitute a Variant, rather than a new Work. An institution will need to set internal policies defining the minimum percentage of a work that has been extensively edited to qualify it as a new Work.

This decision tree is intended to help cataloguers determine when changes in content warrant the creation of a new Work record or a new Variant record. This distinction applies to cataloguing structures using a 4-level hierarchy: Work, Variant, Manifestation, and Item. When using a 3-level hierarchy - Work, Manifestation, and Item – minor changes will indicate new Manifestations rather than new Variants. In all cases, major changes warrant the creation of new Work records.

---

30 Adapted from EN 15907, 4.2 Variant

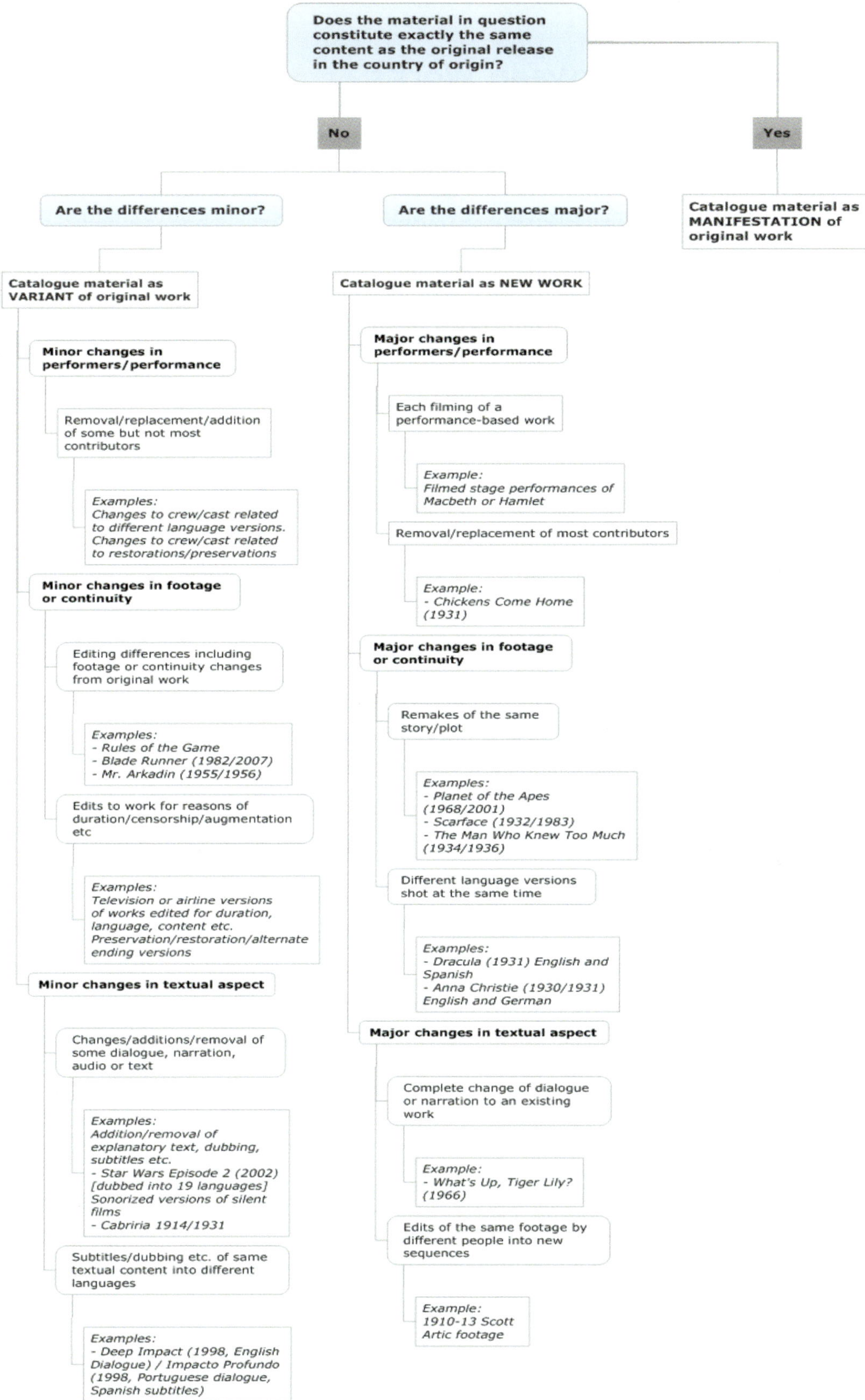

Does the material in question constitute exactly the same content as the original release in the country of origin?
No
Yes
Catalogue material as MANIFESTATION of original work
Are the differences minor?
Are the differences major?
Catalogue material as VARIANT of original work
Minor changes in performers/performance
Removal/replacement/addition of some but not most contributors
Examples: Changes to crew/cast related to different language versions. Changes to crew/cast related to restorations/preservations
Minor changes in footage or continuity
Editing differences including footage or continuity changes from original work
Examples: - Rules of the Game - Blade Runner (1982/2007) - Mr. Arkadin (1955/1956)
Edits to work for reasons of duration/censorship/augmentation etc
Examples: Television or airline versions of works edited for duration, language, content etc. Preservation/restoration/alternate ending versions
Minor changes in textual aspect
Changes/additions/removal of some dialogue, narration, audio or text
Examples: Addition/removal of explanatory text, dubbing, subtitles etc. - Star Wars Episode 2 (2002) [dubbed into 19 languages] Sonorized versions of silent films - Cabriria 1914/1931
Subtitles/dubbing etc. of same textual content into different languages
Examples: - Deep Impact (1998, English Dialogue) / Impacto Profundo (1998, Portuguese dialogue, Spanish subtitles)
Catalogue material as NEW WORK
Major changes in performers/performance
Each filming of a performance-based work
Example: Filmed stage performances of Macbeth or Hamlet
Removal/replacement of most contributors
Example: - Chickens Come Home (1931)
Major changes in footage or continuity
Remakes of the same story/plot
Examples: - Planet of the Apes (1968/2001) - Scarface (1932/1983) - The Man Who Knew Too Much (1934/1936)
Different language versions shot at the same time
Examples: - Dracula (1931) English and Spanish - Anna Christie (1930/1931) English and German
Major changes in textual aspect
Complete change of dialogue or narration to an existing work
Example: - What's Up, Tiger Lily? (1966)
Edits of the same footage by different people into new sequences
Example: 1910-13 Scott Artic footage

1.1.1 Boundaries between Works

These guidelines recognise that real world cataloguing needs and data structures necessitate practical applications of conceptual modelling. To that end, the recommendations made in this chapter about determining boundaries for Works and Variants are based on an approach that emphasizes effective, efficient and economic data creation and maintenance: information that is common to all realisations of a Work or Variant is recorded once and is comprised of the shared information that will not change (for example, title, original creation date, creator, etc.). The Work description or record contains the index terms for describing a Work in the catalogue and fulfills the functions of disambiguation (distinguishes Works containing similar or identical titles) and collocation (brings together all the materials that are related to the Work and all Variants of a given Work). Variations in information describing the Work result in Variants or Manifestations, or new Works.

The boundaries between one Work and another (i.e. where a new Work would be created rather than a Variant) are drawn on the basis of the following alterations to the content:[31]

Change in footage and/or changes in continuity (primary editing)[32]

- remakes of the same story/plot

  Examples:

  The man who knew too much (UK, 1934, Alfred Hitchcock)
  The man who knew too much (UK, 1936, Alfred Hitchcock)

  T'amerò sempre (Italy, 1933, Mario Camerini)
  T'amerò sempre (Italy, 1943, Mario Camerini)

  Planet of the apes (USA, 1968, Franklin J. Schaffner)
  Planet of the apes (USA, 2001, Tim Burton)

  Scarface (USA, 1932, Howard Hawks)
  Scarface (USA, 1983, Brian De Palma)

  Die Dreigroschenoper (Germany, 1931, Georg Wilhelm Pabst)
  Die Dreigroschenoper (Germany,1962, Wolfgang Staudte)

- different language versions shot at the same time, released simultaneously, sometimes with different casts

  Examples:

  Dracula (USA, 1931, Tod Browning, Spanish and English)

31 The types of alterations given here are adapted from Yee, "The Concept of *Work* for Moving Image Materials."
32 Secondary editing results in a Variant.

Anna Christie (USA, 1930, Clarence Brown, English; 1931, German)

Der Fangschuß (France/Germany, 1976, Volker Schlöndorff, German)
Le Coup de grâce (France/Germany, 1976, Volker Schlöndorff, French)

Die Dreigroschenoper (Germany, 1931, Georg Wilhelm Pabst, German)
L'opéra de quat'sous (France, 1931, Georg Wilhelm Pabst, French)

La canzone dell'amore (USA, 1930, Gennaro Righelli, English)
Liebeslied (Germany, 1930, Constantin J. Davis, German)
La dernière berceuse (France, 1930, Jean Cassagne, French)

- editing of the same raw footage by different people into different sequences

  Example:

  Several separate Works made from the footage taken on Captain Robert Falcon Scott's Antarctic expedition, 1910-13.

Change in textual or spoken word aspect

- complete alteration of dialogue and/or narration of an existing work

  Example: What's Up Tiger Lily (1966)

Change in performance/performers

- each cinematographic realisation of a dramatic work

  Examples:

  Moving image representations of theatrical performances of Shakespeare's *Macbeth,* where there is removal and/or replacement of substantially most of the contributors (e.g., cast and/or crew), associated with a work

  Chickens Come Home (1931) where the film was first shot in English, then re-shot with Spanish dialogue and additional Spanish-speaking actors.

If much of the original textual or spoken word material remains, most of the original footage remains in roughly the same continuity, however abridged, and substantially most of the contributors are the same, the existence of alterations more often than not constitute a Variant, rather than a new Work.

1.1.2 Boundaries between Works and Variants/ Manifestations

The boundaries between a moving image Work and its Variant(s) (i.e. where a Variant rather than a new Work may be created) may be drawn on the basis of one or more of the following alterations to the content given below. [33]

Change in footage and/or change in continuity (secondary editing)

- different footage used from the original realisation of the Work, even where footage used was shot at the same time and edited together by the same people, or following the pattern set by original creators.

  Examples:

  The rules of the game (1939): exists only as a Variant of the original Work, made partially from alternate takes to those used in the original release.

  Various re-edited releases of *Blade Runner* (1982, 1986, 1992, 2007)

  Mr. Arkadin (France-Spain-Switzerland, 1955, Orson Welles): eight different Variants between 1955 and 1956, each one with differences in footage and editing. Among them, three have the title *Confidential Report*.[34]

- editing of a Work to create realisations that are shorter in extent/duration

  Examples:

  Große Freiheit Nr. 7 (Germany, 1944) (112 minutes)
  Shortened Variant *Große Freiheit Nr. 7* (109 minutes)

  Works censored or edited for television broadcast, for showing on airplanes, for showing in different parts of the country/world, etc.

  Annie Leibovitz, Life through a Lens (USA, 2007-01-03), broadcast in TV series American Masters
  Shortened Variant (for British television): Annie Leibovitz, Life through a Lens (UK, 2008-06-10), broadcast in TV series Imagine

  Last Tango in Paris (USA, 1972, Bernardo Bertolucci)
  Censored Variant: Ultimo tango a Parigi (Italy, 1988, Broadcast)

- addition of new footage to a Work

  Examples:

  to update informational/educational content; for preservation/resto-

33 The types of alterations given here are adapted from Yee, "The Concept of *Work* for Moving Image Materials."
34 *Il cinema ritrovato 2006. 20. edizione: sabato 1 luglio-sabato 8 luglio* / Cineteca del Comune di Bologna. – Bologna : Cineteca del Comune di Bologna, 2006, p. 154 (*Dossier Mr. Arkadin*).

ration; to offer different endings or alternate takes

Blackmail (UK, 1929, Alfred Hitchcock)
Augmented Variant: UK – 1929 (longer, with some scenes shot on purpose)

Little Shop of Horrors (USA, 1986, Frank Oz)
Augmented Variant: alternate ending of 23 minutes, included in the 2012 Warner Home Video – Blu-ray, DVD edition

Nosferatu. Eine Symphonie des Grauens (Germany, 1922, Friedrich Wilhelm Murnau)
Preservation/Restoration Variant: restoration by Friedrich-Wilhelm Murnau-Stiftung; Luciano Berriatùa (restorer) – Germany – 2005/6 (reconstruction based on different sources)

Change in textual aspect

- partial alteration of dialogue and/or narration of an existing Work, including the removal and/or addition of dialogue (audio and/or intertitles)

  Examples:

  The addition or removal of explanatory text, dubbing, subtitles, etc. Star Wars Episode II: Attack of the Clones (2002) was dubbed into 19 foreign language versions, which were released on the same date as the English language version.[35]

  Cabiria (Italy, 1914, Giovanni Pastrone)
  Sonorized Variant: Italy, 1931

  A dog's life (USA, 1918, Charles Chaplin)
  Sonorized Variant: Vita da cani – sonorized with Italian intertitles – 193?

  The yellow mask (USA, 1930, Harry Lachman)
  Augmented Variant: Il principe corsaro – 1931: only with music, songs and sound effects, plus new Italian intertitles, but without dialogue, according to a 1930 law, which involved the first spoken foreign films distributed in Italy.

  Hallelujah! (USA, 1929, King Vidor)
  Augmented Variant: Alleluia! – addition of music, songs, sound effects, and new Italian intertitles, but without dialogue; Italy, 1930

  La presa di Roma (Italy, 1905)
  Preservation/restoration Variant: addition of stills and explanation texts; Italy, 2007. Restoration by Centro Sperimentale di Cinematografia-Cineteca Nazionale

35 Some institutions may have the 19 foreign language versions as 19 separate Manifestations, rather than create 19 Variant records, particularly if the data relating to specific different dubbing credits is unavailable or deemed of minor importance.

Change in performance/performers

- removal and/or replacement and/or addition of any one or more of the contributors (e.g., cast and/or crew), but not substantially most, associated with a Work

    Examples: restored versions of works often include credits for the responsible individuals and institutions

        Nosferatu. Eine Symphonie des Grauens (Germany, 1922, Friedrich Wilhelm Murnau)
        Preservation/augmented Variant – 2005/6: restoration by the Friedrich-Wilhelm Murnau-Stiftung; Luciano Berriatùa (restorer)

        Die freudlose Gasse (Germany, 1925, Georg Wilhelm Pabst);
        Preservation/augmented Variant – Germany – 2008. Digitale Restaurierung: Filmarchiv Austria, Wien, Stephanie Gratzer in Zusammenarbeit mit der Galerie Krems; Wissenschaftliche Beratung: Stephan Droessler, Nikolaus Wostry; Projectleitung: Ernst Kleininger, Nikolaus Wostry (from the credits on the DVD)

        Kita-kitsune Monogatari (Japan, 1978, Koreyoshi Kurahara); original narrator voice: Eiji Okada; Augmented variant with added prologue and English narration: The Glacier Fox in Search of the Northern Sun – USA – 1979: narrator voice: Arthur Hill.

    Examples: language versions may credit the individuals responsible for dubbing or subtitles

        Senso (Italy, 1954, Luchino Visconti)
        Subtitled Variant: French subtitles – 1955: subtitles by Georges Sadoul

        Cinderella (USA, 1950, Clyde Geronimi, Wilfred Jackson, Hamilton Luske)
        Dubbed variant: Cendrillon, French (spoken language) – France – 1991: Dominique Poulain, voice of Cinderella)

        Sons of the Desert (USA, 1933, William A. Seiter):
        Dubbed Variant 1:I figli del deserto – Italian (spoken language) -1935: Carlo Cassola, voice of Oliver Hardy;
        Dubbed Variant 2:, I figli del deserto – Italian (spoken language) 1946: Alberto Sordi, voice of Oliver Hardy.

When an institution has set a policy not to use Variants, the boundaries will usually be between a Work and Manifestations, i.e., a new Manifestation linked to the Work would be created rather than a Variant, or else a separate new Work, depending on assessment of the level of change or variation.

Boundaries for this decision are akin to the concepts of "versions with major changes" and "variations with minor changes" in the *FIAF Cataloguing Rules for Film Archives (1991)* http://www.fiafnet.org/pages/E-Resources/FIAF-Cataloguing-Rules.html

Example:

Our herring industry (GB, 1932) is the shortened version of Drifters (GB, 1929).

Where a Work/Variant structure exists then *Our herring industry* would constitute a Variant of the Work *Drifters*.

Where no Variant structure exists then the cataloguer would decide whether it constituted a Manifestation or new Work.

It is up to every archive or institution to choose and make its own policy on whether to use Variants or Manifestations.

1.1.3 Boundaries between Variants

It is possible for a moving image Variant to be modified in such a way as to create a new Variant related to the previous one.[36] The boundaries between one Variant and another may be drawn on the basis of the following alterations to the content:[37]

Change in continuity (secondary editing)

- revision or modification of already edited footage of completed work

  Example: In 2007, some in-flight showings of *The Queen* (2006) distributed to Delta and other airlines had all references to the word "God" edited out by an overzealous and inexperienced employee.[38]

- abridgements or additions to existing content

  Example: a release of a dubbed film abridged or augmented

  Il gattopardo (Italy, France,1963, Luchino Visconti)
  Dubbed/ Abridged: The leopard, English (spoken language) -1963 – USA – 161′ (Theatrical distribution in USA, the 20th Century Fox cut 45 minutes);
  Subtitled: The leopard, English (spoken language) -1980 – USA (reintegrates the original running time of 187′)[39].

Change in textual and spoken word aspect

- same dialogue and/or narration rendered in different spoken, sung or written languages

  Example: a release of a foreign film (dubbed), subtitled in a different language

  Die kleine und die grosse Liebe (Germany, 1938, Joseph von Backy)
  Dubbed/Subtitled Variant: Il piccolo e il grande amore, Italian (spoken

36 YCR, Expressions of Expressions, p. 47
37 The types of alterations given here are adapted from Yee, "The Concept of *Work* for Moving Image Materials."
38 Cornick, Michael. (2008). *Modern Film Censorship: Television, Airlines, and Home Entertainment*. p. 44
39 https://en.wikipedia.org/wiki/The_Leopard

language), English (subtitles) – Italy – 1938

Change in performance/performers

- addition, removal and/or replacement of some of the contributors (e.g., cast and/or crew), associated with a Work

  Example: The re-dubbed North American English version of the Japanese movie, *Godzilla 2000: Millennium* (1999), includes the following credits unique to this Variant:[40]

  Dubbing Director: Mike Schlesinger
  Media: Cinema/TV/VHS/DVD
  Dubbing Studio: Tristar Pictures/Sony Pictures Entertainment

Character	Japanese actor	Tristar Pictures English dub
Godzilla	Tsutomu Kitagawa	
Yuji Shinoda	Takehiro Murata	Francois Chau
Yuki Ichinose	Naomi Nishida	Denise Iketani

If much of the original textual and spoken word material remains, most of the original footage remains in roughly the same continuity, however abridged, and substantially most of the contributors are the same, the existence of alterations more often than not constitute a new Variant, rather than a new Work.

1.2 Attributes of a Moving Image Work/Variant

1.2.1 Work/Variant Description Type[41]

The description type establishes the general focus of the Work being catalogued, whether it is a complete Work in one part, a Work made up of several parts, or a physical group or collection of Works. Providing this information helps the cataloguer and user understand the context of the Work/Variant being described, and whether it has any relationships with other Works/Variants. For example, a television series could be catalogued as a Serial, which implies that there could be related Works (episodes) catalogued as Monographs.

Record the level of description of the work being catalogued, for example, "analytic," "monographic," "serial," etc., according to a controlled vocabulary. The terms used in this Manual are derived from traditional bibliographic cataloguing rules and from EN 15907 (and are defined in Appendix D.1), but an institution may choose to create its own list of terms. See D.1 Work/Variant Description Types.

40 Information from IMDb and Wikipedia
41 EN 15907, 4.1.2 Attributes—description Level, p. 8; BFI CID Stylistics Manual, A.1.3 Filmographic Level, pp. 7-8

1.2.2 Variant Type[42]

Identify and describe the kind of change from a Work that gives rise to any instance(s) of a Variant. Selection should be made from a controlled list of values. Examples: Censored; Dubbed; Subtitled; Edited for TV. See D.2 Variant Type.

1.3 Elements of a Work/Variant

This section describes the metadata elements that can be used to describe a Work/ Variant. It is up to each institution to choose which elements are most applicable to describe their collections and according to what their system can support.

This Manual recommends using the qualifier "Type" for several core elements if an institution's system can support it. In these cases, "Type" is used to define the source, function or purpose of the value entered in the main element. Using a "Type" qualifier conforms to its use in Dublin Core and other Dublin Core-influenced standards such as EBUCore and PBCore. Examples of using "Type" include the Identifier, Title, Date, and Description elements.

1.3.1 Work/Variant Identifier

Create an unambiguous reference to the Work/Variant using a unique identifier and indicate the type of identifier. The identifier should be a numerical or alphanumerical reference. This identifier is for the **content** of the Work/Variant, not for a specific Item. Manifestations and Items have their own Identifiers, discussed in later sections. This Work/Variant Identifier is shared by all Manifestations and Items associated to the Work.

In a way, a unique Work/Variant Identifier can have more value than a Work's Title. Titles can confuse through different spellings, translations, and are not unique (i.e., *King Kong*). An Identifier refers to a specific Work/Variant and provides clear disambiguation between Works when there is confusion.

There can be more than one Work/Variant unique identifier for the content. This commonly occurs when institutions have content assigned identifiers by various standards or distribution agencies (ISAN, EIDR), or a government or other official body in the archive's country has assigned an identifier to the work. An institution will likely have its own internal Identifier as well, often auto-generated by an institution's information or asset management system. For example, a Work/Variant may have these associated identifiers:

- International Standard Audiovisual Number (ISAN)[43]
- EIDR (Entertainment Identifier Registry)[44]
- VIAF (Virtual International Authority File).[45]
- Locally-generated

42 EN 15907, 4.2.2 Attributes of a Variant, variant type; YCR, 2.1.1 Nature of modification (change in content) of expression, p. 48

43 www.isan.org

44 www.eidr.org

45 www.viaf.org

Use what makes sense for your institution; there is no recommendation for one particular resource. However, it is recommended that at least one unique identifier be included in the record. It is critical that each Identifier be unique.

Examples:

Cabiria (Italy, 1914, Piero Fosco[46])
Work identifier – ISAN number: ISAN 0000-0000-7B37-0000-J-0000-0000-H

Volver (Spain, 2006, Pedro Almodovar)
Work identifier – ISAN number: ISAN 0000-0001-6B16-0000-Y-0000-0000-9

Metropolis (Germany, 1927, Fritz Lang)
Work identifier – VIAF number: 219448355

The boxer (United States, Ireland, 1997, Jim Sheridan)
Work identifier – EIDR number: 10.5240/5896-B203-017D-11A5-EB7F-W
Work identifier – ISAN number: 0000-0000-60A5-0000-E-0000-0000-W

1.3.1.1 Identifier Type

If an institution's system allows, a "Type" can be applied with an Identifier to define the source of the Identifier. Examples:

The boxer (United States, Ireland, 1997, Jim Sheridan)

Work identifier: 10.5240/5896-B203-017D-11A5-EB7F-W
Identifier type: EIDR
Work identifier: 0000-0000-60A5-0000-E-0000-0000-W
Identifier type: ISAN

1.3.2 Title

Record at least one title, identifying phrase, or name for the moving image Work or Variant. If your institution is applying the use of "Type" qualifiers, use "Title Type" to state the function of a particular title. (see 1.3.2.1 Title Type and Appendix A, Titles and Title Types).

Ideally, the record should at a minimum contain the "preferred title" (also referred to as "main" or "original" title) of the Work or Variant. Generally, it is the title of a moving image Work or Variant when first released, broadcast, published or transmitted (i.e. mounted online) in the country or countries of origin. It may differ from the title found on a particular manifestation of the Work or Variant; the actual title on the Manifestation is noted in the Manifestation Title element (see 2.3.2 Title). See A.2.0 Preferred for additional information.

46 Pietro Fosco is the pseudonym of Giovanni Pastrone used in the ISAN registration.

For creating titles for untitled or unidentified entities see A.2.5 Supplied/Devised Titles. Television programmes and other types of content that are part of a series/serial should have both the series/serial title and the episode title included in the Work record. This may be via use of a "Title type" qualifier. See A.2.6 Titles of series/serials for other options

Examples:

Gone with the wind (USA, 1939, Victor Fleming)
Gone with the wind – Preferred Title of the Work
Via col vento – Variant title – Dubbed (Italian)
Gejaagd door de win – Variant title – Dubbed (Dutch)
Autant en emporte le vent – Variant title – Dubbed – (French)
風と共に去りぬ – Variant title – Dubbed (Japanese)

Аленький цветочек (USSR, 1952, Lev Atamanov)[47]
Аленький цветочек – Title of the Work
Alenkiy tsvetochek: Alternative (transliterated) title of Work/ Variant (Preferred title if systems don't use Cyrillic)
Feuerrotes Blümchen – Variant title – Dubbed (German)
The Scarlet Flower – Variant title – Dubbed (English)

La passeggiata (Italy, 1953, Renato Rascel)
La passeggiata – Preferred Title of the Work
La prospettiva – Alternative title (Working title)[48]

Anathan (Japan, 1953, Joseph von Sternberg)
Anathan – Preferred Title of the Work
The saga of Anathan – Alternative Title of the Work/Variant

Mary Tyler Moore show – Series title
Chuckles bites the dust – Preferred title

See Appendix A.1 Title for fuller titling details and information.

See Appendix E.4 for titling of Aggregates (e.g., compilations).

For guidance on wording, order, spelling, punctuation, accentuation and capitalisation, see Chapter 0. Preliminary Notes.

For sources of information for the Title, see 0.3 Sources of Information

1.3.2.1 Title Type

Where relevant for an institution, if the Work/Variant or Manifestation includes multiple titles, such as a title in another language for a dubbed or subtitled variant, record the relevant Variant titles and associate a "Title Type" to each title for differentiation

47 http://en.wikipedia.org/wiki/The_Scarlet_Flower_(1952_film)
48 *La passeggiata* is a film based on the short story *Nevsky Prospect* (Russian: Невский Проспект, Italian: *La prospettiva Nevskij* by Nikolai Gogol').

between the various types of titles (see Appendix A, Titles and Title Types).

1.3.3 Country of reference

Where known and applicable, record the geographic origin of the moving image Work/Variant. This should be the country or countries where the principal offices or production facilities of the production company or companies are located.[49] Where an official national certificate or designation of a Work exists, use this as the authoritative source, e.g., Italian government department designates what is officially an Italian film.[50] When more than one place is associated with a Work/Variant, choose the place(s) with primary importance.

For institutions who need or require specific ordering of country of reference then the following is a possible example of how this may be achieved.[51]

If the Work is a multi-national production, the countries added to the record should be in order of financial involvement. For example, an Austrian/Italian/French co-production where the Austrian production company/sponsors financed 60%, the Italian 25% and the French 15% then the order of the countries would be: Austria, Italy, France.

If it is not possible to establish clearly the financial percentages of each country's involvement, then consider the nationality of the director of the title and/or the majority of personnel involved with the film and select that as being the main country of origin of the film.

If the production company has branches in more than one country, choose the one responsible for the production of the work.

If the Work is a multi-national production, with production companies in multiple countries, choose the predominant production company if known.

Record the country of origin using the full form of the country name, e.g. United Kingdom rather than UK, by taking the most suitable value(s) from a controlled list. This can be an in-house list but the use of a standard list such as ISO 3166[52] is preferable. If ISO is used, apply the English Short Name that is associated to a code. Optionally, record the country code as found in ISO 3166-1-alpha 2.

If the country name has changed, record the name of the country as it was at the time of production, e.g., Czechoslovakia for a Work/Variant produced in 1970, but Czech Republic or Slovakia for one from 2012.[53]

---

49 EN 15907, 6.5 Country of Reference, p. 19

50 The certification of "Italian nationality" is provided by the law/decree 2004, n. 28, part. 5 (but already provided in the former law 1213/1965). According to the 2004 law, the biggest part of the cast and crew, the locations, and the technical facilities have to be Italian, and 30% of the budget has to be spent in Italy. There is a number of exceptions for artistic reasons and in case of co-productions.

51 This is the formula followed by the British Film Institute. BFI CID Stylistics Manual – 2nd Edition. A.8.1.

52 http://www.iso.org/iso/home/standards/country_codes.htm

53 ISO 3166-3 Codes for the representation of names of countries and their subdivisions -- Part 3: Code for formerly used names of countries, is available for purchase as a PDF on the ISO website: http://www.iso.org/iso/home/store/catalogue_tc/catalogue_detail.htm?csnumber=2130

1.3.4 Year/Date of reference

A year or fuller date (e.g., day/month/year) is essential to identifying a moving image Work and, where applicable, its Variants. A common use of year/date is chronological ordering of lists of Works and their Variants.[54] As explained below, these guidelines recommend, where possible, applying two qualifiers to a Date element: Date Type, and Date Precision.

There is no primary or "preferred" year or date except within the context of the type of Work and, where applicable, its Variants. That is, typically, an original date of release or broadcast is essential for identifying a moving image Work and its Variants. In the absence of a release or broadcast date, provide a year of creation or production.

Record any dates associated with the Work or its Variants formatted according to ISO 8601 or other available resources, such as EDTF (Extended Date Time Format). ISO 8601 prescribes that dates should be formatted hierarchically as Year-Month-Day, using this convention: YYYY-MM-DD. Example: 2015-07-04. This structure eliminates confusion when dates can be formatted with month before day or day before month (e.g., 07/04/2015 or 04/7/2015). Using the ISO format makes indexing and sorting more efficient. Using words (June 11, 2004), while perhaps user-friendly in its narrative construction, are difficult to index as dates. Mixing date formats causes confusion in data retrieval and for users!

Where full dates are not known use Year-Month YYYY-MM or just Year YYYY, as systems permit.

1.3.4.1 Date Type

The year or date should be associated with an event in the life cycle of the Work or its Variants (see 1.4.2 Events). If your system supports it, apply a "Date Type" qualifier to make the date or year purpose clear. Date Type terms should be derived from a controlled vocabulary. For a list of initial terms, see Appendix D.4 Event Types.

For Works, the date is typically related to events such as its creation, availability (i.e., publication, release, distribution, broadcast or transmission) or registration (e.g., for copyright or intellectual property purposes).

For Variants, the date is typically related to its creation, availability, registration or bestowal of an award (e.g. the subtitled version of a foreign language motion picture, or a Variant of the original Work, is the entity nominated for an award).

More than one year or date may be associated with a Work or its Variants. For example, in the case of a Work comprising segments produced in different years (for example, a home movie); list the years, if known, e.g., 1955, 1956, 1959.[55]

Similarly, a Work may have a production date of 1962, a copyright date of December 1963, and a first release date of January 1964. Apply the Date Type qualifier to clarify the purpose of each date.

---

54 EN 15907, 6.6 Year of Reference, p. 20

55 Irish Film Archive, p. 13.

1.3.4.2 Date Precision

Where possible, provide a "Date Precision" qualifier to note if the date is precise, approximate, estimated, or a range. EDTF also provides codes to denote precision. For example, an uncertain or approximate date may be formatted thus: 2004-06~-11 (year and month are approximate; day known). Using a Date Precision qualifier, this Date entry could be entered as:

Date:	2004-06-11
Date Type:	Creation
Date Precision:	Approximate

An institution may choose to use a precision qualifier for imprecise dates.

If ISO formatting and/or the Date Precision qualifier are not applied, then use consistent terms and formatting to note date approximations.

Examples:[56]

1971 or 1972	One year or the other
[1969?]	Probable Year
1969?	
Circa 1969	(with qualifying note to indicate date is probably 1969)
[Circa 1960]	Approximate Year
Circa 1960	
1960 circa	
191-	Decade certain
Decade 1910	
1910 decade	
[191-?]	Probable decade
1910 decade	(with qualifying note to indicate that date is probable decade date)
Decade 1910	(as above)
between 1906 and 1912	Use for time spans, the outside limits of which can be precisely determined
1906 1912	(where system has date start/ date end functionality)

In instances such as these, a note should be given which further explains the Date.

Example:[57]
[Personal record. Eugene Meyer family. Family camping trip through the Canadian Rockies]. -- US, 1926.

56 FIAF, 3.5.4, p. 64.
57

[Note] Year from notes accompanying item, attached to inventory, and from Merlo Pusey's Eugene Meyer, (New York: Knopf, 1974), p.195

1.3.5 Language(s)

A moving image Work is conceived and presented in a particular language or set of languages. Changes to the original language(s), as in the case of dubbing, are considered minor changes and can constitute a Variant of a moving image Work.

Alternatively, such minor changes can constitute a new Manifestation of a moving image Work rather than a Variant. Institutions using cataloguing structures that do not distinguish Variant level information (for example, those that create records primarily at the Manifestation level), should apply this alternative. (See guidelines for language in a Manifestation: 2.3.3 Language)

Indicate the language(s) (e.g., Italian) and usage(s) (e.g., Italian intertitles) in which the moving image Variant/Manifestation is written, spoken or sung, if applicable. More than one language can occur in different forms, depending on how the content is expressed (e.g., French dialogue and English subtitles).

1.3.5.1 Language Term

Record the language(s) by taking the most suitable value(s) from a controlled list of languages.

This can be an in-house list but it is preferable to use a standard language list such as the ISO 639 codes, including ISO 639-2, 693-3 and 639-5 (http://www.loc.gov/standards/iso639-2/langhome.html).

Optionally, record the language code as found in ISO 639, where allowable.

If no language can be determined, the information can be omitted or indicated by a value of "unknown".

1.3.5.2 Usage type

Record the usage type of a language (e.g. spoken, intertitles, subtitles, etc.) by taking the most suitable term from a controlled list elaborated in-house or referring to an existing authoritative list. See D.6 Language Usage Types.

Optionally, record language usage type at the Manifestation/Item level (see 2.3.3 Language). A value of "original" can be added to the Language element here to indicate that statements made about the language(s) for a particular Manifestation/Item are indicative of the language(s) of the "original" Work.[58]

58 The indication of "original" values at the Manifestation level follows EN 15907 attributes of a Manifestation, pp. 10-11

1.3.6 Content description (synopses, shotlists, etc) [59]

Write a concise, objective, non-critical summary of the content of the moving image Work and/or Variant. Content descriptions can be synposes, brief TV guide-like one sentence description, shotlists, etc. There can be more than one type of content description in the record.

The content description should be written in a style that is easy to read. It should not include technical terms, abbreviations, or allusions significant to a specialist audience. Avoid slang expressions and colloquialisms fashionable at the time of writing, and, where several cataloguers are viewing independently, they should, ideally, try to achieve a common written style. Descriptions should be objective and not include subjective commentary on the quality of the content. If acceptable summaries are already available in secondary sources, cataloguers may use these, instead of taking the time to prepare summaries of their own.[60] If using summaries exactly as written, put the summary in quotes and note the source of the summary.

Example[61]

> An historical drama set in 16th century England in which King Henry VIII divorces his wife, Catherine of Aragon, and marries Anne Boleyn, a former lady-in-waiting, who is in love with Sir Thomas Wyatt. After several years, Henry becomes infatuated with Lady Jane Seymour and arranges to have the innocent Anne found in a compromising situation with Sir Thomas. Anne is tried for infidelity, found guilty, and executed.

Example

> Donald Graham, millionaire ex-convict, plans revenge on society
> figure John Cabin Brand, whom he blames for the death of his daughter.

A content description may also be a shotlist or listing of the contents of an aggregate Work/Variant (see Appendix E, Aggregates).

Example:[62]

> Title: Pathe News [Excerpts No. 6]
> Contents: "Newest U.S. Submarine Goes into Commission," Pathe News No. 60 [1921] (160 ft.) -- "Span of New Memorial Bridge to Connect N.H. and Maine," Pathe News No. 57 [1923] (72 ft.) -- "Celebrate 300th Anniversary of Settling of Portsmouth," Pathe News No. 69 [1923] (99 ft.) -- "World's Largest Sub Takes First Plunge," Pathe News No. 93 [1927], (c) 21Nov27; MP4478 (134 ft.) -- "New Memorial Bridge between N.H. and Maine!" Pathe News No. 70 [1923] (105 ft.) -- "Launch Largest Submarine Cruiser," Pathe Sound News No. 1 [1930], (c) 29Dec29; MP1025 (80 ft.).

---

59 Adapted from YCR, 1.2.16 Summary of genre, form, and subject matter of work, p. 38.

60 FIAF 7.2.12. Summary

61 Ibid.

62 FIAF 7.2.16. Contents

Title: Victorian Cinema: 4: Bamforth/Riley/Hepworth
Contents:
Weary Willie (1898) (78ft),
Catching the Milk Thief (1899) (140ft)
The Tramp and the Baby's Bottle (1899) (214ft),
Women's Rights (1899) (289ft),
A Kiss in the Tunnel (1899) (367ft),
Boy's Cricket Match and Fight (1900) (475ft),
[... real example shortened]
End

Title: Magnificent Reproductions of the Great Yorkshire Show in Bradford (1901)

Mitchell & Kenyon 641: Panning shot across a road to the Yorkshire Agricultural Society building with a diffuse crowd of people in front of the building. As the shot passes the building, a number of people can be seen sitting down, including mothers with babies and some older people (00.36). Cut to a close-up shot of the building, with a sign reading "The Yorkshire Agricultural Society. Established 1837" (00.45). Cut to a horse-drawn cart spraying some sort of liquid on the path as it moves along. Lettering on the back of the cart reads "Bradford City Council no. 30" (00.58). Cut to wide steps, with a number of smartly dressed men walking down them (presumably entering the show) (01.14). Cut to a shot of the blades of a windmill as they turn (01.23). Cut to a general shot of the show, with crowds and various stalls (02.07). A marquee in the background has the sign "R. Hornsby & Sons Ltd., Grantham". Another sign reads "Marshall. Sons & Co.". Chimneys and houses can be seen in the background (02.27min).

The content description can be based on a viewing of the work, accompanying documentation, or secondary sources, but the source should be clearly noted.

For unedited Works, where time and resources permit, each scene should be summarized. If there are shots of particular significance or interest – of, for example, prominent people or places – these should be recorded. Otherwise a general description of scenes and sequences will suffice.[63]

If applicable, add information about the content of the moving image Variant where it differs from the content of the Work.

1.3.6.1 Content Description Type

Include a qualifying keyword or otherwise denote the type of summary (e.g. Synopsis, Shotlist, Review).[64]

63 Irish Film Archive, p. 23.
64 EN 15907, 6.17.3 Elements, Description type, p. 30.

1.3.7 Notes

Notes for moving image Works/Variants are annotations providing additional information or clarification relating specifically to Works/Variants attributes and relationships.[65] See Appendix B, Cataloguer's Notes.

1.3.8 History

Record historical information about events of interest in the creation of the original moving image Work/Variant that is of value for your users, such as censorship history, production versions, and the like. This historical information may be recorded in association with instances of Events or Agents.

If desired, institutions may include historical information that crosses over into being about the Manifestation(s) and/or Item(s). This may be done where there is value to the user in keeping all the information together for research or clarification purposes rather than across disparate Manifestation and Item records. This may also be applied where no History fields exist in an institution's system at Manifestation or Item levels, or a no hierarchy one level structure is used.

Example:

> Christopher Columbus (United Kingdom, 1949, David MacDonald)[66]
> There are three documented versions. Version one: which has the shortened reels 3A and 3B; Version two: which has the shorter ending; Version three: which has the long ending (this script is based on the full length reels 3A and 3B and on the short ending, as this is the export version.
> The short ending (version two) has Columbus reinstated by the King and Queen, him leaving their presence and telling Juana he will be remembered longer than the monarchs as he walks down a corridor. The longer version (version three) has a more American feel with two sailors informing Columbus of the great nation his discovery will give rise to, complete with quotes from Jefferson, Lincoln and Roosevelt.

1.3.8.1 Custodial history

If desired, write a brief custodial history of the Work/Variant if known, particularly for rare and unique materials. Indicate the current holding institution of the original or master material if known.

Information on the provenance of the specific Items in an archive's collection should be included in the Item sections.

65 Based on RDA 2.20.1.Basic Instructions on Making Notes on Manifestations or Items
66 Abridged version of fuller Work History note from BFI CID record for the film

1.3.8.2 Censorship history

Document information related to the censorship history of a Work/Variant, including:[67]

- any events in which a Manifestation/Item of a Work/Variant was evaluated by a censorship body or an accredited rating agency
- the geographic region for which the verdict is (was) valid
- any identifier issued by the agency uniquely identifying the act of rating or censorship and associated documents such as censorship visa or rating certificates
- the outcome of the act of rating or censorship

Example:

À bout de souffle (France, 1960, Jean-Luc Godard)

In Italy, this film has three different theatrical distributions, corresponding to three different visas ("visto di censura") from the official censorship body (Ufficio di revisione cinematografica).[68]
Censored Variant: Theatrical distribution in Italy – censorship visa n. 32329 – date: 1960-07-05 – Length 2463m – original French – not for under 16 years
Dubbed, Censored Variant: Theatrical distribution in Italy – censorship visa n. 57609 – date: 1971-01-23 – Length 2440m. – Italian
Dubbed, Censored Variant: Theatrical distribution in Italy– censorship visa n. 64662 – date: 1974-05-20 – Length 2430m. – Italian dubbed

1.3.8.3 Other Work/Variant History

Any other relevant information or clarifications pertaining to the Work/Variant. For example:

- any changes of director, crew, or cast part-way through production

  Tosca (Italy, 1939, Karl Koch)
  The film was started by Jean Renoir, but after beginning, Renoir escaped to France because of World War II. The film was completed by his assistant Karl Koch, with Luchino Visconti as assistant.

- any demise of members of the cast or crew associated with the production

  Foolish Wives (USA, 1922, Erich von Stroheim)
  Actor Rudolph Christians died in mid-shooting; replaced by Robert Edenson who is used mainly as a double.

- explanations regarding length of time between production and release, e.g., due to funding issues, an initial banning, delayed release due to sensitivity over subject matter and world events, etc.

67 EN 15907, 6.13 Decision event, pp. 26-27.
68 http://www.italiataglia.it/tagli_rassegna/_bout_de_souffle_

La porta del cielo (Italy, 1945, Vittorio De Sica)
The shooting of the film lasted almost one year (February–November 1944) throughout the period of Nazi occupation of Rome and served as an excuse to hide and protect Jewish people, anti-fascists, etc...

La grande illusion (France, 1937, Jean Renoir)
The shooting of the film lasted two years (1935-1936) and the first projection was in 1937.

- any other information relevant to the history of the Work and its production

Christopher Columbus (United Kingdom, 1949, David MacDonald)
Location shooting in Barbados was fraught with difficulties. The re-created ship stuck on launch, was then later rammed, suffered mechanical failure and finally caught fire. The stand-in ship was then lost at sea twice. Location shooting was hampered by the heat and the local gaol had to be used to keep the Technicolor film cool. There was also a troublesome parrot that would shout "tea break" during a dramatic scene.[69]

1.4 Relationships of a Work/Variant (links/associations with other entities/records)

A relationship associates an instance of a Work/Variant with another instance of an entity. Entities are described in subsequent sections, but examples of entities are people or companies associated with a Work/Variant (eg, studio, director, cast), events (copyright registration), subjects (other Works/Variants are about the same subject), and records.

Relationships can be implemented in many ways, depending on the purpose, the modelling paradigm, or architectural constraints of the chosen platform. These guidelines are intended to be data structure neutral.[70] Therefore, these guidelines cannot prescribe exactly how to demonstrate relationships. Instead they recommend that certain relationships be established without instruction on how precisely those links be made manifest, i.e., whether by physical associative record linking or "see also" text conventions.

A Work may have relationships with the following:

- Agent(s)
- Event(s)
- Subject(s)/Genre(s)/Form(s)
- Variant(s)
- Manifestation(s)
- Other (including other Works)

69 Abridged version of fuller Work History note from BFI CID record for the film.
70 EN 15907 8.1 Relationships. General

A Variant may have relationships with the following:

- Agent(s)
- Event(s)
- Subject(s)/Genre(s)/Form(s)
- Work(s)
- Manifestation(s)
- Other (including other Variants)

1.4.1 Agents (e.g. Cast, Credits, Person, Organisation, etc.)

An Agent is defined as an entity that is involved in the creation, realisation, curation or exploitation of a Work/Variant and who is considered to have major responsibility for, or be of major importance to, the Work/Variant. Typical distinctions between Agent types are Person, Corporate Body, Family and Person Group.[71] This includes cast and credits for the Work/Variant.

Agent(s) may also have relationships to an instance of a specific Event or of an "Other" relationship in connection with the Work/Variant.

Because responsibility for moving image materials is most often complex and highly diverse, institutions - particularly those with special interests - should determine the types of activities they wish to include. These activities may vary from institution to institution according to the types of moving image material held. For example, an institution holding primarily television material may consider the activity of producer more important than that of director. Institutions whose collections are primarily composed of motion picture material may value equally the activities of directors and producers. Provide access to Agents when they have made an important contribution to the particular Work or Variant, even when the type of responsibility (credit function) is one that may not be considered major in other Works/Variants or types of Works/Variants.[72]

Agents may be described in two ways: as discrete index points, and/or merged into one field where the credits are listed in order of role importance or as transcribed from the Work.

Optionally, record multiple instances of Agent, e.g., cast and credits, associated with aggregated Works/Variants (See E.6 Credits (i.e. Agents) for Aggregates).

For recording the attributes of Agents (e.g. first name, last name, nationality, etc.), refer to authoritative sources such as AACR2, applicable RDA chapters for recording attributes of Persons, Families, and Corporate Bodies or tools such as the Virtual International Authority File (VIAF) (viaf.org), Library of Congress Name Authority File (authorities.loc.gov), Library of Congress Linked Data Service (id.loc.gov), Getty Union List of Artists Names (ULAN), International Standard Name Identifier (ISNI).

71 EN 15907, 5.1 Agent

72 1991 FIAF Cataloguing Rules for Film Archives – Statements of Responsibility, p. 35.

It is also recommended where possible to register key Agents with any of the aforementioned authority bodies if they are not already included.

Optionally, if the Agent is credited under a name that is not identical with the preferred name from an authority file, record the name as used in the current instance of the related entity.

Examples:

Bob Robertson (pseudonym/screen name used by the director Sergio Leone at the beginning of the career)

Terence Hill (pseudonym/screen name used by the actor Mario Girotti in the most known part of his career)

Sofia Lazzaro (first pseudonym/screen name used by the actress Sophia Loren, whose birth name is Sofia Villani Scicolone).

1.4.1.1 Agent Activity

This describes the activity or role of the Agent in relation to the moving image Work/Variant (e.g. credit terms).

Record one or more Agent Activity terms, for example, "animator," "cast," "choreographer," etc., to express the nature of the agent's relationship to the Work or Variant. Choose the single most specific term, if possible. Selection should be made from a controlled list of terms, such as the FIAF Glossary of Filmographic Terms[73].

If no suggested terms apply, compose a term to describe the relationship between the Agent and the Work/Variant being catalogued. If the relationship is ambiguous, use a value to indicate this, for example, "unknown" or "on-screen participant" to indicate a person appearing on screen in a capacity that is indeterminate or not covered by typical terms.[74] Optionally, when the role performed by an Agent is probable but not certain, provide the function name followed by a question mark.

Besides the principal Agent Activity suggested, institutions, particularly those with special interests, should create and apply in-house value lists of other specific Agent Types, which may vary from institution to institution.

Record in a note any additional details that cannot be expressed through controlled terms. (e.g. "appears only in final scene", etc.). If a name is known to be fictitious, or requires clarification, make a note giving the actual name.

Give the Agent(s) and Agent Activity in the terms and language in which they appear, either in the sources of information or in the language of the institution, or both. If more than one Agent is associated with a particular role connected with a Work/Variant or

73 http://www.fiafnet.org/publications/GlossaryMasterComboMarch2015.html.htm

74 List of relator terms are a combination of those found in YCR, 1.3.2. Other creators, pp. 42-43; and, OLAC TF, Part II, Core Attributes and Relationships, Commonly-Occurring Roles, pp. 16-18.

Event, where possible or desirable, record the names in the order indicated by the sequence, layout, or typography of the names on the source of information. Preserving the ordering of the credited persons should be determined by the requirements of individual institutions.[75]

Examples:

Les Enfants du paradis
réalisation, Marcel Carné
scenario et dialogue, Jacques Prevert
musique, Maurice Thiriet

OR

Enfants du paradis, Les
director, Marcel Carné
script and dialogue, Jacques Prevert
music, Maurice Thiriet

Star wars
Director, George Lucas
Executive Producer, George Lucas
Producer, Gary Kurtz
Screenplay, George Lucas

If Agents are added as index points rather than listed or described in order of importance, an organisation may choose to put the Agent Activity or role term(s) at the end of the name.

Examples:

Les Enfants du paradis
Carné, Marcel, réalisation
Prevert, Jacques, scenario, dialogue
Thiriet, Maurice, musique

Star wars
Lucas, George, director, executive producer, screenplay
Kurtz, Gary, producer

1.4.2 Events (e.g., IPR registration, screenings, awards, etc.)[76]

An Event characterises occurrences in the lifecycle of a moving image Work or its Variants. Instances of any Event type can have Agent and "Other" relationships.

Record one or more Event type, for example, "publication," "copyright/IPR registration," "festival showing," etc., to express the nature of the Event's relationship to the

75 FIAF, 1.6.2, pp. 36-37.
76 EN 15907 5.2 Event

Work/Variant. Selection should be made from a controlled list of terms. A suggested list, which is open and not exhaustive, can be found in D.4 Event Types.

1.4.3 Subject/Genre/Form terms

Provide access to the Work by means of subjects (or subject identifiers) that describe the content of the Work (i.e., what the Work is *about*). Use an existing data value standard such as *Library of Congress Subject Headings (LCSH)*.[77] Alternatively, or additionally, use standards such as Universal Decimal Classification (UDC), Dewey Decimal Classification (DDC), or equivalent in country in which you are working, or an in-house data value standard.

In addition, access to the Work can be provided by means of genre(s) and/or form(s) (or identifiers) of which the Work is an example (i.e., what the Work *is*). Form describes the format and/or purpose of a Work, e.g., "non-fiction", "short" and "animation" are particular forms or identifiers. Genre describes categories of Works, characterized by similar plots, themes, settings, situations, and characters. Examples of genres are "westerns" and "thrillers".[78] Use an existing and widely used data value standard such as *Library of Congress Thesaurus for Genre/Form Terms in Libraries and Archives (LCGFT)*[79], or equivalent in country where work is being done, or an in-house controlled vocabulary genre thesaurus.

Examples:

Main title	A trip down Market Street before the fire / [Miles Brothers].[80]
Published/Created	United States. [United States : Miles Brothers, 1906].
Summary	The following is a scene-by-scene description of the film: [Frame: 0300 (part 1)] The film begins looking northeast on Market Street just west of the intersection of Hyde, Grove and 8th streets. The dark building at right is the Odd Fellows Hall and the grey building beyond (across 8th St.) is the Grant Building (1905). A white postal service automobile is at left center. The three large buildings receding down Market Street at left are [0319 (part 1)] the Murphy Building (1889), [0353 (part 1)] the Donohoe Building (1890), and the Flood Building (1905). [etc.; this is an excerpt from the full record.]
Subjects	Market Street (San Francisco, Calif.) Street-railroads--California--San Francisco. Horse-drawn vehicles--California--San Francisco. City traffic--California--San Francisco. Pedestrians--California--San Francisco. Automobiles--California--San Francisco.

---

77 Adapted from YCR, 1.3.3. Subjects, pp. 43-45

78 Frequently Asked Questions about Library of Congress Genre/Form Terms for Library and Archival Materials (LCGFT), Revised June 6, 2011, http://www.loc.gov/catdir/cpso/genre_form_faq.pdf

79 http://id.loc.gov/authorities/genreForms

80 For full record see http://lccn.loc.gov/00694408

Form/Genre	Actualities (Motion pictures) Short films. Silent films. Nonfiction films.

Main title	Mardi Gras parade -- US : Thomas A. Edison, Inc. [producer, distributor], [190-?].
Summary	Early actuality footage, shot from a single location on a street in New Orleans, showing a Mardi Gras parade. Mule drawn floats, children and adults in costumes, and brass bands march down the street, as crowds of spectators mill about the sidewalks, sometimes spilling into the street.
Subjects	1. Carnival -- Louisiana -- New Orleans. 2. Parades -- Louisiana – New Orleans. 3. Holidays.
Genres	1. Actualities. 2. Shorts.

Main title	British Canadian Pathe news. No. 83A / L.E. Ouimet presents. -- CA : British Canadian Pathe News [producer], 1919 ; CA : Specialty Film Ltd. [distributor], 1919.
Contents	London: Ilford Municipal Market proves great success (43 ft.) -- Yarmouth, Eng.: Happy hours by the sea (46 ft.) -- Lauzon, Que.: World's largest drydock (84 ft.) -- Toronto: Cycle racing at Exhibition Park (218 ft.) -- Kingston: [Geo. Vernot, Canadian swimmer, demonstrates strokes] (140 ft.) -- Fresno, Cal.: [Staged train wreck at fair] (69 ft.) -- Gary, Ind.: [Federal troops in big steel centers as result of recent riots] (150 ft.) -- Getting together, an animated cartoon by Bert Green (65 ft.) – A Review of events in Great Britain: Yarmouth: Deutschland, German Navy ship, now tourist attraction; London: "Pussyfoot" Johnson trying to make Britain "dry;" Doncaster: horse racing; Manchester: statue of Abraham Lincoln unveiled, gift of the U.S. to England's great Cotton City (123 ft.).
Subjects	1. Markets -- England -- London. 2. London (England) -- Description. 3. Seaside resorts -- England. 4. Yarmouth (Isle of Wight) -- Description. 5. Drydocks -- Canada. 6. Saint Henri (Quebec) -- Description. 7. Bicycle racing -- Canada. 8. Swimming -- Canada. 9. Strikes and lockouts -- Steel industry -- United States. 10. Prohibition -- England. 11. Horse-racing -- England. 12. Doncaster (South Yorkshire) -- Description. 13. Lincoln, Abraham, 1809-1865 -- Statues. 14. Manchester (Greater Manchester) -- Description.
Genre	1. Newsreels.

Main title	O Beijo da mulher aranha = Kiss of the spider woman / director, Hector Babenco ; producer, David Weisman ; screenplay, Leonard Schrader. -- BR : HB Filmes [producer], 1895 ; US Sugarloaf Films [producer], 1985 ; US : Island Alive [distributor], 1985.
Summary	Molina, a homosexual window-trimmer convicted on a morals charge, shares a dreary prison cell with Valentin, a clandestinely-held politically active journalist who has been endlessly tortured by prison authorities in a vain attempt to extract information about his activities. Both men could not be farther apart in personal attitudes, lifestyles, and emotional makeup: Molina is a glib raconteur, who dwells in a fantasy world of glamorous movies from yesteryear, of romantic screen heroes and tragic heroines. Valentin is a self-disciplined intellectual who is devoted to the cause of human rights and his political concerns. [etc. ; this is an excerpt from the full record]
Subjects	1. Prisoners -- Drama. 2. Interpersonal relations -- Drama. 3. Homosexuality, Male -- Drama. 4. Political prisoners -- Drama. 5. Torture -- Drama.
Genres	1. Drama. 2. Features.

1.4.4 Other relationships[81]

If desired or appropriate, express relationships that are not covered by the Agent, Subject, and Event relationships, including all kinds of aggregation and re-use of Works and their Variants. (See Appendix E, Aggregates.)

Commonly-occurring relationships include:[82]

- Work(s) that the moving image Work is based on (e.g. moving images adapted from novels, plays, etc.)

  The grapes of wrath (USA, 1940, John Ford), based on the homonymous novel by John Steinbeck (1939).

- Work(s) that the moving image Work is a performance of (moving image recordings made of live stage presentations of music, plays, dance, etc.

  Pink Floyd: live at Pompeii (Belgium,West Germany, France, 1972, Adrian Maben), concert filmed in the old Pompeii amphitheatre.

- Work(s) that the moving image Work forms part of (e.g. series/serials, aggregations/compilations)

  Fantômas contre Fantômas (Serial in 4 episodes, Louis Feuillade 1914, production Société des Etablissements Gaumont).

81 EN 15907 8.5 HasAsSubject; YCR, 1.2.7 Relationships With Other Moving Image Works or Other Kinds of Works

82 OLAC TF, Part I, Moving Image Work Definition and Boundaries, Commonly-Occurring Relationships, p. 16.

Fiddlesticks, Ub Iwerks, 1930, episode of the animation series Flip the Frog (Celebrity Pictures, distr. Metro Goldwyn-Mayer, 1930-1933 (38 issues).

- Work(s) that the moving image Work has a sequential relationship with (e.g. sequels, prequels, serials)

  The Godfather Part I
  The Godfather Part II
  The Godfather Part III
  Francis Ford Coppola (USA, 1972- 1974-1990)

- Work(s) about the moving image Work (e.g. documentary about the making of a feature film or TV programme)

  La ciociara quarant'anni dopo (Italy, 2001, Stefano Landini), documentary on the restoration of La ciociara (Italy, 1960, Vittorio De Sica).

  Reise nach Metropoli (Germany, 2009, Artem Demenok), documentary on the restoration of Metropolis (Fritz Lang, 1927).

- Work(s) that are promotional material of the moving image Work (e.g. Trailers)

  Wuthering Heights (Film Trailer) (USA, 1939) is the trailer for Wuthering Heights (USA, 1939, William Wyler)

- Non-moving image Works that the moving image Work has a relationship with (e.g. Books, articles, scripts, posters, documents, etc)

  Kes (United Kingdom, 1969, Ken Loach), book "Life after Kes: an anthology of the film Kes", by Simon W. Golding. GET Publishing, 2005. ISBN. 0954879333

  Land and freedom (United Kingdom, 1995, Ken Loach), script Land and freedom (c.1993) (script for 'Land and freedom', with opening sequence different from earlier scripts).

  Carry on camping (United Kingdom, 1969, Gerald Thomas), archival documents - general production correspondence including notes from the pre-production meeting, studio agreement, final screen credits, and draft trailer script).

  The wicked lady (United Kingdom, 1945, Leslie Arliss), costume

Record one or more "Other" relationship type terms to express the nature of the relationship to the Work/Variant, choosing the most specific term possible from a controlled list of values , for example, "based on," "contained in," etc. . A suggested list, which is open and not exhaustive, can be found in Appendix D.17.1 Work/Variant Other Relationship Types.

Or, compose a term to describe the relationship between the Work being catalogued and the related Work.

In a note, add any additional information concerning the relationship considered relevant.

Describe or demonstrate Work-to-Work relationships through linking to the Work identifier of the related Work, through the usage of relator terms, or according to the confines of the institution's data structure.

Remember, a Work based on a pre-existing Work should be identified as a Variant of the same Work unless it has been so significantly changed as to have become a new related Work.[83] See 1.1.1 Boundaries between Works and 1.1.2 Boundaries between Works and Variants/Manifestations for determining when a Work should be identified as a new, but related Work and when it should be identified as a Variant of the original Work.

1.4.5 Variants

Express the relationship between a moving image Work and a moving image Variant (e.g., Part/part of). Describe or demonstrate Work-to-Variant relationships through linking to the Work identifier, through the usage of relator terms, or according to the confines of your data structure.

1.4.6 Manifestations

Express the relationship between a moving image Work or Variant and a moving image Manifestation (e.g., Part/part of). Describe or demonstrate Work-to-Manifestation relationships through linking to the Work identifier, through the usage of relator terms, or according to the confines of your data structure.

83 YCR, 1.1.7 Works based on previous works, pp. 24-25.

2. Moving Image Manifestations

2.0 Definition

A moving image Manifestation is the embodiment of a moving image Work/Variant. Manifestations usually include all analogue, digital and online media associated with a particular embodiment of a Work/Variant.

A Manifestation possesses common characteristics with respect to shared intellectual content and physical format, e.g., releases, broadcasts, etc.

It may be whole or incomplete or a fragment.

A Manifestation is not exclusively bound to a single Work/Variant, since it can be an aggregate for reasons connected to the publication, to the commercial release, or for mere convenience. A Manifestation can therefore be associated or linked to more than one Work/Variant, where an institution's system allows.

For Aggregate Manifestations see Appendix E, Aggregates.

2.1 Boundaries between Manifestations

The boundaries between one Manifestation and another are drawn on the basis of two criteria: changes in the publication context and changes in format.[84] The distinction between one Manifestation and another can be made according to one of the two criteria or the presence of both.

2.1.1 Changes in the publication context

If the embodiment of a Work/Variant involves contextual changes, related to the publication or release process, the resulting product is a new Manifestation, e.g., a change from theatrical release to home video distribution.

In this case, create a new Manifestation and characterise it according to a controlled list. A suggested list, which is open and not exhaustive, can be found at D.5 Manifestation Types

2.1.2 Changes in the format

If the embodiment of a Work/Variant involves changes in format, the resulting product is a new Manifestation, e.g., a change from 70mm to 35mm.

Create a new Manifestation when there is evidence of at least one (or more than one) of the following changes from the original format:

- Changes to the physical format or the digital file on which it is fixed;
- Changes to the display characteristics (i.e. in aspect ratio, sound or colour characteristics, etc.);
- Change in the container (i.e. cassette to cartridge as container for a tape).

Include and describe any of the distinguishing physical changes according to the guidelines in 2.3.4 Format.

The example below shows a number of possible Manifestations of the original Italian version of Il gattopardo (Italy, France, Luchino Visconti, 1963).

Example: change in format

Il gattopardo (Italy, France, Luchino Visconti, 1963) [85]
Theatrical release, 35mm, Cinemascope – aspect ratio 2,35 : 1
Theatrical release, 70mm, Cinemascope – aspect ratio 2,20 : 1

Example: change in format and publication context

---

84 The definitions that individuate a "new" M. I. Manifestation and distinguish one from another are mainly based on YEE 2008 (draft), 81.

85 Information about the cinematographic process and aspect ratio is taken from: http://www.imdb.it/title/tt0057091/technical.

Il gattopardo (Luchino Visconti, 1963)
Home video publication, DVD – aspect ratio 2,21 :1 – Medusa Video, Italia, 00/00/2009

In-house copying of an institution's holding onto a different format, e.g. a video transfer of a 35mm film does not necessitate creation of a new Manifestation. In this case there is also the option of simply creating an Item for the copy, and linking it to the same Manifestation as the source Item.

This option depends on an institution's policy. Some may choose always to create a new Manifestation, whilst others may decide to create a new Manifestation where change in format and change in distribution/publication coincide but just create a new Item where change in format is as a result of in-house copying.

It is for an institution to decide on which approach it prefers and apply consistently.

2.2 Attributes of a Manifestation

2.2.1 Manifestation Type

As previously mentioned, a Manifestation is defined on the basis of two criteria: changes in the publication context and changes in format. The element Manifestation Type describes the specific type of change.

The Manifestation Type is expressed by a phrase denoting the relationship between the Manifestation and the associated Work/Variant, for example, "pre-release," "theatrical distribution," "not for release," "original," etc.

Record the Manifestation Type by taking the most suitable term from a controlled list. A suggested list, which is open and not exhaustive, can be found in D.5 Manifestation Types.

If it is impossible to determine the specific Manifestation Type the information can be omitted or indicated by a value of "unknown."

Statements made about Language, Format and/or Extent may have an added value of "original" to indicate characteristics of an "original Work," where such a concept is required or desired.[86] Associating the value of "original" with a particular Manifestation indicates it has privileged status in relation to other possible Manifestations.

2.3 Elements of a Manifestation

2.3.1 Identifier

Create an unambiguous reference to the Manifestation, such as a specific standard

86 The indication of "original" values at the Manifestation level follows EN 15907 attributes of a Manifestation, pp. 10-11.

number issued by an official body (i.e. V-ISAN[87] or DOI[88]), or a system-automated assigned ID number. These should be different identifiers than those for Works/Variants, since they are for specific embodiments of the Work/Variant.

If one or more identifiers are available, record each according to its standardised syntax, where allowable. The following examples reflect both 3 and 4 level hierarchies, i.e. ones that use Variants and ones that do not have Variants but utilise Manifestations instead.

Example:

Lola rennt (Germany, 1998, Tom Tykwer)
Work identifier: ISAN 0000-0000-606A-0000-0-0000-0000-3
Variant identifier (original German): ISAN 0000-0000-606A-0000-0-0000-0002-0
Manifestation identifier: Home video publication (2007) – Run Lola Run – DVD – English – V-ISAN: ISAN 0000-0000-606A-0000-0-0000-0001-1 (DVD-31943)

Shichinin no samurai (Japan, 1954, Akira Kurosawa)
Work identifier: ISAN 0000-0001-61AE-0000-1-0000-0001-W
Variant identifier (Dubbed Spanish – Castellano): *Los Siete Samurai*: ISAN 0000-0001-61AE-0000-1-0000-0001-W

Les chevaliers du ciel (France, 2005, Gérard Pirès)
Manifestation identifier: Home video publication – DVD – Fox Pathé Europa (publisher) – 2006 – ISAN 0000-0001-8CFA-0000-I-0000-000-

8 1/2 (Italy, 1962, Federico Fellini) Otto e mezzo – Alternative title of the Work
Work identifier: ISAN 0000-0000-161F-0000-W-0000-0000-F
Manifestation identifier: V- ISAN 0000-0000-161F-0000-W-0000-0002-B – Italian (spoken); Japanese (subtitles) – DVD – Blu-ray – 2013/01/11 – Japan)

2.3.1.1 Identifier Type

If an institution's system allows, as with the Work/Variant Identifiers a "Type" can be applied with an Identifier to define the source of the Identifier.

2.3.2 Title

Record at least one title, identifying phrase, or name for the Manifestation Title. This is a transcribed element, reflecting the actual title as it appears on screen. The original release title would be added under the Work/Variant Title field.

If multiple titles are recorded, where allowable, associate a "Title Type" to a title for differentiation between the various types of titles (see 2.3.2.1 Title Type and A.2 Title Types).

87 The V-ISAN represents the third segment of the ISAN number, which consists of a 96-bits number structured as follows: the first is the root, which identifies the work, the second is the episode section, which identifies the part within a multi-part work, the third is the so-called version section, which identifies variants and *Manifestations* (particularly as far as format changes and "media embodiments", such as Blu-Ray, digital files, tapes, etc.., are concerned): see http://www.isan.org/docs/isan_user_guide.pdf, Version 2.2.2. February 2012, 13/49.
88 DOI (= Digital Object Identifier): see http://www.doi.org/.

The title of a Manifestation can sometimes differ, either slightly or wholly from the title of the Variant or Work to which it is linked. This may be the case, for example, with the acquisition of an incomplete Manifestation lacking a title or with a title added by the source of the acquisition.

See Appendix A.1 Title for further titling details and information.

For creating titles for untitled or unidentified entities see A.2.5 Supplied/Devised Titles

See Appendix E.4 for titling of Aggregates.

For guidance on wording, order, spelling, punctuation, accentuation and capitalisation, see Chapter 0. Preliminary Notes.

For sources of information for the Manifestation Title, see Section 0.3 Sources of Information.

2.3.2.1 Title Type

Where relevant for an institution, if the Manifestation includes multiple titles, such as a title in another language for a dubbed or subtitled variant, record the relevant titles and associate a "Title Type" to each title for differentiation between the various types of titles (see Appendix A, Titles and Title Types).

2.3.3 Language

"Language" should ideally be presented as a set of two elements: the language term, and its usage in a particular Manifestation. Language can be present in a Manifestation as written, spoken or sung. Its usage qualifies whether the specific language is dialogue, dubbed, subtitles, intertitles, etc.

2.3.3.1 Language terms

Where possible, record the language(s) using the full form of name, e.g., French, Italian, etc. rather than abbreviations or codes, by taking the most suitable value(s) from a controlled list. This can be an in-house list but it is preferable to use a standard language list such as ISO 639 (http://www.loc.gov/standards/iso639-2/php/code_list.php).

Optionally, record the language code as found in ISO 639.

If no language can be determined, the information can be omitted or indicated by a value of "not known".

2.3.3.2 Usage type

More than one language can occur in different forms, depending on how the content is expressed: the usage type of the languages defines the form with which the language is expressed, for example, spoken, sung, written, etc.

Record the usage type of a language by taking the most suitable value from a controlled list. A suggested list, which is open and not exhaustive, can be found in D.6 Manifestation Language Usage Types.

If usage type(s) cannot be determined, indicate a value of "unknown".

Examples:

> Caccia tragica (Italy, Giuseppe De Santis, 1947)
> Not for release (archival) – 35mm – Italian (spoken), Romanian (intertitles)
>
> New York stories, (USA, Woody Allen, Francis Ford Coppola, Martin Scorsese, 1989
> Home video publication – DVD, English (spoken); – Italian, German; English, Italian, German, French, Spanish (subtitles) – Buena Vista (publisher), 2002/05/16
>
> The Bridge. Episode 1 (Sweden, Denmark, Charlotte Sieling, 2011)
> TV broadcast – United Kingdom, 2012-04-21 - Swedish (Dialogue (original)), Danish (Dialogue (original)), English (Subtitles)

2.3.4 Format of a moving image Manifestation

As previously mentioned, a Manifestation is defined on the basis of two criteria: changes in the publication context and changes in format. The format of a Manifestation is the description of the physical artefact or the digital file on which it is fixed. The concept of format as applied to Manifestations is the "ideal" representation of all the physical items or computer files that bear the same characteristics and descend from a common Work/Variant, regardless of what is actually held in a collection.

A majority of the physical and digital description elements of moving image Manifestations are intended to be inherited by the Items, as they serve as the exemplars of Manifestations. In some databases, selection of a physical carrier type initiates provision of element fields relevant to that type at a Manifestation level, or an Item level, or both (e.g. in a 2-Level hierarchy. See "Shallow hierarchy model: 2 levels" found at 0.2.1 Elements of description across Works, Variants, Manifestations, and Items).

Ideally the information need only be recorded once irrespective of where in the data structure an institution must place it. Therefore guidelines for the treatment of high-level physical and digital description elements are explained fully in the Manifestation chapter. The Item chapter contains a detailed listing of item-specific elements. Physical properties such as Extent and Format at the Manifestation level represent the "ideal," and item-specific elements will capture where it differs from this "ideal" at the Item level.

The information about the format of a Manifestation plays a relevant role because any change in format represents a criterion to determine the boundaries between one Manifestation and another (see 2.1 Boundaries between Manifestations).

Record a new Manifestation of a Work/Variant when there is evidence of at least one, or more than one, of the following changes associated with the format:

- Changes to the physical artefact or the digital file on which it is fixed
- Changes to the display characteristics (i.e. in aspect ratio, sound or colour characteristics, etc.)
- Change in the container (i.e. cassette to cartridge as container for a tape).

In a note (See Appendix B, Cataloguer's Notes), explain the format changes used to determine the Manifestation in hand as different and "new" in comparison with any other, already identified and described Manifestation.

The description of the format of a Manifestation is articulated in the following elements:

- **Carrier type**
- **Projection characteristics**
- **Sound characteristics**
- **Colour characteristics**

2.3.4.1 Carrier type of a Manifestation

Carrier type is the medium on or the encoding format in which the Manifestation is fixed.

Its description consists of a **general carrier type**, which describes the basic properties of the Manifestation's physical format, for example, film, video tape, digital file, etc., and a **specific carrier type**, which corresponds to the gauge, in case of films and tapes, and for digital files, to the physical carrier on which the file is stored.

2.3.4.1.1 General Carrier Type

The broad media type of the Manifestation (e.g., film, video, audio, optical, digital file). Recording this high-level information will enable simple searching for only film, video, digital, etc. elements rather than searching by all possible formats and carriers.

A suggested list, which is open and not exhaustive, can be found in D.7.2 Manifestation/Item Specific Carrier Type.

For reasons of clarity and to avoid redundancy, optionally, institutions can decide to skip the general carrier type description, since it is already implicit in the specific carrier type.

2.3.4.1.2 Specific Carrier Type

Record the **specific carrier type**, by indicating

1) For film and video: the width of the film stock or of the magnetic tape on which the Manifestation is fixed;

2) For digital files: The physical carrier storing the digital file.

For digital files, it is most important for users to immediately identify the file container or wrapper (MXF, MOV, DPX, etc.) rather than the physical media on which it is stored. Physical media storing a file can change, but that does not necessarily mean that the file format has changed. For purposes of distinguishing the format change that constitutes a new Manifestation, it is the digital file format that is the important distinguishing factor. Information on the specific codecs and resolution are captured in Item elements.

For optical media, only add commercially produced media here. If the optical media is "writable" and is being used to store a digital file, put the digital file format in the general carrrier type, and the optical storage media in specific media type.

Select the value from a suitable controlled list. A suggested list, which is open and not exhaustive, can be found in D.7.2 Manifestation/Item Specific Carrier Type.

2.3.4.2 Projection characteristics of a Manifestation

The projection characteristics of a Manifestation include aspect ratio and aperture or image format.

Aspect Ratio

The aspect ratio (also known as projection ratio) is the projected image area visible on screen, expressed as a value of width to height (the value of height always being "1"), for example, 2.34:1, 2.39:1. Selection should be made from a controlled list of values. A suggested list, which is open and not exhaustive, can be found in D.7.14 Aspect Ratio.

The aspect ratio reflects the compositional intentions of the original content makers and the intended presentation of the moving image content.[89] If the aspect ratio of a Work/Variant is altered, moving image information is lost, creating a Manifestation/ Item with different moving image content.[90] The Manifestation should reflect the projected image of the Work/Variant that it represents, rather than that on the Item. Institutions may record variations in projection characteristics as Item-specifics, rather than create multiple Manifestations.

Aperture/Image Format

The actual exposed image or picture area as it appears on the moving image itself, for example Academy, Full screen, Widescreen, etc. The image format does not necessarily bear any relation to the preferred projection ratio (aspect ratio) of the moving image.[91] Selection should be made from a controlled list of terms. A suggested list, which is open and not exhaustive, can be found in D.7.15 Aperture.

89 This definition from Academy Film Archive in-house glossary of terms, and OLAC, Moving Image Works, Part 3a: Operational Definitions (08/09) (PDF Document), http://olacinc.org/drupal/capc_files/MIW_3a.pdf.
90 OLAC, Moving Image Works, Part 3a: Operational Definitions (08/09) (PDF Document), http://olacinc.org/drupal/capc_files/MIW_3a.pdf
91 This definition from Academy Film Archive in-house glossary of terms.

2.3.4.3 Sound characteristics of a Manifestation

Sound characteristics are technical specifications relating to the placement of sound on a Manifestation.[92]

Its description consists of a statement about the presence or absence of sound, and optionally, in case of presence, of the description of the method with which the sound has been fixed.

Indicate the presence or absence of sound in the Manifestation, i.e. "sound," "silent," "mute". Selection should be made from a controlled list of terms. A suggested list, which is open and not exhaustive, can be found in D.7.4 Manifestation/Item Sound Type.

Optionally, use a flag-type value indicating if the Manifestation includes recorded sound or not (i.e.: has sound: yes/no).

2.3.4.3.1 Sound systems

Describes the technical or proprietary system used to record the sound on a Manifestation/Item, for example, Dolby SR, Dolby Digital, etc. Select from a controlled list. A suggested list, which is open and not exhaustive, can be found in D.7.13 Item Sound System.

2.3.4.3.2 Sound Channel Configuration

If the Manifestation has sound, note here the track configuration (e.g., mono, stereo, etc.). Selection should be made from a controlled list of terms.

In case of presence of sound, optionally, if considered relevant, record the name of the physical principle of sound recording, for example, "Needle,", "Optical," "Magnetic," etc. Selection should be made from a controlled list of terms. A suggested list, which is open and not exhaustive, can be found in D.7.5 Manifestation/Item Sound Fixation Type.

If the Work/Variant associated with the Manifestation in hand had sound originally, but the Manifestation lacks sound, describe it as silent (or mute) and give a note to that effect.[93]

If the Work/Variant associated with the Manifestation in hand was silent originally, but the Manifestation has sound added, describe it as sound and make a note to that effect.

2.3.4.4 Colour characteristics of a Manifestation

The presence of colour(s), tone(s), etc. in a Manifestation.[94]

Colour is also the specific colours, tones, etc. (including black and white) present in a moving image contained in a Manifestation.[95]

---

92 RDA 3.17. 01
93 Based on AMIM2 5C3.
94 RDA 7.17.3 Colour of Moving Image
95 RDA 7.17.3 Colour of Moving Image

It consists of a designation of the colour state and, optionally, of the description of the colour system.

Record the colour state of a Manifestation, for example, Black and white (tinted), Colour, Colour + Black & White, etc. Selection should be made from a controlled list of terms. A suggested list, which is open and not exhaustive, can be found in D.7.11 Manifestation/Item Colour Type.

Optionally, if considered relevant, describe the system or process by which colour is fixed on the carrier or as part of the digital encoding, for example, Pathécolor, Technicolor, RGB, , etc. Selection should be made from a controlled list of terms. A suggested list, which is open and not exhaustive, can be found in D.7.12 Manifestation/Item Colour Standard.

2.3.5 Extent of a Manifestation[96]

The concept of extent as applied to Manifestations is the "ideal" **logical, physical, or temporal (duration)** units and not a description of a real physical object. Actual objects in the collection are described at the Item level.

The extent of a Manifestation must be recorded as a reference for the completeness of all the related Items, using appropriate authoritative secondary sources where feasible.

2.3.5.1 Logical extent of a Manifestation

Logical extent is the number of discrete logical **units** which make up the Manifestation, both for analogue (e.g. reels, cassettes, discs) and digital (cassettes, discs, files), considering that the digital Manifestations may be bound to a physical carrier (such as DVD) or exist without a defined carrier (such as online streaming media, podcasts, etc.).

For digital Manifestations, there can be two extents: one for the number of files, and one for the extent of the carrier (e.g., 2 LTO6 tapes).

Example:

A home video publication: DVD in 2 discs
A theatrical print: in 6 reels
A hard-disk stored film in 3 files

Record the number of the logical units of a Manifestation in Arabic numerals, and, if necessary, specify the type of unit, for example, reel, roll, disc, file, etc. Selection should be made from a controlled list of terms. A suggested list, which is open and not exhaustive, can be found in D.7.6 Manifestation Unit Types.

If the number of the logical units of a Manifestation is uncertain, use a question mark following the unit count[97] or record the uncertain number preceded by "approximately."[98]

---

96 Partially based on EN 15907, 6.8 except for the physical components/units number, which is not provided for in the standard._
97 AMIM2, 5B5, p.9
98 RDA: 3.4.0.4

If the number of the logical units of a Manifestation is indeterminate, record the information using a value of "unknown."

Alternatively, provide for a distinguishing "precision" field specifying if the unit number is exact, approximate or unknown.

2.3.5.2 Physical extent of a Manifestation[99]

Physical extent is the total "ideal" **length or footage** of the medium carrying the moving image Manifestation (using appropriate authoritative secondary sources where feasible such as filmographies, censorship visas, etc.).

The actual length is a characteristic of a singular Item since it can be different for multiple Items exemplifying the same Manifestation.

Record the total length in Arabic numerals, in metres or feet.

For digital Manifestations, record the total storage of all files that comprise the Manifestation. Use Arabic numerals followed by MB, GB, or TB as appropriate.

The Unit of Measurement (feet, metres, GB, etc.) can be provided in a separate field. This could be two separate fields side by side – one for numbers and one for size measurement.

If the length of a Manifestation is uncertain, use a question mark following the unit count or record the uncertain number preceded by "approximately." In a note, give an explanation for the estimated footage or metre count, where known. Estimating the total storage size for a digital Manifestation can be particularly difficult, since storage can vary depending on technical characteristics of the file(s).

If the length of a Manifestation is unknown, record the information using a value of "unknown."

Alternatively, provide for a distinguishing "precision" field specifying if the length is exact, approximate or unknown.

2.3.5.2.1 Physical extent of an Aggregate Manifestation

For Aggregate Manifestations record the length or footage of the whole, i.e. the total in feet or metres of all the units that constitute the Aggregate. In addition there is the option to qualify this with details of the physical extent of each individual unit in either a Notes field, or in multiple occurrences of the duration fields, depending on what systems used permit or an institution decides.

For more information about aggregates, seeAppendix E, Aggregates.

99 Based on FIAF 1991, 5.3.4.1, 87.

2.3.5.3 Duration of a Manifestation[100]

This is the total **duration/running time** under normal or specific playback conditions (e.g. a specific frame rate). It represents the concept of "ideal" duration/running time (i.e., the duration reported on the moving image Manifestation itself – i.e., on the container, on the accompanying material, on the wrapper of metadata in a digital file or reported by authoritative secondary sources such as filmographies, censorship visas, etc.). In cases where it is known that the time on the Manifestation is incorrect and all Items will inherit the same incorrect duration, record the accurate duration and make a note about the error/discrepancy found on the Manifestation.

The actual duration is usually considered a characteristic of a singular moving image Item, since it can differ among multiple Items exemplifying the same Manifestation.

Record, in Arabic numerals, the total duration/running time in minutes, normally rounded off to the nearest minute. Optionally, include minutes and seconds, or, for a higher level of precision and to enable calculations, use the format HH:MM:SS. This numeric format will help to calculate estimated digital storage in analogue-to-digital transfer projects.

If the duration/running time of a Manifestation is uncertain, use a question mark following the unit count or, if the system allows, use the qualifier "Duration Precision" and add the term "approximate." (see 2.3.5.3.4 Duration Precision)

In a note, give an explanation for the estimated duration/running time, if such information applies.[101]

If the duration/running time of a Manifestation is unknown, record the information using a value of "unknown."

2.3.5.3.1 Duration of an Aggregate Manifestation

For Aggregate Manifestations record the duration of the whole, i.e. the total running time of all the units that constitute the Aggregate. In addition there is the option to qualify this with details of the duration of each individual unit in either a Notes field, or in multiple occurrences of the duration fields, depending on what systems used permit or an institution decides.

Example:

DVD "The Audrey Hepburn Collection" contains 3 films, all with extra features. The running times for each of those 3 units are given on the container.

---

100 Based on FIAF 1991, 5.3.4.2.
101 Based on FIAF 1991, 5.3.4.2.

The total running time of these may be added as duration, with an additional clarifying note detailing the running times of the individual units.

For more information about Aggregates see Appendix E, Aggregates.

2.3.5.3.2 Duration of a Manifestation associated with a Work/ Variant of the silent era

When recording duration of Manifestations of a Work/Variant of the silent era, take into account that the rate of frames per second varied over the years and between Variants/Manifestations. Also take into account the so-called "stretch frame" practice, adopted after the silent era, which "increases the number of frames printed on a film to enable films shot at silent speeds to be projected at sound speed and retain the original temporal characteristics."[102]

In a note, indicate the frame rate on which the duration is based or if the Manifestation is the result of a "stretch frame" practice.[103] (See also 3.1.5.12 Frame Rate)

2.3.5.3.3 Duration of a Broadcast Manifestation associated with a Work/Variant

When recording duration for Broadcast Manifestations there are two potential sets of data: a Slot Duration and an Actual Running Time. If the system allows, note the type of duration in the Duration Type element (see 2.3.5.3.5 Duration Type).

Slot Duration relates to information from TV listings or publicity information for the programmed "slot" on the TV channel, whereas Actual Running Time relates to the exact running time of the entity when it was broadcast, excluding any inserted advertisements, etc. Thus, for example, an episode of the soap opera "Coronation Street" may have a Slot Duration of 30 minutes, but an Actual Running Time of 24 minutes.

Similarly, record the start and end time of the broadcast, ideally using 24-hour clock notation, e.g. 23:00 rather than 11:00pm. This may also involve two potential sets of data: a whole slot start and end time, or the actual more precise start and end time of the broadcast.

It is for an institution to choose whether to record both sets of data in each instance or limit to either just slot or actual broadcast/running times.

2.3.5.3.4 Duration Precision

In this qualifier, note whether the duration is exact, approximate, or estimated. Items can apply the additional "stock maximum."

102 Definition of "Stretch frame" taken from: http://www.nfsa.gov.au/preservation/glossary/stretch-frame.
103 Adapted from FIAF 5.3.4.2.

2.3.5.3.5 Duration Type

Where appropriate, add the type of duration being described. For example, broadcast materials could have "Slot Duration" and "Actual Duration."

2.3.6 Notes for Manifestations

Notes for Manifestations are annotations providing additional information relating specifically to Manifestation attributes and relationships.[104] See Appendix B, Cataloguer's Notes.

2.4 Relationships of a Manifestation

A relationship associates an instance of Manifestation with another instance of an entity.

Relationships can be implemented in many ways, depending on the purpose, the modelling paradigm, or architectural constraints of the chosen platform. These guidelines are intended to be data structure neutral.[105] Therefore, these guidelines cannot prescribe exactly how to demonstrate relationships. Instead they recommend that certain relationships be established without instruction on how precisely those links be made manifest.

A Manifestation may have relationships with the following:

- **Agent(s)**
- **Event(s)**
- **Other**
- **Item(s)**
- **Work**
- **Variant**

2.4.1 Agent(s)

An Agent for moving image Manifestations is defined as an entity that is involved in the exploitation (release, distribution, broadcasting), publishing, manufacturing or preservation of a Manifestation and who is considered to have major responsibility for, or be of major importance to, the Manifestation. Typical distinctions between agent types are Person, Corporate Body, Family and Person Group.[106]

Work/Variant Agent(s) tend to be involved in the original creation of the Work/Variant so are not repeated in the Manifestation record. Only "new" Agents that contributed to the Manifestation as described above are included in the Manifestation record.

Agent(s) may also have relationships to an instance of a specific Event or of an "Other" relationship in connection with the Manifestation.

---

104 Based on RDA 2.20.1.Basic Instructions on Making Notes on Manifestations or Items

105 EN 15907 8.1 Relationships. General

106 EN 15907, 5.1 Agent

Because responsibility for moving image materials is most often complex and highly diverse, institutions - particularly those with special interests - should determine the types of roles they wish to include. These roles may vary from institution to institution according to the types of moving image material held. For example, an institution holding television material would probably consider, for Manifestations, the function of *broadcaster* more important than that of *distributor*. The opposite would be the case for institutions whose collections are composed of motion picture material. Provide access to Agents when they have made an important contribution to the particular Manifestation, even when the type of responsibility (credit function) is one that may not be considered major in other Manifestations.[107]

In the case of aggregate Manifestations, if desirable and applicable, record multiple instances of Agent associated with the aggregated content.

2.4.1.1 Agent Activity

Describes the activity of the Agent(s) to make explicit the relationship(s) between the Agent(s) and the Manifestation.

Record one or more Agent activity terms, for example, "distributor," "broadcaster," "broadcast channel," etc., to express the nature of the agent's relationship to the Manifestation. Selection should be made from a controlled list of terms. A suggested list, which is open and not exhaustive, can be found in D.8 Manifestation Agent Types.

Choose the single most specific term in each case, if possible. If no suggested terms apply, compose a term to describe the relationship between the creator and the Manifestation being catalogued. If the relationship is ambiguous, use a value to indicate this, for example, "unknown" to indicate a person performing in a capacity that is uncertain or not covered by typical terms.[108] Optionally, when the activity performed by an Agent is probable but not certain, provide the function name followed by a question mark.

Besides the principal Agent Activities suggested, institutions, particularly those with special interests, should create and apply in-house value lists of other specific Agent activities, which may vary from institution to institution.

Record in a note any additional details that cannot be expressed through controlled terms. (e.g. "appears only in final scene", etc.). If a name is known to be fictitious, or requires clarification, make a note giving the actual name, etc.

For recording the attributes of Agents (e.g. first name, last name, nationality, etc.), refer to authoritative sources such as *Functional requirements for authority data: a conceptual model* or tools such as the Library of Congress Name Authority File.[109] Optionally, if the Agent is credited under a name that is not identical with the preferred name from an authority file, record the name as used in the current instance of the related entity.[110]

---

107 YCR, 1.3.2. Other creators, p. 42.
108 List of relator terms are a combination of those found in YCR, 1.3.2. Other creators, pp. 42-43; and, OLAC TF, Part II, Core Attributes and Relationships, Commonly-Occurring Roles, pp. 16-18.
109 Patton, Glenn E. 2009. *Functional requirements for authority data: a conceptual model*. München: K.G. Saur.
110 RDA 2.20.7.3

Give the Agent(s) and Agent Activity in the terms and language in which they appear, either in the sources of information or in the language of the institution, or both. If more than one Agent is associated with a particular role connected with a Manifestation or Event, where possible or desirable, record the names in the order indicated by the sequence, layout, or typography of the names on the source of information. Preserving the ordering of the credited persons should be determined by the requirements of individual institutions.[111]

Example:

Broadcaster: CBS

Broadcast Channel: BBC1

Distributor: GUO Film Distributors

Publisher: Buena Vista International

2.4.2 Events

An Event characterises occurrences in the life cycle of a moving image Manifestation. Instances of any Event type can have Agent and "Other" relationships.

Record one or more Event type, for example, "decision," "manufacture," etc., to express the nature of the Event's relationship to the Manifestation. Selection should be made from a controlled list of terms. A suggested list, which is open and not exhaustive, can be found in D.4 Event Types.

2.4.3 "Other" relationships

Expresses relationships that are not covered by the Agent and Event relationships. Aggregation relationships are expressed at the Work/Variant level (see Appendix E, Aggregates).

Commonly-occurring relationships include:

- Manifestations that the moving image Manifestation forms part of (e.g. series/serials)

  Le cryptogramme rouge (35mm print, m 984, m 48' (18fps)
  3° episode of the serial Les vampires (L. Feuillade, 1915).

- Manifestation(s) that the moving image Manifestation has a sequential relationship with (e.g. series/serials)
- Manifestation(s) that are promotional material(s) (i.e. trailers) for a particular Manifestation

  Rashomon (Japan, 1950, A. Kurosawa)

111 FIAF, 1.6.2, pp. 36-37.

"has as promotional material": Rashomon, Italian trailer (35mm), of the Italian theatrical release (1952).

- Non-moving image Works/Manifestation(s), about or relating to the moving image Manifestation (e.g. objects, articles, documents such as a review relating to a DVD home video publication, advertising materials referring to a specific theatrical distribution, related materials such as censorship visas, laboratory technical papers, etc.)

    Metro. Issue 157. June 2008. "DVD review: Blade Runner: The Final Cut", by Steven Aoun.

    Der Dritte Mann (German film poster for the German-language Release Manifestation of the film The third man (United Kingdom, 1949, Carol Reed)

- Pre-release Manifestation(s) relating to a Release Manifestation

    Blow-up (UK-Italy, 1966, Michelangelo Antonioni)and
    Blow-up censorship cuts (35mm) of the Italian theatrical release (1967).

    Othello, Orson Welles, USA- Italy-Morocco-France, 1952 and
    Otello, dailies and rushes, positive silent and some with sound, 35mm, containing shots included in only a very limited extent in the first theatrical release (their title proper in Italian is: Otello).

Record one or more "Other" relationship type to express the nature of the relationship to the Manifestation, choosing the most specific term possible from existing relator terms lists, for example, "commentary on," "review of," etc. Selection should be made from a controlled list of values. A suggested list, which is open and not exhaustive, can be found in Appendix D.17.2 Manifestation Other Relationship Types.

Or, compose a term to describe the relationship between the Manifestation being catalogued and the related Manifestation.

In a note, add any additional information concerning the relationship considered relevant.

Describe or demonstrate Manifestation-to-Manifestation relationships through linking to the Manifestation identifier of the related Manifestation, through the usage of relator terms, or according to the confines of your data structure.

If the cataloguing system allows the procedure, attach a digital file that reproduces any associated "document."

2.4.4 Item(s)

Express the relationship between a moving image Manifestation and a moving image Item (e.g. Part/part of).

Here could be listed the unique Item identifiers associated to this Manifestation, noting their "part of " relationships to the Manifestation.

2.4.5 Work

Express the relationship between a moving image Manifestation and a moving image Work (e.g., Part/part of). Describe or demonstrate Manifestation-to-Work relationships through linking to the Manifestation identifier, through the usage of relator terms, or according to the confines of your data structure.

2.4.6 Variant

Express the relationship between a moving image Manifestation and a moving image Variant (e.g., Part/part of). Describe or demonstrate Manifestation-to-Variant relationships through linking to the Manifestation identifier, through the usage of relator terms, or according to the confines of your data structure.

3. Moving Image Items

3.0 Definition

A moving image Item is the physical or digital product of a Manifestation of a Work or Variant, i.e. the actual copy of a Work or Variant. Whereas the Manifestation record describes the "ideal" of a particular format or publication, the Item record represents the actual holding in a repository's collection.

An Item may consist of one or more components, i.e. the whole Item may consist of 1 reel or 5 reels, 2 VHS tapes or 1 DVD. An Item record may contain fields or scope for separate barcodes and condition information for each component of the item (each reel for example) if required.

The Item may be whole or incomplete or a fragment. In the case of purely digital media, an Item is defined as the availability of the computer file, irrespective of the number of backup copies that may exist.[112]

112 Digital medium definition taken from CEN's "Film Identification – enhancing interoperability of metadata. Element sets and structures. FprEN 15907:2010 (E)

3.1 Elements of a moving image Item

A majority of the physical and digital description elements of moving image Items are intended to be inherited from the Manifestations, as they serve as the exemplars of Manifestations. In some databases, selection of a physical carrier type initiates provision of element fields relevant to that type at a Manifestation level, or an Item level, or both (e.g. in a 2 Level hierarchy. See "Shallow hierarchy model: 2 levels" in 0.2.1 Elements of description across Works, Variants, Manifestations, and Items).

Ideally the information need only be recorded once irrespective of where in the data structure an institution must place it. Therefore guidelines for the treatment of physical/digital description elements are explained fully in the Manifestation chapter.

This chapter contains Item-specific physical/digital description elements beginning at Section 3.1.5 (see 3.1.5 Item Specifics/Extent (e.g. physical/Digital description). For example, properties such as Extent and Format at the Manifestation level represent the "ideal," and item-specific information will capture where it differs from this ideal. Only elements that are considered Item-specific have guidelines for the recording of data. Physical/digital description elements that are considered Manifestation-specific, but which may be repeated at the Item level, contain hyperlinks to the relevant sections in the Manifestation chapter.

3.1.1 Identifier

Create an unambiguous numerical or alphanumerical reference to the moving image Item, such as a call number, barcode, shelf mark or similar, to uniquely identify the copy.[113] This may be in addition to separate Acquisition and Accession number(s) or identifier(s).

For digital files, the filename is not an identifier since filenames can change. Instead, the filename is tracked as part of the technical metadata associated with a digital item.

As with Work and Manifestation Identifiers, an Item can have more than one Identifier. For example, a film Item may have a barcode for the can and a shelf number for its location. Note the type of Identifier using Identifier Type.

3.1.1.1 Identifier Type

If an institution's system allows, a "Type" can be applied with an Identifier to define the source of the Identifier. Examples: Barcode, Shelf mark, Accession number.

3.1.2 Title

Record at least one title, identifying phrase, or name for the moving image Item Title.

113 EN 15907, "Inventory number," p. 12

If multiple titles are recorded, where allowable, associate a "Title Type" to a title for differentiation between the various types of titles (see A.2 Title Types).

In most cases the title of an Item will be the same as that of the Manifestation to which it pertains.

The title of an Item can sometimes differ, either slightly or wholly from the title of the Manifestation, and/or Work/Variant to which it is linked. In particular, this may be the case where an incomplete physical product of the Manifestation has been acquired. For example, if a film in the collection is missing the first reel where opening title credits usually appear, the Item will not have a title to be transcribed.

For creating titles for untitled or unidentified entities see A.2.5 Supplied/Devised Titles

For the treatment of Aggregates (e.g. compilations of whole Manifestations) as applied to Items, see Appendix E.4 Titling of Aggregates for titling of Aggregates.

For guidance on wording, order, spelling, punctuation, accentuation and capitalisation, see Chapter 0. Preliminary Notes.

For sources of information for the Title, see Section 0.3 Sources of Information.

3.1.2.1 Title Type

Items can have more than just the title transcribed from the opening credits. There can be title information written on leader, cans, and video containers. Sometimes this information is different to what is in the credits; sometimes it is the only source of information to help identify an Item's content.

Note the source of title information. For Items where the only title information is found on a can or leader, use an Acquisition Title Type(s) (see A.2.4.1 Alternative title types) or descriptive words such as "Title on can" or "Title on leader."

3.1.3 Holding institution[114]

Record the name of the institution possessing the moving image Item or authorised to make it available.

Optionally, if available, record a suitable repository identifier or a registered namespace identifier for the institution.

3.1.4 Item Element type[115]

Record the nature or function of the moving image Item, describing its place in the photochemical or digital production or duplication process, for example, "original nega-

114 Based on EN 15907, Holding institution
115 Based on EN 15907, Instantiation type

tive," "duplicate negative," etc. Selection should be made from a controlled list of terms. A suggested list, which is open and not exhaustive, can be found in D.7.8 Item Element Type.

3.1.5 Item Specifics/Extent (e.g. physical/Digital description)

All moving image Item descriptions should contain details of the physical/digital characteristics of the Items, their location, treatment and condition.

Institutions with archival moving images need to describe their holdings accurately for preservation, copying and reconstruction purposes. Often there will be physically separate Items, for example image, track, music, different colour bases, etc., which are all essential parts of a single moving image.[116] Descriptive terminology covering all areas of physical description and attributes should be established in controlled lists of terms, to be applied in the relevant categories. The range of these and what they are can be established in-house or utilising an established list, for example, the FIAF Glossary of Technical Terms.

Each Item should have its own description, whether the physical/digital characteristics between Items differ in one way or another, for example, in length, gauge, base, sound, etc., or, the Items acquired are duplicate identical copies.

Institutions may record as much technical information as they wish or need, but the Physical and Digital Description elements of an Item should ideally consist of the elements listed in the sub-sections below where discernible.

Further data relating to the condition, preservation, location, and, acquisition, accessioning, and source of the Item are also recommended elements for the Item (see 3.1.6 Access conditions).

These may be either added to the Item description itself or, where this is not possible, related to other separate files or databases, via physical link or text indication.

3.1.5.1 Carrier Type

Carrier type is the medium on or the encoding format in which the Item is fixed.

Its description consists of a **general carrier type**, which describes the basic properties of the Item's physical format, for example, film, video tape, digital file, etc., and a **specific carrier type**, which corresponds to the gauge, in case of films and tapes, and for digital files, to the physical carrier on which the file is stored.

116 See The FIAF Cataloguing Rules for Film Archives (1991). 5. Physical Description. Introduction

3.1.5.1.1 General Carrier Type

The broad media type of the Item (e.g., film, video, audio, optical, digital file). Recording this high-level information will enable simple searching for only film, video, digital, etc. elements rather than searching by all possible formats and carriers.

Record only if this information is not captured at the Manifestation level or if required at the Item level by the system in use.

A suggested list can be found in D.7.1 Manifestation/Item General Carrier Type.

For reasons of clarity and to avoid redundancy, optionally, institutions can decide to skip the general carrier type description for film and video, since it is already implicit in the specific carrier type.

3.1.5.1.2 Specific Carrier Type

Record the **specific carrier type**, by indicating

1) For film and video: the width of the film stock or of the magnetic tape on which the Item is fixed;

2) For digital files: The physical carrier storing the digital file.

For digital files, it is most important for users to immediately identify the file container or wrapper (MXF, MOV, DPX, etc.) rather than the physical media on which it is stored. Physical media storing a file can change, but that does not necessarily mean that the file format has changed. It is the digital file format that is the important distinguishing factor. Information on the specific codecs and resolution are captured in other Item elements.

For optical media, only add commercially produced media here. If the optical media is "writable" and is being used to store a digital file, put the digital file format in the general carrrier type, and the optical storage media in specific media type.

Record the **specific carrier type,** selecting from a suitable controlled list. A suggested list, which is open and not exhaustive, can be found in D.7.2 Manifestation/Item Specific Carrier Type.

3.1.5.2 Item Status

Description of the preservation or access status of the Item, for example Master, Viewing, etc. Select term from a controlled list. A suggested list, which is open and not exhaustive, can be found in D.7.3 Item Preservation/Access status.

3.1.5.3 Sound

Technical specifications relating to the fixation of sound in a moving image Manifestation/Item (see 2.3.4.3 Sound characteristics of a moving image Manifestation). This element is for high-level description of sound on the item; i.e., noting whether it has sound, is silent, etc.

Indicate the presence or absence of sound in the Manifestation/Item, i.e. "sound," "silent," "mute", "combined" or "mixed" etc. Selection should be made from a controlled list of terms. A suggested list, which is open and not exhaustive, can be found in D.7.4 Manifestation/Item Sound Type.

Record only if this information is not captured at the Manifestation level or if required at the Item level by the system in use.

3.1.5.4 Sound Channel Configuration

If the Item has sound, note here the track configuration (e.g., mono, stereo, etc.) Selection should be made from a controlled list of terms.

3.1.5.5 Sound System

See also 2.3.4.3 Sound characteristics of a Manifestation

Describes the technical or proprietary system used to record the sound on a Manifestation/Item, for example, Dolby SR, Dolby Digital, etc. Select from a controlled list. A suggested list, which is open and not exhaustive, can be found in D.7.13 Item Sound System.

3.1.5.6 Colour

For full instructions, see 2.3.4.4 Colour characteristics of a Manifestation.

The presence of colour(s), tone(s), etc. in an Item.[117]

Record only if this information is not captured at the Manifestation level or if required at the Item level by the system in use.

3.1.5.7 Unit number

For full instructions see 2.3.5.1 Logical extent of a Manifestation

The number of discrete logical units that make up the moving image Item. Item unit number(s) may differ from that of the associated Manifestation. The unit number in Manifestation relates to the ideal, whereas the Item unit number refers to the actual units held by the institution, e.g. an institution may have only acquired 3 reels of a 4-reel film.

117 RDA 7.17.3 Colour of Moving Image

3.1.5.8 Extent

The actual physical/digital extent is a characteristic of a singular Item, since it can be different for multiple Items exemplifying the same moving image Manifestation.

For film, record footage for the film reel in feet or metres. This footage represents actual length, rather than the "ideal" length, which is recorded for Manifestations (see 2.3.5.2 Physical extent of a Manifestation). If your system allows, provide the Unit of Measurement – feet or metres – in another element. Having separate numeric fields can facilitate calculations in determining the amount of footage that will be preserved.

For digital files, enter the numerical measurement indicating the size of the digital asset's file(s), in KB, MB, GB, or TB.

As above, the Unit of Measurement (feet, metres, GB, etc.) may be provided in a separate field. This could be two separate fields side by side – one for numbers and one for size measurement. A suggested list, which is open and not exhaustive, can be found in D.7.9 Item File Size – Digital.

If the length of an Item is uncertain, use a question mark following the unit count or record the uncertain number preceded by "approximately." In a note, give an explanation for the estimated footage or metre count, where known.

If the length of an Item is indeterminate, record the information using a value of "unknown."

Alternatively, provide for a distinguishing "precision" field specifying if the length is exact, approximate or unknown.

3.1.5.9 Projection characteristics

For full instructions, see 2.3.4.2 Projection characteristics of a Manifestation

The projection characteristics of a Manifestation/Item include aspect ratio and aperture or image format.

Record only if this information is not captured at the Manifestation level or if required at the Item level by the system in use.

3.1.5.10 Broadcast standard - Video

The broadcast standard for a video or DVD/BluRay: NTSC, PAL, SECAM.

3.1.5.11 Duration

Duration in minutes of the moving image(s) contained in the Item, not the total duration of the Manifestation. Optionally, include minutes and seconds, or, for a higher level of precision and to enable calculations, use the format HH:MM:SS. This numeric format will help to calculate estimated digital storage in analogue-to-digital transfer projects.

This duration represents actual temporal extent, rather than the "ideal" temporal extent, which is recorded for Manifestations (see 2.3.5.3 Duration of a Manifestation). Actual duration is a characteristic of a singular Item, since it can differ among multiple Items exemplifying the same Manifestation.

If the duration/running time of an Item is uncertain, use a question mark following the unit count or record the uncertain number preceded by "approximately." If necessary, in a note, give an explanation for the estimated duration/running time, where known.

If the duration/running time of an Item is indeterminate, record the information using a value of "unknown."

Alternatively, provide for a distinguishing "precision" field specifying if the duration/running time is exact, approximate or unknown. If the Item is a video or audio tape where the tape stock maximum duration is identified (e.g., Fuji M321-SP 30M is a Betacam SP tape of 30 minutes duration), that maximum duration can be noted in the "precision" field as "stock maximum." This information can be helpful since it implies the Item cannot be longer than the maximum duration of the stock.

3.1.5.11.1 Duration Precision

In this qualifier, note whether the duration is exact, approximate, estimated, or stock maximum.

3.1.5.12 Frame Rate

Selection should be made from a controlled list of terms. A suggested list, which is open and not exhaustive, can be found in D.7.18 Item Frame Rate/Transfer Speed.

Frame rate is the native frame rate for the Item. Information related to the frame rate used during a digitisation process is added to Transfer Speed (see 3.1.5.23 Transfer Speed).

Frame Rate and Transfer Speed can sometimes be the same thing, and at other times different, depending on whether it is an Item that is being scanned into a digital file or an Item that is a digital file to start with. For example, a silent film that was shot at a 16 fps frame rate could be transferred at 23.98 fps. In this case, the resulting digital file would have a frame rate of 23.98, even though the original film is 16 fps.

Precision can be added to this element by adding a "Type" qualifier to note if the frame rate is original, or the transfer rate.

Note that in digital cinema, a film can have Variable frame rates.

3.1.5.13 Base

The physical material or video format on which the Item is captured, for example, describing the flexible transparent material that supports a film items' emulsion or a magnetic track, (e.g., acetate, nitrate, CTA, etc.). Select from controlled list of terms. A suggested list, which is open and not exhaustive, can be found in D.7.7 Item Base – Film or Video.

3.1.5.14 Stock

Describes the specific stock/brand on which the Item is captured, for example, Eastman Kodak, Fuji, 3M, etc. This element should be used for all media: film, video, audio, optical, digital tape, external hard drives. Selection should be made from a controlled list of terms. A suggested list, which is open and not exhaustive, can be found in D.7.16 Item Stock.

3.1.5.15 Stock batch

The stock batch number of the media the Item is captured on. This can be a video, audio, optical media, or digital tape stock. Identifying the batch number can assist in identifying problems related to specific manufactured batches.

3.1.5.16 Video Codec

The video compression standard used in the digital video Item, for example, D10, MP4, etc.

Video and digital cinema formats contained in wrappers have separate audio files contained in the format with the video file. For example, DCPs (contained in MXF files) are comprised of a JPEG2000 video file and a WAV audio file (along with textual information in an XML file), The audio codec is described separately.

Select from controlled list of terms. A suggested list, which is open and not exhaustive, can be found in D.7.10 Item Code type – Digital. Other lists include:

PBCore essenceTrackEncoding vocabulary:
http://metadataregistry.org/concept/list/vocabulary_id/156.html

EBUCore Video Compression Code:
https://www.ebu.ch/metadata/cs/web/ebu_VideoCompressionCodeCS_p.xml.htm

3.1.5.17 Audio Codec

The audio compression standard used in the audio file, whether it is contained in a wrapper with a video file or as a standalone audio file.

Select from controlled list of terms. A suggested list, which is open and not exhaustive, can be found in D.7.10 Item Codec type. Other lists include:

PBCore essenceTrackEncoding vocabulary:
http://metadataregistry.org/concept/list/vocabulary_id/156.html

EBUCore Video Compression Code:
https://www.ebu.ch/metadata/cs/web/ebu_VideoCompressionCodeCS_p.xml.htm

3.1.5.18 Resolution

Note whether the Item's resolution is Standard Definition, High Definition, etc. Selection should be made from a controlled list of terms. A suggested list, which is open and not exhaustive, can be found in D.7.19 Item Resolution.

3.1.5.19 Line standard – Video

Describes the number of scan lines which make up the image and indicates the resolution, for example, 405, 525, 1080. Selection should be made from a controlled list of terms. A suggested list, which is open and not exhaustive, can be found in D.7.21 Item Line Standard – Video.

3.1.5.20 Bit Depth

Selection should be made from a controlled list of terms. A suggested list, which is open and not exhaustive, can be found in D.7.17 Item Bit Depth – Digital.

Note that bit depth can be used in describing both video and audio files.

3.1.5.21 Source Device

Record the source playback device used in transfer projects. This can be a video deck, film printer, or hardware.

Selection should be made from a controlled list of terms. A suggested list, which is open and not exhaustive, can be found in D.7.20 Item Source Device – Digital D.7.20 Item Source Device – Digital.

3.1.5.22 Source Software

Record the source software used in playing a digital file.

3.1.5.23 Transfer Speed

Selection should be made from a controlled list of terms. A suggested list, which is open and not exhaustive, can be found in D.7.18 Item Frame Rate/Transfer Speed – Digital.

If the Transfer Speed is the same as the Frame Rate (3.1.5.12 Frame Rate), these values should be the same. However, silent films might be transferred at a higher speed than the original frame rate. For example, a silent film that was shot at a 16fps frame rate could be transferred at 23.98 fps. It is important to note the transfer speed so an institution can identify how the transferred Item compares to the source Item. If the transfer speed is faster than the source frame rate, the target Item could have a shorter duration than the source Item.

3.1.6 Access conditions

Record any information on how and to whom the moving image Item can be made available, including details of the condition of the Item and of its treatment, preservation or restoration Events. This creates a condition and preservation history for the Item, and is also important for assessing conservation conditions and establishing and prioritising collections care and preservation activities.

3.1.6.1 Item condition

Observations about conditions will typically happen in the course of an Event such as inspection of an Item. These observations should aim to be as clear and concise as possible, avoiding abbreviations and initials, and as far as possible using controlled vocabulary. For example, establish whether to use "scratched", "scratches" or "scratch marks" and be as consistent as possible. This enables better searching and accessibility of data.

Record these actions as an Event (see 3.3.2 Events), with the person or entity performing the action as an Agent (see 3.3.1 Agent(s)).

Ideally, elements covering information and details regarding the condition of an acquired Item would include those listed below.

This could be recorded using single or multiple specific headed fields (i.e., covering Base, Emulsion, Image, Perforations, etc.), and then sub-sections of the latter, to incorporate data ranging from graded scales designations (either numerical or alphabetical, for example 1-5, A-G, Perfect – Very Poor) with clear definitions of what each designation means; condition terms selected from a controlled list; free text additional qualification or clarification in observations or comments sections; identification of technical assessor; and, dates.

Record the condition of the Item including its base and/or emulsion and/or perforations, where applicable. Selection should be made from a controlled list of terms, for example, "brittle", "buckled", "tears," etc. A suggested list, which is open and not exhaustive, can be found in D.16 Manifestation/Item Condition, Preservation and Restoration.

Capture the date on which the condition of the Item was recorded (using ISO standard[118]). The identification of the individual who carried out the technical assessment and has recorded the condition should also be given. Any names should be given in full, rather than initials or abbreviations. As stated above, people or companies performing inspections are Agents.

Note any indication that the Item is in need of servicing prior to being accessed for use.

---

118 ISO 8601

3.1.6.2 Item location

Item descriptions should indicate a storage location number in order to provide access and retrieval. Movements and changes of location should also be logged in order to ascertain the precise location of an Item at any given time. If possible, use the Item Identifier and Identifier Type fields to note an Item's location (see 3.1.1 Identifier).

This could be a single simple field, or could include multiple fields to reflect various electronic package or barcode numbers that may be attached to each individual can or container, shelf, or whatever is applicable to an individual institution.

3.1.7 Notes for Items

Notes for Items are an annotation providing additional information relating specifically to Item attributes and relationships.[119] See Appendix B, Cataloguer's Notes.

3.2 Boundaries between Items

The boundaries between moving image Items is determined primarily by the boundaries between Manifestations (see 2.1 Boundaries between Manifestations). There may be multiple Items associated to a Manifestation that are, for all intents and purposes, exact copies, but which may have small differences that do not necessitate representation as a Manifestation. For example, an institution may have two DVD-R copies of the same Manifestation, with cosmetic differences in their labels.

3.3 Relationships of an Item

A relationship associates an instance of an Item with another instance of an entity.

Relationships can be implemented in many ways, depending on the purpose, the modelling paradigm, or architectural constraints of the chosen platform. These guidelines are intended to be data structure neutral.[120] Therefore, these guidelines cannot prescribe exactly how to demonstrate relationships. Instead they recommend that certain relationships be established without instruction on how precisely those links be made manifest.

An Item may have relationships with the following:

- Agent(s)
- Event(s)
- Other
- Manifestation

119 Based on RDA 2.20.1.Basic Instructions on Making Notes on Manifestations or Items
120 EN 15907 8.1 Relationships. General

3.3.1 Agent(s)

An Agent for moving image Items is defined as an entity that is involved in the acquisition, movement (for loans, inspection, storage, etc.), or preservation of a moving image Item and who is considered to have major responsibility for, or be of major importance to, the moving image Item. Typical distinctions between Agent types are Person, Corporate Body, Family and Person Group.[121]

Agent(s) may also have relationships to an instance of a specific Event or of an "Other" relationship in connection with the Item.

Because responsibility for moving image materials is most often complex and highly diverse, institutions - particularly those with special interests - should determine the types of functions they wish to include in this area. These functions may vary from institution to institution according to the types of moving image material held.

3.3.1.1 Agent Activity

Describes the activity of the Agent to make explicit the relationship(s) between the Agent and the Item.

Record one or more Agent activity terms, for example, "preservationist," "curator," "acquisition source", etc., to express the nature of the Agent's relationship to the Item. Selection should be made from a controlled list of terms.

Choose the single most specific term, if possible. If no suggested terms apply, compose a term to describe the relationship between the Agent and the Item. If the relationship is ambiguous, use a value to indicate this, for example, "unknown." Optionally, when the role performed by an Agent is probable but not certain, provide the function name followed by a question mark, or by a qualifying note.

Besides the principal Agent Activities suggested, institutions, particularly those with special interests, should create and apply in-house value lists of other specific Agent activities, which may vary from institution to institution.

Record in a note any additional details that cannot be expressed through controlled terms. If a name is known to be fictitious, or requires clarification, make a note giving the actual name, etc.

For recording the attributes of Agents (e.g. first name, last name, nationality, etc.), refer to authoritative sources such as *Functional requirements for authority data: a conceptual model* or tools such as the Library of Congress Name Authority File.[122] Optionally, if the Agent is credited under a name that is not identical with the preferred name from an authority file, record the name as used in the current instance of the related entity.[123]

---

121 EN 15907, 5.1 Agent

122 Patton, Glenn E. 2009. *Functional requirements for authority data: a conceptual model.* München: K.G. Saur.

123 RDA 2.20.7.3

Provide access to the Agent(s) and Agent Activity in the terms and language in which they appear, either in the sources of information or in the language of the institution, or both. If more than one Agent is associated with a particular role connected with an Item or Event, where possible or desirable, record the names in the order indicated by the sequence, layout, or typography of the names on the source of information. Preserving the ordering of the credited persons should be determined by the requirements of individual institutions.[124]

3.3.2 Events

An Event characterises occurrences in the life cycle of a moving image Item. Instances of any Event type can have Agent and "Other" relationships.

Record one or more Event types, for example, "preservation," "inspection," "acquisition", etc., to express the nature of the Event's relationship to the Item. Selection should be made from a controlled list of terms. A suggested list, which is open and not exhaustive, can be found in D.4 Event Types.

3.3.3 Other Relationships

Express relationships that are not covered by the Agent and Event relationships. These may include compilations of convenience, i.e. where an institution has transferred copies of two or more films onto one reel/tape/DVD etc. for convenient storage.[125]

- Item(s) associated with the moving image Item

It is possible for a moving image Item to have a horizontal relationship with another Item as a related object. Such associative relationships are more prevalent and varied at the Work level, but there are instances where Items need to be related, for example, where an institution has separate Items for Yellow, Cyan and Magenta Separation Negatives, each of which have to be combined in Technicolor Three Colour Strip Process to make a new colour print. Or, hold separate sound and image Items that would both be needed to make a new print. Similarly, in the case of restorations where separate Items or elements have been used to create a new restored Item.

> The Wizard of Oz (USA, 1939, Victor Fleming)
>
> Yellow Separation Negative
> Cyan Separation Negative
> Magenta Separation Negative
>
> Local hero (United Kingdom, 1983, Bill Forsyth)
>
> DPX sequence
> WAV audio file

- An Item that contains other Items (e.g. two or more separate Items are held on

124 FIAF, 1.6.2, pp. 36-37.
125 See Appendix E.2 Identifying Aggregates

the same reel/tape/DVD etc. for convenient storage).

Selezione Fregoli 2002

Compilation of 16 short Fregoli films, spliced together for projection convenience.

Laughing gas (USA, 1914, Charlie Chaplin)
Those love pangs (USA, 1914, Charlie Chaplin)
(two Charlie Chaplin short comedies spliced together on one reel - for storage convenience).

- Item that is the source of a moving image Item (e.g. In-house copying of an Item to create a new Item for preservation or access)

  35mm CTA Duplicating Postive copy of Carnival (c.1927) made from a 35mm Nitrate Negative copy of Carnival (c.1927)

- Non-moving image Works/Items (e.g. Objects, documents, etc. relating to a specific Item)

  Shots of 1932 (United Kingdom, 1932) (home movie) 9.5mm Safety film Item related to paper donor agreement

Record one or more "Other" relationship type terms to express the nature of the relationship to the Item, choosing the most specific term possible from existing relator terms lists, for example, "accompanied by," "contained in," etc. Selection should be made from a controlled list of values. A suggested list, which is open and not exhaustive, can be found in D.17.3 Item Other Relationship Types.

In a note, add any additional information concerning the relationship considered relevant.

If the cataloguing system allows, attach a digital file that reproduces any associated "document".

3.3.4 Manifestation

Express the relationship between a moving image Manifestation and a moving image Item (e.g. Part/part of).

Appendix A, Titles and Title Types

A.1 Title

The following general guidelines for recording Titles largely apply across all the WVMI (Work, Variant, Manifestation, Item) entities, and all Title Types. Certain guidelines are specified as applying to one or more of the WVMI entities where pertinent.

When recording a title, apply the guidelines on capitalisation, numbers, diacritical marks, initial articles, spacing of initials and acronyms, and abbreviations, in Chapter 0. Preliminary Notes. If those guidelines refer to an appendix, apply the additional instructions in that appendix, as applicable.[126]

A.1.1 Language[127]

Record titles for Works/Variants in the language and script in which they appear on the sources from which they are taken.

Transcribe titles for Manifestations/Items in the language of the title frames or screens. Otherwise, record titles for Manifestations/Items in the language and script in which they appear on the sources from which they are taken.

Optionally, record a transliterated form of the title for any of the WVMI entities either as a substitute for, or in addition to, the form that appears on the source.

A.1.2 Reflecting graphics of on-screen Titles

For graphics reasons, many moving image titles appear on screen all in capitals (e.g. 'ALIEN', 'LAWRENCE OF ARABIA'), or all in lower case (e.g. 'archipelago') and some are mixed ('ORANGES and SUNSHINE', 'young Hearts Run Free').

It may be important to your institution to differentiate between a graphics decision and a linguistic decision. In some cases, the filmmakers specify that a title is meant to be written a certain way, and in those cases you may choose to follow the filmmakers' wishes (e.g. 'sex, lies and videotape' is not capitalised; 'GoodFellas' takes a capital 'F' though the word is all capitals on screen.)[128]

A.1.3 Statements of responsibility

If the title on the Manifestation or Item includes a statement of responsibility, the name of a company, or a cast member, etc., do not include it as part of the title regardless of linguistic construction.

---

126 Adapted from RDA 6.2.1.3 General Guidelines on Recording Titles of Works

127 Adapted from RDA 5.4 Language and Script

128 BFI CID Stylistics Manual, A.2.3 Words not to be capitalised (unless the last word of the title), p. 10

If the predominant form of the title in reference works includes a possessive statement of responsibility (e.g., "Il Casanova di Federico Fellini"/"Fellini's Casanova"), the cataloguer may include it as part of the title. In doubtful cases, do not include the possessive statement of responsibility as part of the title. In most cases the statement of responsibility or name was not intended to be part of the title, but was included for publicity purposes. Create alternative titles for cases where, in the judgment of the cataloguer, such titles would be helpful points of access.

Examples:

Work
Preferred title: Victor/Victoria
Alternative title: Blake Edwards' Victor/Victoria (title from onscreen)

Work
Preferred title: Il Casanova di Federico Fellini
Alternative (Parallel) title: Fellini's Casanova
Alternative title: Casanova

Variant
Preferred title for English language version: Fellini's Casanova (Research indicates that the possessive form of proper name is part of the English release title.)
Alternative (Parallel) title for English language version: Il Casanova di Federico Fellini
Alternative title: Casanova

Work/Variant/Manifestation/Item
Preferred title: Fisherman's luck?
Alternative (Part) title: Gandy Goose in Fisherman's luck?

A.1.4 Possessives

Do not confuse possessive forms, or other grammatically related phrases, for statements of responsibility with such phrases or forms, which are not statements of responsibility, e.g., character names. Treat possessive forms as part of the title.

Examples:
Fatty's wedding day
Eliza's Romeo
Billy Bunter's double

A.1.5 Other characters/unusual symbols

Where numbers, symbols (e.g. ½, &, +, %) or other characters (e.g. £, $, °) exist as part of the title, these should appear as they are on screen.[129]

129 BFI CID Stylistics Manual, A.2.4.4 Numerals in the title; A.2.4.5 & (ampersand) occurring in a title; A.2.4.6 Other characters; A.2.4.7 Unusual symbols not on the system

An alternative title should also be added giving the numbers, symbols or characters in writing (in the language of origin) to assist in searching and sorting for list production.

Examples:

8½ [Preferred/Title Proper]
Otto e mezzo [Alternative]

Catch-22 [Preferred/Title Proper]
Catch Twenty-two [Alternative]

37°2 le matin [Preferred/Title Proper]
Trente sept deux degrees le matin [Alternative]
Trente-sept deux le matin [Alternative]
37.2 degrees in the morning [Alternative]

The £25,000 kiss [Preferred/Title Proper]
The twenty five thousand pounds kiss [Alternative]

Se7en [Preferred/Title Proper]
Seven [Alternative]

Where possible a word should be used as a substitute when creating the title if a symbol or graphic design used cannot be replicated, with a note explaining this. See Notes 1.3.7.

Example
I [heart] Huckabees [Preferred/Title Proper]
I love Huckabees [Alternative or Non-preferred]
(Onscreen title shows a heart symbol for the middle word.) [Note]

A.2 Title Types

This manual recommends a title + title type approach for the treatment of various titles that may be associated with any Moving Image Work, Variant, Manifestation or Item (WVMI).

This would be done with separate title and title type fields in close proximity.

However, this approach is optional, considering that not all systems may be able to accommodate title types in fields that establish the relationship of the title type to the title. Additionally, not all systems will be able to represent clearly the WVMI entities. In such cases, where possible or considered useful, it is recommended that the title + title type include an additional element or description intended to denote the entity to which it belongs. The underlying philosophy is to associate as many titles to the respective entities as possible, within the bounds of time/resources and systems, to facilitate discovery.

The different titles types have been combined in a single section to aid in real-world cataloguing, where one may have an item-in-hand but be making assessments about the title of the Work or Variant associated with the Item, as well as physical characteristics that are particular to the Item but which do not signal a change in the content itself. This is often the case for archival moving images where titles can be readily changed, misidentified by a well-meaning collector, or completely eliminated before the material reaches an institution.[130]

For guidance on wording, order, spelling, punctuation, accentuation and capitalisation, see Chapter 0. Preliminary Notes.

For sources of information for the Title, see 0.3 Sources of Information.

Primary Title Types[131]

Title Types			
Work	Variant	Manifestation	Item
Identifiying	Identifiying		
Preferred	Preferred		
		Title Proper	Title Proper
Other title information	Other title information	Other title information	Other title information
Alternative	Alternative	Alternative	Alternative
Supplied/Devised	Supplied/Devised	Supplied/Devised	Supplied/Devised

A.2.0 Preferred

The title of a moving image Work or Variant when first released, broadcast, published or transmitted (i.e. mounted online) in the country or countries of origin (see 1.3.3 Country of reference.

The preferred title is the chief name (also referred to as "main" or "original" title) of any moving image Work or Variant. The preferred title may include part title and series/serial information for moving image materials issued in multiple parts, e.g., episodes in a film or TV serial. See A.2.7 Moving images with probable or questionable titles.

In cases where the preferred Work/Variant title cannot be determined but there is a title on the Manifestation/Item, the title on the Manifestation/Item being catalogued may be used as the preferred title for the Work or Variant.

If the preferred title is ascertained at some point and is different from the Manifestation/Item title, the Manifestation/Item title may then be added to the Work or Variant as an alternative title.

When no title at all can be found for a Work or Variant, follow the procedure set out in the A.2.5 Supplied/Devised Titles section.

130 FIAF Cataloguing Rules, p. xiii

131 For simplicity's sake, this table does not present sub-types of Title Types, i.e., sub-types of Alternative and Supplied/Devised titles. Suggested sub-types and definitions can be found under the headings for the primary Title Types.

A.2.1 Identifying (i.e. Uniform or Display)[132]

A title that differentiates Works or Variants and which is designed for identification and differentiation purposes in display, i.e. the title which displays in search results.[133]

An identifying title is designed to identify the entity it represents quickly and concisely to as many users as possible, including users both familiar and unfamiliar with the entity being identified. This type of title will not be necessary in all systems, such as those utilising unique identifiers (e.g., ISAN or EIDR), or those that index other distinguishing elements in separate fields that will display with the title in search results, e.g., Year of reference. In those cases the Identifying and Preferred title will often be one and the same.

Where separate fields do not exist, create an identifying title using the preferred title of the Work/Variant as the starting point (if no title, see A.2.5.1 Partially Supplied/Devised Titles).[134]

Add whatever additions to the title are necessary to identify the Work/Variant and distinguish it from other Works/Variants with the same title.[135] These types of additions are traditionally made within the title field itself (in parentheses or brackets) although other punctuation separators, e.g. full stop may also be used. Use multiple additions where necessary. If multiple additions must be made to the title field in order to identify the Work/Variant, distinguish each addition (e.g., through the use of punctuation such as space colon space, or space full stop space).

For example:
Blade runner. Final Cut. 1982

Possible qualifiers include content terms (see for example D.18 List of form terms for Supplied/Devised titles), corporate bodies that are not principal creators of the Work/Variant but are closely associated with the Work/Variant and useful for identification of it, place of publication/release/distribution/broadcast, and date of publication/release/distribution/ broadcast.[136]

Example:

Works

A Star is born (Motion picture : 1954)

A Star is born (Television programme : 1961)

---

132 Term "Identifying title" corresponds with EN 15907. This is the equivalent of "Uniform title" in FRBR and "Preferred title" in RDA.

133 OLAC TF, Part 3a, p. 5.

134 Both YCR (0.9.3 Normalized human-readable identifiers or headings) and EN 15907 (6.4 Identifying Title) recommend the construction of a human-readable identifier for result list displays, with disambiguation using data such as Genre, Year, etc.

135 YCR, 0.9.3 Normalized human-readable identifiers or headings, p. 8

136 YCR, 1.1.2.3 Unique identifiers for works identified by title, pp. 21-22

Variants

Police story III – Supercop. English subtitled version

Blade runner (Motion picture. 1982. 2007 version)

Blade runner (Motion picture. 1987. 25th anniversary edition)

It is not necessary to append Variant information to the Work identifying title for every type of Variant; many of the types of modifications that lead to Variants are too complex to include and much of the data that identifies a particular Variant will consist of data elements that form part of the Variant description.

A.2.2 Title Proper

The title of a moving image Manifestation or Item. This is a transcribed element, reflecting the title as it appears onscreen.

Manifestations

The title proper corresponds to that of the Manifestation of a Work/Variant, i.e. the title used for a theatrical 35mm release, the title used for a DVD release, the title used for a Television broadcast, the title used for an Internet release, etc. It may reflect the title used in secondary sources or the title as viewed by the cataloguer from a moving image Item belonging to the considered Manifestation. It is the chief name of any Manifestation and represents the primary access point.[137]

Ideally record in a note or dedicated field the source of the title proper.

If it is impossible to determine the title proper or if the Manifestation is the embodiment of a Work not intended to have a formal title, construct a supplied/devised title (see A.2.5 Supplied/Devised Titles).

Specify in a note or dedicated field if the title proper is not determinable or if the Manifestation embodies a Work not intended to have a formal title.

Items[138]

Ascertaining the Title Proper of Items differs from ascertaining those for Works, Variants and Manifestations in that what is on or affixed to the Item or physical copy itself takes precedence.

The title of an Item may differ, either slightly or wholly, from the title of the Manifestation and/or Work/Variant to which it is linked hierarchically. In particular, where an

137 In this FRBR-based context, the title of a moving image Manifestation corresponds strictly to the traditionally ISBD concept of "title proper". Vice versa, in the previous FIAF Rules the title proper was defined as "the title of the original release in the country the origin", which, in a FRBR-based approach, corresponds to the "preferred title" of a Moving Image Work.
138 Item Title Types and definitions taken from BFI CID Stylistics Manual. 2nd Edition. May 2012

incomplete physical product of the Manifestation has been acquired (see A.2.6.3 Analytics/Components of identified newsreels/cinemagazines).

If it is not possible to establish a title from either the Item or its container then secondary sources or a supplied/devised title can be used.

Titles should be transcribed in accordance with the cataloguing guidelines and stylistics applied to Works/Variants and Manifestations.

Items may also have title-like information on film leader, cans, and containers.

Ideally, the title proper of an Item is determined by the following:

i) The title frame or frames, or title screen or screens, or title that is permanently printed on, affixed to, or embedded in the resource.

ii) If the resource contains none of (i), then use any label bearing a title that is physically affixed to or within the container of the item, or printed on accompanying textual material.

iii) In the absence of either (i) or (ii), and if catalogued within a WVMI structure, then replicate the title of the Manifestation to which the Item will be linked.

iv) In the absence of either (i) or (ii), and **either** not catalogued within a WVMI structure, **or** Work and Manifestation have not yet been identified, then a supplied/devised title should be created. In the latter instance, any subsequently created Work and Manifestation to be linked to the Item record should have the same title and a supplied/devised title type (See A.2.5 Supplied/Devised Titles).

A.2.3 Other Title information[139]

Other Work/Variant/Manifestation/Item title (WVMI) information is defined as a word or phrase appearing in conjunction with, and subordinate to the title, and which qualifies, explains, or completes the title to which it applies or which is indicative of the character, contents, etc., of the WVMI, or the motives for, or occasion of, its production or publication.

Other title information includes subtitles, avant-titres, etc., but does not include alternative titles.[140] Cataloguers may constitute subordinate phrases as part of the Work or Vari-

139 Adapted from FIAF, 1.4. Other title information, p. 25.

140 FIAF glossary and FIAF 1992, 1.4: "Other title information: a word or phrase, or a group of characters appearing in conjunction with, and subordinate to, the title proper of the item. Other title information also occurs in conjunction with and subordinate to: parallel titles, variations of the title proper, episode titles, contents titles, titles of series, or of subseries. Other title information qualifies, explains or completes that title to which it applies, or is indicative of the character, contents, etc. of the item or the Works contained in it, or is indicative of the motive for, or the occasion of, the item's production. The term includes subtitles and avant-tîtres."

Differently, in the RDA glossary and RDA 2.3.4: "Other title information is information that appears in conjunction with, and is subordinate to, the title proper of a resource. It may include any phrase appearing in conjunction with the title proper that is indicative of the character, content, etc. of the resource or the motives for, or occasion of, its production of publication. Other title information includes subtitles, avant-titres, etc., but does not include variations on the title proper such as spine titles, sleeve titles, etc. (see 2.3.6) or designations and/or names of parts, sections, or supplements (see 2.3.1.7)."

ant title when, in their judgment, such phrases form an integral part of the preferred title.

If other title information appearing on the Manifestation/Item is considered to be important (either for identification or for access), transcribe it as it appears on the source of information, following the principle of transcription and according to the general guidelines on transcription given in F.3 Relationship of FIAF Cataloguing Rules to Functional Requirements of Bibliographic Records (FRBR), Resource Description and Access (RDA) and The European Standards Committee (CEN) Cinematographic Works Standard EN 15907, section entitled "Representation (or principle of transcription).

Examples:

Dr. Strangelove, or, How I learned to stop worrying and love the bomb
Film d'amore e d'anarchia, ovvero, Stamattina alle 10 in Via del Fiore nella nota casa du tolleranza
Claymation: three dimensional clay animation
This Britain: Heritage of the sea

Distinguish the other title information through the use of spacing or punctuation, or a separate or dedicated field. If a general material designation is used, place it after the preferred title and before other title information.[141]

Examples:

Claymation [motion picture]: three dimensional clay animation
This Britain [motion picture]: Heritage of the sea

A.2.3.1 Abridging or omitting other title information

If other title information is lengthy or of very minor importance, either give it in a note or omit it. See Appendix B, Cataloguer's Notes. Abridge other title information only if this can be done without essential loss of information.[142]

If other title information is clearly of very minor importance, for example a newsreel slogan, or it is an avant-titre which grammatically cannot follow the title proper, place it in a note.[143]

Examples:[144]

CBS news special. Challenge in the coal mines : (*other title information*) men against their union

But:
(without separation into "title proper" and "other title information"):

141 FIAF, 1.4.1.1, 1.4.1.2., 1.4.1.3., pp. 25-26.
142 FIAF, 1.4.2, p. 26.
143 Based on FIAF 1.4.2
144 FIAF 1991, 1.4.1.1

Berlin – Die Sinfonie der Großstadt
Pompeii, frozen in Fire

A.2.4 Alternative[145]

Ensures that users can search under any variation of the title that has been used for a Work, Variant, Manifestation or Item, and be led to the content or particular physical object that they seek.

Alternative titles for the Work differ from uniform, preferred, and other title information and may be encountered in the course of cataloguing its Variants, Manifestations and Items. If the Work could reasonably be sought under the title(s) of one of these Variants/Manifestations, the alternative title should be indexed in such a way that a user who searches on it is led to the Work.

Alternative titles for the Manifestation differ from the title proper or other title information.[146]

Alternative titles on a Manifestation can have a different nature, expressing the possible different designations of the Manifestation during its production, release, publication or archival history that may be different from the title proper or parallel titles.

Ideally record in a note the source(s) for the alternative title(s).

Some institutions may wish to name the type of alternative title. Record the Alternative Title Type by taking the most suitable term from a controlled list elaborated in-house or referring to an authoritative existing list.

If no specific alternative title type is known, the information can be omitted.

A controlled list, not exhaustive and open to further and continued implementation, is suggested below:

A.2.4.1 Alternative title types

- **Working**: A provisional title, given during the production or the manufacturing process.[147]
- **Acquisition title**: A title under which a moving image was acquired, with no other discernible title discovered.
- **Pre-release title**: A provisional title, given to the Manifestation before the release or publication with the definitive title of the related Work.[148]

145 Adapted from YCR, 1.3 Work access, p. 39.
146 The definition is based on the explanation of the "Variant title" title given in RDA (glossary and 2.3.6), but in this case, to avoid confusion with the "Variant" entity, the term "Alternative" has been adopted. The main reference and reason for this choice is the FIAF Glossary where "Alternative title" is in parallel with the RDA "Variant title" and practically with the same meaning: FIAF Glossary, 2008 revision, A.1.12 "Alternative Title, Alternative title. Any title by which a film is known other than the Original Title".
147 Based on FIAF 1.3.
148 Ibid.

- **Abbreviated title**: A title given in order to designate it quickly by the institution.[149]
- **Translated title**: A title given to designate the Manifestation in the language of the institution, in a literally translated form (not to be confused with the Parallel title).[150]
- **Transliterated title**: A title given to designate the Manifestation in the alphabet of the institution, following international standards of transliteration, such as ISO 9 (not to be confused with the Parallel title).[151]
- **Corrected title**: A title given in the corrected form by the institution, when it is recorded incorrectly in the sources of information, if it is considered to be important (either for identification or for access).[152]
- **Help/Search**: Titles which may or may not have been used in verified sources but which clearly help when searching. Use the "Help/Search" title type for stylistic variations including, abbreviations (e.g., Dr./Doctor), numerals (e.g., 45/forty five), acronyms (e.g., FIAF/International Federation of Film Archives) symbols and other characters (e.g., &/and, £/pound), different spelling (Southsea/South Sea).[153]

  Examples:

  The fast & the furious 5
  The fast and the furious 5
  The fast & the furious 5 Rio heist
  The fast and the furious 5 Rio heist
  Fast & furious 5
  Fast and furious 5
  Fast & furious 5 Rio heist
  Fast and furious 5 Rio heist
  The fast & the furious five
  The fast and the furious five
  The fast & the furious five Rio heist

- **Series/Serial title**: the series/serial title of a Work that constitutes an episode/part

  Example:

  Mary Tyler Moore show = Series/Serial Title
  Chuckles bites the dust = Preferred Title

  (see 1.3.2 Title)

- Parallel title : the title in another language or script.

In most cases, a Parallel title correlates to Variants for different language versions.

---

149 Ibid.
150 Ibid.
151 Based on FIAF 1.3.
152 Based on RDA 2.3.6.
153 CID Stylistics Manual – 2nd edition. BFI. 2011.

For archival moving image cataloguing, the concept of a parallel title includes any title qualifying as a preferred title but which is not used as the preferred Work title (e.g. parallel titles for international co-productions, a title which cannot be reproduced) and any title by which the Work is commonly known to users and researchers.

Parallel titles are recorded with wording and spelling as established by an appropriate principal source. Where this involves transcription between scripts, use an appropriate standard for transliterations.[154]

Example: Chandralekha
[No English language title translation available; archive holds Indian release copy – title is romanized.]

When a title is an international co-production, or is produced in a bi- or multi-lingual country of origin, and is released simultaneously under separate titles in the languages of the country of origin or countries of co-production as well as in other languages, record all the parallel titles in the languages of the countries of co-production and in the language of the copy the institution holds, if it is in an additional language.

If it cannot be determined whether the Work was released simultaneously or the release order cannot be determined, the cataloguer should select one of the qualifying titles in accordance with a consistent policy (for example from a list of languages in the institution's preferred order, or by reference to an authoritative source.) [155] [156]

Historically, parallel titles have been placed within the title field itself, following the preferred title and an equal sign to represent the title frame (i.e., the fact that both titles appear onscreen). These guidelines recommend the use of separate fields that distinguish between the preferred title and any subsequent parallel title(s) but if this is not possible, the older approach is acceptable.

Example:

Der Fangschuss = Coup de grâce
[Work is a German-French co-production. The Work was released in the U.S. under the French title.]

Der Fangschuss (Preferred Title)
Coup de grâce (Parallel Title)

Alternatively, an institution may opt to have fewer Title Types and simply use Preferred

154 FIAF, 1.3. Parallel title, p. 22.
155 FIAF, 1.3.4., pp. 23-24.
156 Such lists will normally give preference to the languages most familiar to researchers in the country of the archive. For example, the standard list for archival moving image cataloguing in the United States is:
1. U.S. title (if an American company is involved in the production).
2. U.K. title (if a British company is involved in the production).
3. Other English language title (if an English language speaking country is involved in the production).
4. French title (if a French company is involved in the production).
5. German title (if a German-speaking country is involved in the production).
6. Other Romance language title (if these language companies are involved in the production).
7. Other Germanic language title (if these language companies are involved in the production).

and Alternative Title Types (i.e., designating parallel titles as Alternative Title Types). For example, with co-productions, a Preferred title for the Work is established with all other language titles added both as Alternative title types to the Work and as the Title Proper/Other Title of an associated Variant and/or Manifestation.

A parallel title of a Manifestation corresponds to the title proper in another language or script.[157]

Record in a note the source of the parallel title, as appropriate. Institutions may choose to distinguish between distinct Parallel and Alternative title types or adopt a wider definition of "Alternative" which incorporates both.

For parallel titles of a Manifestation distributed in distinct geographical regions, record the region(s) to which the parallel title applies.

(For the treatment of the geographical names, see Getty Thesaurus of *Geographic Names* (TGN), or some other recognised standard.)

A.2.5 Supplied/Devised Titles (i.e. Creating titles for untitled/unidentified entities or production material)

A title "made up" or assigned by the cataloguer. This is often applied to untitled or unidentified entities or production material.

This section helps in the construction of both partially or fully supplied/devised titles for Works, Variants, Manifestations and Items.

Partially or fully supplied/devised titles facilitate the discovery and identification of moving images without formal title. The title itself should be descriptive, describing the Work as succinctly as possible.[158]

Supplied/Devised titles are implemented for:

- moving image entities (i.e., WMVI) intended to have a formal title but the title cannot be determined from any other source (i.e. moving image entities with "no titles")
- moving image entities that were not intended to have a formal title (i.e. "untitled" moving image entities such as home movies)
- moving image entities that are unidentifiable.

The moving images may be monographic, multi-part or component part. They may also be edited, partially edited, or unedited; complete or incomplete.

157 Differences between FIAF 1992 and RDA: FIAF expands the concept of Parallel title to any title qualifying as an original but not used as a title proper (the attempt was to include as many alternative titles as possible), but gives to the archives the responsibility to decide whether to enter them in the appropriate area or in the Notes area. RDA makes a distinction among the different characteristics of a title and considers the parallel title strictly as "the title proper in another language or script". In this context the RDA approach has been considered more appropriate.
158 Based on OLAC (2009), Part 3a, pp. 8-9.

These guidelines do not explicitly address the construction of supplied/ devised titles for collection-level records, although the principles would be the same. For collections of material based on the principle of provenance, refer to other standards such as *General International Standard Archival Description* (ISAD(G)) or *Describing Archives: A Content Standard* (*DACS*).

It is recognised that in real-world cataloguing, the creation of supplied/devised titles must begin with an examination of the moving images (i.e. the sound and picture) on a Manifestation/Item.

Where appropriate, the supplied/devised title for Works and Variants will be inherited directly from the supplied/devised titles constructed for the Manifestations/Items (i.e., the "things" under consideration) from information sourced from the Manifestations/ Items alone or in combination with accompanying documentation, or secondary sources.

NOTE: The guidelines for the construction of partially or fully supplied/devised titles have traditionally incorporated display concerns by recommending the consistent placement of different components of data in the title field of a record. Current data content standards, such as RDA, mean to separate display from content rules. These guidelines straddle the middle by providing recommendations for concatenating data in the title field, or allowing a more atomized way of indexing.

Additionally, some institutions place the partially or fully supplied/devised titles in square or rounded brackets. Traditionally, the presence of brackets indicates information taken from a place other than the Item being catalogued. Use the practice of your institution. Where possible, use a Title + Title Type approach. This approach effectively removes the need for brackets by establishing the Title is supplied/devised by the cataloguer. If there is no Title Type field then a Notes or other field could be utilised.

It is recommended that archive titles are devised following a pattern of:

Who/what: persons, events or objects
What: activity
Where: location
When: time period
Who/what: name of source or collection

The above elements can be combined with a form qualifier if relevant: i.e. Commercial, Rushes, Interview, or Screen test, etc.

Not all the above information has to be in the archive title if not discernible, but incorporating as many as possible using a consistent will aid identification.

Examples:

Lawrence of Arabia. Rushes
Tram journey through Southampton 1902
Warships. 1920s
Tango. Orange genie. Commercial
Jones Collection footage. No. 5

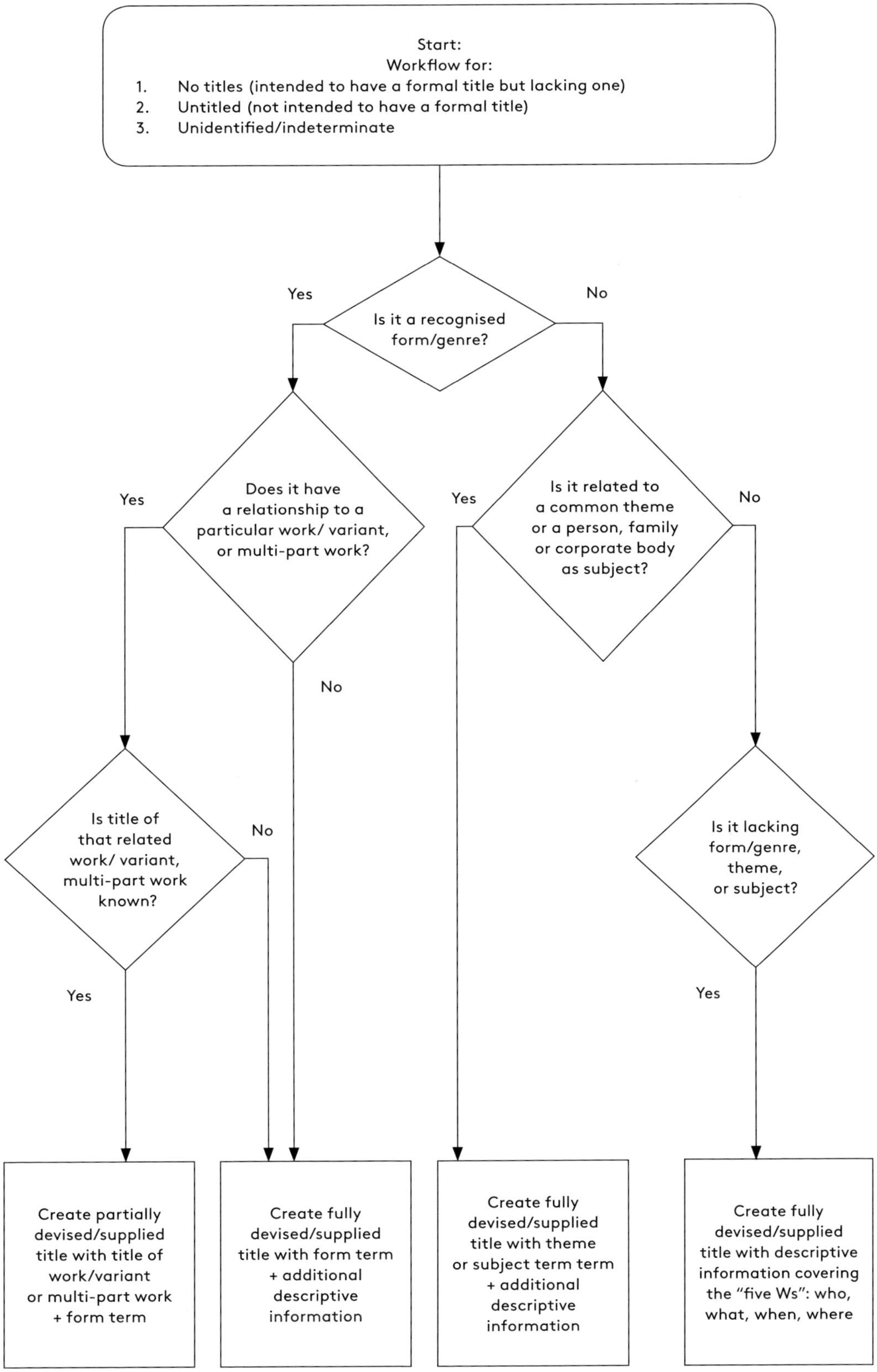
Start:
Workflow for:
1. No titles (intended to have a formal title but lacking one)
2. Untitled (not intended to have a formal title)
3. Unidentified/indeterminate
Is it a recognised form/genre?
Yes
No
Does it have a relationship to a particular work/ variant, or multi-part work?
Yes
No
Is it related to a common theme or a person, family or corporate body as subject?
Yes
No
Is title of that related work/ variant, multi-part work known?
No
Yes
Is it lacking form/genre, theme, or subject?
Yes
Create partially devised/supplied title with title of work/variant or multi-part work + form term
Create fully devised/supplied title with form term + additional descriptive information
Create fully devised/supplied title with theme or subject term term + additional descriptive information
Create fully devised/supplied title with descriptive information covering the "five Ws": who, what, when, where

A.2.5.1 Partially Supplied/Devised Titles[159]

Partially supplied/devised titles are applied in cases where the moving image content from a Manifestation/item has:

- a recognised form

and

- a relationship with, or is dependent upon, a particular moving image Work or Variant, or a multi-part Work.

Therefore, partially supplied/devised titles may be created for edited content that is a Work in its own right (e.g. trailers or a compilation of trailers) but connected to a larger Work; or unedited content that is derived from or otherwise has a dependent relationship to a Work (e.g. rushes).

Partially supplied/devised titles are basically augmented preferred titles for a Work/ Variant. This augmentation traditionally appends a form term to the title itself, (e.g., Gone with the wind. Trailer).

Optionally, form terms may be left out of the title field and indexed as an attribute of the Work/Variant where possible or preferable.

Partially supplied/devised titles may be provided in cases of unidentified moving image content. For example, a Work may have a partially supplied/devised title in instances where a series/serial title is known but the episode or chapter title is not (e.g., The Mighty Boosh. Unidentified episode). Unedited footage from a known, named television programme (e.g. a compilation of outtakes from 60 Minutes) is another case where a Work may have a partially supplied/devised title.

Institutions should rely upon in-house lists of standardised form terms to be used as additions to/indexed as an attribute of such related titles, or utilise established standardised lists such as Library of Congress Genre/Form Terms for Library and Archival Materials (LCGFT), or rely upon the "form terms" list provided in D.18 List of form terms for Supplied/Devised titles.

General guidelines for Partially Supplied/Devised titles[160]

Formulate the Partially supplied/devised title by recording in the order suggested, the following three components, in a manner that it will clearly and uniquely identify the content being catalogued.

i) The TITLE of the particular moving image Work or Variant, or multi-part Work to which the content has a recognised form and relationship with

---

159 This section, including form terms and examples, is based on or taken from FIAF 1.4.3 Additions to titles;Y-ee/UCLA 5.1.2; AMIM2 1F1.1

160 This section, including form terms and examples, is based on or taken from FIAF 1.4.3 Additions to titles;Y-ee/UCLA 5.1.2; AMIM2 1F1.1

And

ii) The FORM qualifier, e.g. Commercial, Interview, Rushes, Screentest, etc.

And/Or

iii) The NAME of Persons/Events/Objects, activity, location, time period (Who, What, Where, When)

Optionally, associate a form term with the Work through indexing the form term in a specific field(s).

Where applicable, more than one form term can be used, e.g., Frenzy. Promotional film. Rushes.

If the order or the number of the components cannot be met as prescribed, optionally, use a local practice that presents the data in a standardised way, even if such standardised presentations must be developed on a case-by-case basis, depending on the material itself as well as the context of an institution's collection. A level of consistency can be maintained by following the general principles of description laid out in these guidelines.

When there is more than one Manifestation/Item with the same supplied/devised title, and there are no other means of further disambiguation, use a number to distinguish them.

The source(s) of information of the supplied/devised title should be made clear, whether in notes or through some other structured method for correlating data to its source(s).

A relationship between the title and the title type should be established such that the title constructed by the cataloguer is named and identified as "supplied" or "devised," whether within the title itself or via a juxtaposed field such as "Title Type." If there is no Title Type field then a Notes or other field could be utilised.

Some archives place the entire sequence of components in the title field in brackets. Other archives place only the qualifying form term in square or round brackets.

EXAMPLES:

Le Cercle Rouge. Theatrical trailer

OR

Le Cercle Rouge (Theatrical trailer)

OR

[Le Cercle Rouge. Theatrical trailer]

OR

Title: Le Cercle Rouge

Form: Theatrical trailer

The misfits. TV trailers

OR

The misfits (TV Trailers)

OR

[The Misfits. TV trailers]

OR

Title: The Misfits

Form: TV trailers

L'armée des ombres. Rushes

OR

L'armée des ombres (Rushes)

OR

L'armée des ombres [Rushes]

OR

Title: L'armée des ombres

Form: Rushes

Le samourai. Excerpt

OR

Le samourai (Excerpt)

OR

[Le samourai. Excerpt]

OR

Title: Le samourai

Form: Excerpt

For constructing partially supplied/devised titles where the moving image is a component part of a known larger Work, but the title of the component part is not known:

If the content probably was released or broadcast or published with a title, but the title is missing, supply/devise a title with the word "unidentified." If it is known that the content falls into a form category, add a form term as listed in the "form term" list.[161]

Descriptive phrases, which are short statements summarising the moving image, can also be used in association with a titled Work, in conjunction with the form term.

161 Taken almost wholly from Yee/UCLA, 5.2.2.1. Unidentified materials released or broadcast with a title

Any further description may be added following a period, or a dash.[162] For example, the type of test (screen test), the person tested, or the particular sequence(s) in an excerpt, may be specified in the title field where necessary or warranted.

Optionally (or additionally), this data can also be indexed in specific fields dedicated to this content.

Use numbers to distinguish separate content when there is more than one unidentified segment in a particular descriptor category.

EXAMPLE

The Mighty Boosh. Unidentified episode

OR

Series Title: The Mighty Boosh

Episode Title: Unidentified episode

Flash Gordon conquers the universe. Unidentified episode.

OR

Series Title: Flash Gordon conquers the universe

Episode Title: Unidentified episode

This hour has seven days. Unidentified episode. International espionage. 196?

OR

Series Title: This hour has seven days

Episode Title: Unidentified episode

Summary/Content description: International espionage

Year: 196?

Heckle and Jeckle. Unidentified cartoon.

OR

Series Title: Heckle and Jeckle

Episode Title: Unidentified episode

A.2.5.2 Fully Supplied/Devised Titles

Fully supplied/devised titles are applied in cases where the moving image content from a Manifestation/Item has no formal title and a formal title cannot be established from the entity itself or accompanying documentation, or other secondary sources.

162 The punctuation used is less important than following a consistent order and conforming to standard terminology.

General guidelines for FULLY Supplied/Devised titles

Formulate the FULLY supplied/devised title by recording in the order suggested, the following TWO components, in a manner that will clearly and uniquely identify the content being catalogued.

1) The NAME of Persons/Events/Objects, activity, location, time period (Who, What, Where, When)

AND/OR

2) A FORM qualifier, e.g. Commercial, Interview, Rushes, Screentest, etc. [Either added as a component to the title itself, or indexed in specific field(s)]

Where ascertainable, when the content being described consists of one specific form, supply the form using standardised vocabulary.[163]

Optionally (or additionally), establish a link with the form index adopted by the archive.

Institutions should rely upon in-house lists of standardised form terms, or utilise established standardised lists such as Library of Congress Genre/Form Terms for Library and Archival Materials (LCGFT), or rely upon the list provided in D.18 List of form terms for Supplied/Devised titles.

EXAMPLES:

Announcements
Bloopers
Commercials
Home movies

If the content being described consists of two or more forms, record the one or two most predominate forms followed by the phrase "and other content,"[164] or "and other segments" or something similar as long as consistency is achieved.

EXAMPLE:

CBS bloopers, commercials and other content

It is recommended that institutions stipulate within the supplied/devised title that the footage is unedited (e.g. "unedited footage" or "unedited content"), as an overall way of characterising the form of the content. This may not be appropriate in all cases.[165]

EXAMPLES:

Animals. Unedited footage
Boulder transmission line tests. Unedited footage

163 Adapted from DACS, 2.3.18, pp. 20-21.
164 Adapted from DACS, 2.3.18, pp. 20-21.
165 Based on Yee/UCLA, 5.2.3

Cattle herd. Stock footage
Kennedy presidential campaign. Arrival, Boston. Unedited footage
Trains, night clubs, Santa Ana Freeway. Stock shots
Unedited. Kleine Collection footage
Unedited. Jones Collection footage. No. 5

Where ascertainable, supply standardised or controlled terms or phrases that most precisely and succinctly characterise what the content is about (e.g. persons, corporate bodies, objects, activities, events, geographical area).

Where ascertainable, record the name(s) of the person(s), family (families) or corporate body (bodies) predominately responsible for the creation, assembly, accumulation and/or maintenance of the content.[166] An agent relationship should be associated with a Work, Variant or Manifestation/item depending on the type of contribution involved.

Record or index the name(s) in the form by which the creator/collector/assembler, etc. is generally known in natural language order.[167]

If no name has been recorded, but the subject of the content is a person, family or corporate body, express the title in a way that clearly indicates that the subject of the content is the named person, family or corporate body.[168]

EXAMPLES:

Compilation on Emmanuelle Devos
Early balloon footage.
World War I patriotic marches. No. 3
Ads and tours of Seattle industry
Ponselle, Rosa. Screentests.
Theodore Roosevelt. 1905 inaugural ceremony. Speeches
James Cagney, ca. 1965. Interviews
ABC Network fall season preview. 1964-65 season. Unedited footage
optionally: Unedited footage. ABC Network fall season preview. 1964-65 season
Academy Awards, 17th. Best actor and actress. Unedited footage
optionally, Unedited footage. Academy Awards, 17th. Best actor and actress
optionally, Unedited 17th Academy Awards footage. Best actor and actress
Academy Awards. Award presentation, Conrad Nagel. Unedited footage
Anna Held. Unedited footage
CBS logo reel
Eddie Cantor and others. Unedited footage
World Series, 1956. Game no. 7. Unedited footage

For unidentified moving images, use the term "unidentified" in the title. Use numbers to distinguish separate content when there is more than one unidentified segment in a particular descriptor category.

166 DACS, 2.3.4, p. 18.
167 DACS, 2.3.4, p. 18.
168 Adapted from DACS, 2.3.22, p. 22.

EXAMPLES:

Unidentified cartoon
Unidentified cartoon. Warner Brothers
    optionally: Unidentified Warner Brothers cartoon
Unidentified short about Africa
Unidentified film. James Cagney/Joe E. Brown
Unidentified equestrian film
Unidentified films. Excerpts
Unidentified film. Kay Kyser musical
    optionally: Unidentified Kay Kyser musical
Unidentified film. Warner Brothers. Outtakes
    optionally: Unidentified Warner Brothers outtakes
Unidentified film. Western
    optionally: Unidentified Western
Unidentified newsreel. Excerpts. Auto race subjects, 1930s
Unidentified newsreel. Native American ritual dances, fifth wheel car, Fremont High game
Unidentified newsreel, Russian
    optionally: Unidentified Russian newsreel
Unidentified shorts
Unidentified television programme. Wrestling. DuMont prod. no. 1757
Travelogue. Greenland expedition. Unidentified excerpts
Unidentified television series. Quiz show. Unidentified episodes

For a more comprehensive list of form terms to use with for FULLY or PARTIALLY Supplied/Devised titles, see D.18 List of form terms for Supplied/Devised titles.

A.2.6 Titles of series/serials

The guidelines and principles laid out in this section can be applicable across all the categories of Works, Variants, Manifestations and Items (WVMI).

For monographic Works that are an episode within a series or serial[169], and have their own individual title, the individual episode title may be used as the preferred title for the Work or Variant, or the title proper for the Manifestation and Item. However, the series/serial title should also be indicated.

The series/serial title may be indicated within (i) the title field itself, or (ii) reflected in a linked hierarchical relationship with an individual Serial Work level record, i.e. a Work assigned the Description Type "Serial[170]; or (iii) added as a Title Type; or (iv) a combination. Individual institutions should select which is most appropriate for their own systems and for clarity of identification and retrieval.

---

169 Serial = something which is a continuing story, for which it is necessary to have seen previous episodes to follow the story line, e.g. Pride and Prejudice, The Black Arrow, Brideshead Revisited. Series = something which contains programmes or episodes which are complete in themselves (although they may have characters in common) for which it is not essential to have seen previous episodes in order to understand the story line/content, e.g. Cadfael. Midsomer Murders, World in Action.. BFI SIFT Inputting Manual.
170 See Appendix D.1 Work/Variant Description Types for EN 15907/BFI definitions of Serial as Description Type.

Example:

Work (Serial) – Mary Tyler Moore show

Work (Monographic) – Chuckles bites the dust

Manifestation – Chuckles bites the dust

Item – Chuckles bites the dust

OR

Work (Serial) – Mary Tyler Moore show

Work (Monographic) – Mary Tyler Moore show. Chuckles bites the dust

Manifestation – Mary Tyler Moore show. Chuckles bites the dust

Item – Mary Tyler Moore show. Chuckles bites the dust

OR

Work (Monographic) – Chuckles bites the dust (Preferred title)
Mary Tyler Moore show (Series title)

Manifestation – Chuckles bites the dust

Item – Chuckles bites the dust

A.2.6.1 Numbered episodes of a series/serial

With series/serials that contain episode or part numbers and individual episode titles the same principles apply. The preferred title/title proper of the WVMI may incorporate all these for clarity and retrieval purposes, or an institution's systems may allow for use of the episode title combined with separate specific Part field(s) for parts and numbers, or both. Alternatively, an institution may choose to use one form for Work/Variants and another for Manifestation and/or Items. With television series additional numbered season details may also be required as well as episode/part numbers.

Any or either of the forms may be used in combination as an institution chooses, although this should be within the context of an institution establishing a clear standard in-house practice rather than individual cataloguer preference and choice.[171]

It is worth bearing in mind that serials are always intended to be viewed in a specified order. Therefore serial title, episode numbers, and episode titles are usually included on

171 The 1991 FIAF rules stipulated that such titles should have a comma separator between the part element and individual title components of the Title, e.g., Flash Gordon's trip to Mars, Chapter 12, Ming the Merciless. However, the trend seems to be to distinguish the different elements of such component types of titles with a full stop separator, e.g., Flash Gordon's trip to Mars. Chapter 12. Ming the Merciless.

the Item itself or in secondary sources, and should be reflected in the record to aid in discovery and identification.

Example: Flash Gordon's trip to Mars. Chapter 12. Ming the Merciless

Work (Serial) – Flash Gordon's trip to Mars

Work (Monographic) – Ming the Merciless

Manifestation – Ming the Merciless

Item – Ming the Merciless

[with "Chapter 12" element being added to a separate relevant Part field]

OR

Work (Serial) – Flash Gordon's trip to Mars

Work (Monographic) – Flash Gordon's trip to Mars. Chapter 12. Ming the Merciless

Manifestation – Flash Gordon's trip to Mars. Chapter 12. Ming the Merciless

Item – Flash Gordon's trip to Mars. Chapter 12. Ming the Merciless

OR

Work (Serial) – Flash Gordon's trip to Mars

Work (Monographic) – Ming the Merciless

Manifestation – Flash Gordon's trip to Mars. Chapter 12. Ming the Merciless

Item – Flash Gordon's trip to Mars. Chapter 12. Ming the Merciless

The same principle can be applied to episodes of a series/serial that do not have their own individual titles but have numbered parts.

Example:

Work (Serial) – Pride and prejudice

Work (Monographic) – Pride and prejudice. Part One

Manifestation – Pride and prejudice. Part One

Item – Pride and prejudice. Part One

Reflect the Part term used in any source of information, for example, "part," "chapter," "episode," etc. Equally, if the number is in numerals then use those, and if alphabetical, i.e. One, Two, Three, etc., use those.

A.2.6.2 Episodes of a series/serial with no individual title or numbered parts

For episodes of a series/serial that have neither individual episode titles nor numbered parts, a date can be added to the title field, with the option of utilising square brackets for clarity. It is recommended to use the release/production/transmission date of the Manifestation to which the Item or Work/Variant pertains.

If a repeat broadcast of a television programme with no individual title or numbered parts has been acquired, then a new Manifestation and Item should be created with the repeat broadcast date appended to their titles. Within the hierarchical structure this new Manifestation would link to the Work that may incorporate an earlier original broadcast date within its preferred title.

The new Manifestation/Item title could be added to the Work level as an Alternative title type.

Example:

Work (Serial) – Panorama

Work (Monographic) – Panorama [2011-01-23]

Manifestation 1 – Panorama [2011-01-23]

Item – Panorama [2011-01-23]

Manifestation 2 – Panorama [2011-05-03]

Item – Panorama [2011-05-03]

In the above example the Manifestations "Panorama [2011-01-23] and "Panorama [2011-05-03]" both link hierarchically to the same Work, entitled "Panorama [2011-01-23]" as they are broadcasts on different dates of exactly the same programme.

Alternatively, the cataloguer can supply the type of unit and number, with the option of utilising square brackets for clarity.

Example:

Work (Serial) – Panorama

Work (Monographic) – Panorama. [Episode 1]

Manifestation – Panorama. [Episode 1]

Item – Panorama. [Episode 1]

Manifestation – Panorama. [Episode 1] (repeat broadcast)

Item – Panorama. [Episode 1] (repeat broadcast)

In the above example, the Manifestations with different broadcast dates both link hierarchically to the same Work. The original broadcast date can be entered in the Date field for the Work, and the repeat broadcast date can be entered in a Date field for the Manifestation/Item, should one exist, or in a Notes field for the Manifestation/Item.

A.2.6.3 Analytics/Components of identified newsreels/ cinemagazines

Where a complete newsreel issue has been acquired and the newsreel series has been identified, then titling follows the same principles and guidelines above.

Newsreels and cinemagazines can often be acquired as incomplete. The incomplete Items acquired may have a different title than the Manifestation and Work to which they are related. Such Items should be linked to a Work/Manifestation reflecting the whole issue, (see "British Paramount News" examples given below).

Newsreels and cinemagazines[172] usually consisted of several separate reports that were all analytics/components of a particular issue, and also usually had inter-title headings within the newsreel itself.

If an institution acquires only a part of a newsreel issue, then any inter-title heading that is on the acquired print may be used as the title of the Item, particularly in cases where the title of the newsreel issue as a whole (i.e. the Work/Manifestation) is unknown.

For example, *British Paramount news No. 856* contains the inter-titled headed segments *President Roosevelt opens World Fair; 70th birthday of US coast to coast railway*; and, *Princesses play with baby pandas*.

Should an institution only acquire a reel of the segment *President Roosevelt opens World Fair*, then this can be designated as the title of the Item.

Where it is known with which particular newsreel issue or series the acquired segment belongs then there is also the option to incorporate the newsreel series/issue title within the title assigned to the segment, for example:

British Paramount news No. 856. President Roosevelt opens World Fair

OR

172 BFI definitions: Newsreels = Films dating from 1910 to 1979, which report on local and international events and which were regularly screened at cinemas, e.g. Pathé News 1910-1970; Warwick Bioscope Chronicle 1910-1915; Topical Budget 1911-1931; Newsreel Flying Machine Compilation 1910. Cinemagazines = Short magazine film including more than two interest items, e.g. Aussie Oddities (1948), This Week in Britain (1950-1980)

British Paramount news. President Roosevelt opens World Fair

Within a hierarchical structure, the Item *President Roosevelt opens World Fair* would be linked as "part of" the Theatrical Manifestation *British Paramount news No. 856*, i.e. the whole newsreel issue, which in turn would be linked to the Work record for the whole issue also with the title *British Paramount news No. 856*.

Example:

Work (Series) – British Paramount news

Work (Monographic) – British Paramount news. No. 856

Manifestation – British Paramount news. No. 856

Item – President Roosevelt opens World Fair

OR

Work (Series) – British Paramount news

Work (Monographic) – British Paramount news. No. 856

Manifestation – British Paramount news. No. 856

Item – British Paramount news. No. 856. President Roosevelt opens World Fair

At the Work level each of the titled analytics/components making up the whole, i.e. the separate news reports, can be added as additional alternative titles.

Alternatively, the component titles can be listed in a Summary or Description field for the Work.

Should the Item acquired incorporate more than one inter-titled component, for example only reel 2 of a 2 reel Item is acquired that includes both *70th birthday of US coast to coast railway* and *Princesses play with baby pandas*, then a different approach may be taken. This would involve using the title of the appropriate Manifestation pertaining to the whole newsreel issue and adding qualifying details, optionally in square brackets, as a second element of the title to create a title for the Item, for example

British Paramount news No. 856. [Reel 2]

OR

British Paramount news No.856. Reel 2

British Paramount news No.856. [Incomplete]

OR

British Paramount news No.856. Incomplete

with any inter-title designations on the print then added as alternative type titles, for example:

Preferred Title: British Paramount news No. 856. [Reel 2]

Alternative Title : 70th birthday of US coast to coast railway

Alternative Title : Princesses play with baby pandas

If deemed necessary or helpful for the purposes of discovery, the alternative titles added to Items should also be added to the Work level record.

Alternatively, the titles of each analytic/component may be included in a notes and/or contents field.

Square brackets may be used within titles for encasing necessary extra qualifying or clarification elements that are not on the actual print.

A.2.6.4 Analytics/components of unidentified news-reels/ cinemagazines

Where only an analytic/component of a copy pertaining to a whole Work has been acquired as an Item, and the Serial Work to which it belongs is unable to be identified (i.e., the Item acquired is clearly a section of newsreel but the newsreel series has not been identified), then the title assigned to that Item should also be used to create the title for the Manifestation and Work records, which will then be related to each other hierarchically.

The Item title is assigned in accordance with 3.1.2 Title and A.2.5 Supplied/Devised Titles.

The following paragraphs relate to Archive systems that are using the CEN structure:

Work level titles created in this way would be described as having the CEN attribute of "Analytic" and indication that the title is a supplied/devised title type. Further clarifications could then be put into synopsis/description or notes fields areas of the Work.

Should the whole Work of which the Item is a part subsequently be identified, then the Analytic record can be either modified or deleted and the Item linked via a "part of" relationship to a whole issue Theatrical Manifestation, which is in turn "part of" a whole Work, or Monographic Work.[173]

173 See Appendix D, Value Lists for CEN categories and definitions used by BFI

A.2.6.5 Fragments/segments of unidentified moving images (film or television programmes)

Similar principles apply to any unidentified and incomplete segments or fragments of films or television programmes that have been acquired.

For example, a reel of a silent fiction film with no title given on either the print or can, or any indication of what it is, other than it is clearly part of a longer film, should be assigned a relevant Item title in accordance with the guidelines in A.2.5 Supplied/Devised Titles, for example:

Unidentified silent film segment

or where possible following the who/what/where/when ordering principles in creating a devised title.[174]

Medieval battle segment. Unidentified silent film

OR

Unidentified silent film. Medieval battle segment

The Item title would then be utilised to create the Manifestation and Work level records as well.

In such cases the Work would be assigned the attribute Monographic. Analytic is only used for a whole component rather than a fragment of a whole.

Square brackets around a whole devised title are optional, as this can alternatively be inferred by use of a Supplied/Devised Title Type designation. Many electronic systems can be punctuation sensitive, so presence of square brackets [], particularly at the start of a title, could impact on searchability.

A.2.7 Moving images with probable or questionable titles[175]

There are instances where the title from a Manifestation/Item may not be inherited by the Work or Variant. Such is the case when a Manifestation/Item contains a probable or questionable title.

If the Manifestation/item contains a probable or questionable title, this title may be included as a component in constructing the supplied/devised title, or it may be used alone as the supplied/devised title for the Work. (See A.2.5 Supplied/Devised Titles). The probability or questionable nature of the title, and its source, should be made clear in a note.

174 See A.2.5 Supplied/Devised Titles (i.e. Creating titles for untitled/unidentified entities or production material) and examples of titling
175 Based on AMIM2, 1F2.1.

For example, an Item may have a probable or questionable title but the title is not the preferred title for the Work and the preferred title for the Work cannot be discovered. Some institutions may choose to record a probable or questionable title as the title proper, or preferred title, for the Manifestation/Item, but not as the preferred title for the Work or Variant. Some institutions may use the probable or questionable title as the preferred title for the Manifestation/item and Work (or Work and Variant).

For example:[176]

> Archive contains a copy of the Italian version of an unidentified American silent comedy, with Italian intertitles[177].
>
> > Primary Title on Item: Title proper – Nipote Modello
> > Primary Title for Manifestation: Title proper – Nipote Modello
> > Primary Title for Variant: Preferred title – Nipote Modello
> > Primary Title for Work: Supplied/devised title – Unidentified film. Silent American comedy
> >
> > OR
> >
> > Primary Title on Item: Title proper – Nipote Modello
> > Primary Title for Manifestation/Item record: Title proper – Nipote Modello
> > Primary Title for Variant record: Preferred title – Nipote Modello
> > Primary Title for Work: Supplied/devised title – Unidentified silent American Comedy. Nipote Modello
> >
> > OR
> >
> > Primary Title on Item: Title proper – Nipote Modello
> > Primary Title for Manifestation/Item record: Title proper – Nipote Modello
> > Primary Title for Variant record: Preferred title – Nipote Modello
> > Primary Title for Work record: Preferred title – Nipote Modello

The treatment of probable or questionable titles may vary among institutions. Many institutions' catalogues contain a mixture of Collection-, Work-, Variant-, and Manifestation-level records that function as the "parent" record or the topmost "node", to which the units of moving image material are associated. In the absence of a Work or information about a Work, many institutions represent what they have.

For purposes of discoverability, accessibility, and standardisation, it is recommended that a Work is always represented in the catalogue, even if it means utilising and repeating information more strictly related to a Variant, Manifestation or Item.

The Work can take the title of the Item, Manifestation or Variant, until such time as further research or identification assists in establishing the preferred title for the Work. The crucial factor is coupling the title with a descriptive identifier denoting that it is

---

176 Many archives place information found on the Manfestation/Item in quotes to indicate the data is transcribed from the physical item itself or the audiovisual content of the entity. This practice is not recommended unless required by local cataloguing rules or local system requirements.
177 This example has since been identified as the film Grandpa's Girl (USA, 1924 – Gil Pratt)

"supplied" or "devised," whether within the title itself or via a juxtaposed field such as "Title Type." If there is no Title Type field than a Notes or other field could be utilised.

Examples of partially and fully supplied titles for a variety of scenarios can be found in the "form terms" list provided in D.18 List of form terms for Supplied/Devised titles.

A.3 Titling of Aggregates

Titling of aggregates follows the same principles as that of other types of entities as detailed in Appendix A.1 and A.2 sections above.

Appendix B, Cataloguer's Notes

A cataloguer's note is any annotation that might be helpful to those using or revising the cataloguing data. It includes information that does not readily fit into dedicated fields or other areas of the description. The extent and specificity of notes will depend upon factors such as staff, viewing facilities, documentation, system designs, etc.[178]

Take information recorded in notes from any suitable source. When creating the note, apply the guidelines in Chapter 0. Preliminary Notes on capitalisation, quotations, references, etc.

Institutions may establish more rigorous, local guidelines as to the order of information in the notes area. For example, when recording notes which further describe data elements already catalogued, some institutions may stipulate the order of notes follow a particular sequence wherever possible, e.g., title, statement of responsibility, edition/version/variation, production, distribution, etc.; or, when uniformity of presentation assists in the recognition of the type of information being presented or gives economy of space without loss of clarity.[179]

Examples:[180]

> Title, Country of reference, Year/Date and Language(s) verified by telephone call to production company, 2013-07-01.
>
> Intended audience: secondary school students.

In general, make the following notes, if they are considered to be important:[181]

- notes on the specific instructions applied in creating headings/access points, or otherwise justifying the choice and form of name and title
- notes limiting the use of the heading/access point
- notes differentiating persons, families, or corporate bodies with similar names
- notes differentiating WVMI entities with similar titles

Examples:

> sex, lies and videotape (USA, 1989)
> Title represented onscreen in lower-case.
>
> Herr der Ringe Die Zwei Türme (Germany, New Zealand, USA, 2002, Peter Jackson)
> Part II of trilogy. Majority German financing nationality confirmed, thus German title assigned as Preferred title and The Lord of the Rings The Fellowship of the Ring as Alternative.

---

178 Based on FIAF 7. Notes Area, Introduction and RDA 29.7.1.1 Scope, 29.7.1.2 Sources of Information
179 FIAF 7.1.3 Form of notes
180 Adapted from FIAF 7.1.3 Form of notes
181 Based on RDA 5.9.1.3 and 8.13.1.3 Making Cataloguer's Notes

Le cœur de la France (France, 1967, Roger Leenhardt)
The word "cœur " does not actually appear in the title, but is represented by a heart-shaped symbol.

Carlyle Films (production company)
Not to be confused with Carlyle Corporate Communications who also trade as Carlyle Films

Harrison Ford (actor)
Silent film actor, retired from the screen in 1932.

Harrison Ford (actor)
Not to be confused with the silent movie actor of the 1920s of the same name.

The following instructions for notes should be considered neither all-inclusive nor mandatory. The number and type of notes included in a description must be dictated by the moving images being described and the needs of the individual institution.[182]

B.1 Boundaries

Provide additional or explanatory information that clarifies boundary decisions, particularly in cases where the system used does not allow for the clear representation of all the WVMI entities.

Examples:[183]

Version information (re-editing and new narration) from copyright descriptive material.

Censored version.

Remake of the 1941 motion picture, Here comes Mr. Jordan.
Originally developed for ABC-TV.

Teaching version includes questions for discussion about the novel's theme and philosophy presented in a classroom setting at the end of the film; discussion is 10 min. in length.

B.2 Attributes

Provide additional or explanatory information for any WVMI attributes as desired, particularly in cases where this information is not recorded elsewhere in dedicated fields.

182 Based on FIAF 7.2. Notes
183 FIAF 7.2.7. History of edition/version/variation

Examples:

Archive holds copies of both original German 1931 release (copy 1) and 1978 reissue with new English language subtitles (copy 2).[184]

Parts 1-3 (ca. 45 min.) are also included in: Oil spill contingency planning series.[185]

B.3 Elements

Provide additional or explanatory information for any WVMI elements, particularly in cases where this information is not recorded elsewhere in dedicated fields. This is offered for users that do not have the option of structuring this information as described in these guidelines.

Title

The source or function of a title, the date the title was viewed and who viewed it, variations in titles, inaccuracies, deletions, etc., or other information relating to a title, if this information is not recorded elsewhere in dedicated fields.[186]

Examples:[187]

Works

Commonly known in moving image reference sources under title Mon oncle.

Title from publisher's catalogue.

Title devised by cataloguer.

Title from title screen.

Title supplied by donor, Mrs. Pare Lorentz (Elizabeth Meyer).

Title from Moving Picture World 3:122.

The word "Love" in the title is represented by the drawing of a heart.

Parallel title, Mad about money, is American release title.

Variants/Manifestations/Items

Title on containers of parts 3 and 5–6 varies slightly.

Subtitle varies.

184 FIAF 7.2.8.2. Names and Functions
185 FIAF 7.2.12. Series
186 RDA 2.20.2.1 Scope
187 Examples taken from RDA 2.20.2.3 Title Source, 2.20.2.4 Title variations, Inaccuracies, and Deletions; RDA 5.9.1.3 Making Cataloguer's Notes; and FIAF 7.2 Notes

Title from container.

Title from descriptive insert.

Caption title.

Title from menu.

Tentative title taken from label on nitrate can.

Incorrect title spliced on film: Days of glory.

Year of reference

Relevant information which further explains the year/date and the source(s) of information.

Examples:

Personal record. Eugene Meyer family. Family camping trip through the Canadian Rockies -- US, 1926.

[Note] Date from notes accompanying item, attached to inventory, and from Merlo Pusey's Eugene Meyer, (New York: Knopf, 1974), p.195. [188]

French language edition ©1982.
Copyright date recorded as copyright 1987. Resource described is a translation of the French language edition.[189]

Title of work is clearly, Ten nights in a bar room; however, several versions of this film were produced between 1910-1931. It is probable that this work is the 1921 version, but due to vagueness of available plot summaries and disappearance of copyright descriptive material for the 1921 version, date cannot be verified at this time.[190]

Language[191]

Give the language or languages of the spoken, sung, or written content of the WVMI unless they are apparent from the rest of the description or data contained in specific language and usage fields.

Examples:

In Arabic with English subtitles.
English language credits and narration.
Main title, credits, and preface in French; dialogue in special languages created by Anthony Burgess.
Sound track dubbed in English.

188 FIAF, p. 65
189 RDA 2.20.10.3 Details Relating to Copyright Dates
190 FIAF 7.2.7. History of edition/version/variation
191 Based on FIAF 7.2.2. Language

English translation voice-over.

Content description

A note appearing in conjunction with a content description. Cite the source(s) of information for the summary of the content of a Work/Variant.

Format changes

Explain the format changes used to determine the moving image Manifestation in hand as different and "new" in comparison with any other, already recognised and described moving image Manifestation.

Sound characteristics

If the moving image Work/Variant associated with the moving image Manifestation in hand had sound originally, but the Manifestation lacks sound, describe it as silent (or mute) and give a note to that effect.[192]

If the moving image Work/Variant associated with the moving image Manifestation was silent originally, but the Manifestation has sound, describe it as sound and give a note to that effect.

Physical extent

If the length of a moving image Manifestation/Item is uncertain, give an explanation for the estimated footage or metre count, where known.

Duration

If the duration/running time of a Manifestation/Item is uncertain, give an explanation for the estimated duration/running time, if such information applies.[193]

Indicate the frame rate on which the duration is based or if the moving image Manifestation is the result of a "stretch frame" practice.

Item condition

Note any indication that the Item is in need of servicing prior to being accessed for use.

B.4 Relationships

Agent

Include information on the agents (person, family, or corporate body) that are not named in a statement of responsibility but that have been attributed responsibility ac-

192 Based on AMIM2 5C3.
193 Based on FIAF 1991, 5.3.4.2.

cording to other (non-preferred) sources; on the variant forms of names, on possible changes in statements of responsibility or on every other details relating to a statement of responsibility.[194]

Record any additional details that cannot be expressed through controlled terms. (e.g. "appears only in final scene", etc.). If a name is known to be fictitious, or requires clarification, make a note giving the actual name.

Event

Record details on place and date of an event, or information on any other possible related changes.

Production

Record details on producer, place of production, date of production or on any other possible related changes.[195]

Publication

Record details on publisher (distributor, etc.), place of publication (includes place of distribution, release, etc.), date of publication, or on any other possible related changes.[196]

Manufacture

Record details on the manufacturer (i.e. laboratory, studio, etc....), place of manufacture, date of manufacture, or on any other possible related changes.[197]

"Other relationships"

Record any additional information concerning all those relationships that are not covered by the Agent and Event relationships, the so-called "Other relationships" (see D.17 Other Relationships for Works, Variants, Manifestations, Items).

194 Based on RDA 2.20.3 Note on Statement of Responsibility
195 Based on RDA 2.20.6 Note on Production Statement
196 Based on RDA 2.20.7 Note on Publication Statement
197 Based on RDA 2.20.9 Note on Manufacture Statement

Appendix C, Sources of Information

See 0.3 Sources of Information

Appendix D, Value Lists

The value lists provided in this appendix are usually limited to a minimum of five examples if more comprehensive lists are available. If no pre-existing and authoritative lists are available, a non-exhaustive but more comprehensive set of terms is provided.[198]

D.1 Work/Variant Description Types

The Types below reflect terms used in CEN standard EN15907.

Analytic (component part): content that is contained in another content. A component part may itself be either monographic or serial.

Examples:

Work [Monographic] – Harry wird Millionär

Variant [Analytic (component part)] – Harry wird Millionär. Incomplete German version
Manifestation 1: Internet – digital file – [2013] – Deutsches Filminstitut – DIF (internet publisher))
http://www.filmportal.de/en/node/640472/video/1227323 – 0 h 16′ 59″
Item – Harry wird Millionär

Variant [Analytic (component part)] – Harry wordt Millionair. Incomplete Dutch version
Manifestation 1: Internet – digital file – [2013] – Deutsches Filminstitut – DIF (internet publisher))
http://www.filmportal.de/en/node/27915/video/1227322 – 0 h 15′ 44″
Item – Harry wordt Millionair

Variant [Monographic] – Harry wird Millionär. Reconstructed version
Manifestation 1: Internet – digital file – [2013] – Deutsches Filminstitut – DIF (internet publisher))
http://www.filmportal.de/en/node/27915/video/1227166 – 0 h 38′ 56″
Item – Harry wird Millionär

198 It is recognised that vocabulary lists often require frequent updates, additions or amendments. For this reason, should resources permit, it would be ideal to separate value lists from the rules and locate them in a central, online repository, like metadataregistry.org. RDF-based repositories like this can supply up-to-date vocabularies on demand and have additional advantages over traditional value lists such as those found in this Appendix.

Monographic: Complete content in one part or intended to be completed in a finite number of parts.

This is also applicable to television episodes. The record for the television series itself is catalogued as a Serial.

Examples:

Coronation Street [1960-12-09]
Spaced. Series 1 Episode 1. 1999-09-02

Serial: Content issued in successive parts and intended to be continued indefinitely, or across a span of time. A Work record for a television series is catalogued as a "Serial." Individual episodes may be catalogued as a Monographic record.

Examples:

Gaumont British News (1934-)
Flash Gordon's Trip to Mars (1938)
Chemistry Essentials (1996)
Breaking Bad (2008-01-20 – 2013-09-29)

Collection: Content issued in several independent parts; an 'umbrella' work title covering a number of different Works/Variants/Manifestations[199].

Examples:

Pleasure (Joan Littlewood, c1963) (Footage shot on behalf of Joan Littlewood as part of her 'Fun Palace' project.)

The 'Dogme' films (Each individually numbered.)

Shadows of progress: documentary film in post-war Britain 1951-1977

Other uses for **Collection:**[200]

Archive-acquired collections of works not originally intended for general release or broadcast all have component parts that form the collection as a whole, usually acquired on a series of numerous film reels or videotapes, etc. each with an identifying title.

Examples:

David Lean home movies
William Butlin personal films
Hollywood interviews (unedited production material for series Hollywood)
BFI London Film Festival Awards 2010 – production material, etc.
Fifties features (videotape collection of production material, with each of the

199 This aligns with EN15907 definitions relating to Work types and is different and distinct from Collection Aggregates
200 BFI CID Stylistics Manual, A.1.3 Filmographic Level, p. 8

tapes given an identifying acquisition title:
B1-3 Sylvia Syms I/V
B4-6 Sylvia Syms I/V & Jill Craigie I/V

"David Lean home movies," "Fifties features," etc. would be the Work titles for the collection-level description, with **Collection** as its description level.

The individual components of this collection would also be created as individual Works with Work titles at the **Analytic** level of description.

For example:

Egypt
India
India no.2
Kenya

These titles should then be linked to the collection-level description and assigned "part of" relationship.

Aggregate compilation videos/DVDs that are collections of individual works existing as entities in their own right, e.g. *Portrait of a miner* is a DVD of various *Mining review* shorts which had their own individual release as complete entities or works.

- *Portrait of a miner* would be created as the work title, with the description level of **Collection**.
- Each of the *Mining review* Works used in *Portrait of a miner* would then be linked to it and assigned a "contained in" relationship (see Appendix E.5 Modelling Aggregates).

Provide a list of the compiled works contained in the Collections Work in its Synopsis or Summary field.

D.2 Variant Type[201]

Censored
Dubbed
Subtitled
Abridged/Condensed (e.g. for television)
Augmented (where additional content is added, such as director's cuts with restored scenes, or alternate endings, commentaries)
Preservation/Restoration
Different sound track
Sonorized
*Colourized
*Black and white copy of work originally issued in colour

201 YCR, 2.1.1 Nature of modification (change in content) of expression

* A change in colour, which is a physical property, expresses a different Manifestation according to the data model this manual follows. However, it is recognised that in practice, institutions who employ the Variant entity may consider changes to colour to provoke the creation of a Variant because the colourisation of a black and white Work represents a fundamental change to the visual aspects of the original Work.

D.3 Work/Variant Agent Types[202]

Examples:

Cast (or actor/actress)
Cinematographer/Director of Photography/Videographer
Presenter
Producer
Director
Production company
See FIAF Glossary of Filmographic Terms[203]

D.4 Event Types

Event Types			
Work	**Variant**	**Manifestation**	**Item**
Publication	Publication	Publication	
Award(s) or Nomination(s)	Award(s) or Nomination(s)	Award(s) or Nomination(s)	
Production	Production		
Rights/Copyright/ IPR Registration	Rights/Copyright/ IPR Registration	Licensing	Licensing
	Preservation	Preservation	Preservation
	Decision	Decision	
		Manufacture	
			Inspection
			Acquisition

D.4.1 Publication

For Works/Variants, a Publication Event corresponds to the first verified release or availability of the Work or Variant, whether theatrical, straight-to-video, broadcast or online transmission, etc.

For Manifestations, a Publication Event corresponds to a screening, broadcast or the

202 More relator terms can be found in YCR, 1.3.2. Other creators, pp. 42-43; and, OLAC TF, Part II, Core Attributes and Relationships, Commonly-Occurring Roles, pp. 16-18.
203 http://www.fiafnet.org/pages/E-Resources/Glossary.html

release of the Manifestation of a Work/Variant on a physical distribution medium or online.

A Publication Event may be associated with instances of Agent in the role of e.g., publisher, distributor, broadcaster[204], etc. See D.8 Manifestation Agent Types and D.3 Work/ Variant Agent Types.

A Publication Event may be associated with instances of "Other" relationship(s) (e.g., promotional material of the theatrical distribution, the advertising of the home video publication, etc.).

Record all the existing relationships of a Publication Event, if the information is known and considered of relevance.

Publication Event information consists of the following sub-elements:

- Publication type
- Publication date
- Region

- **Publication type**

For Works/Variants, record the type of Publication Event for Works/Variants, for example, publication, release, distribution, broadcast, online transmission. Selection should be made from a controlled list of values. See D.10 Manifestation Publication Types.

Record the Publication type for Manifestations, for example, "pre-release," "theatrical distribution," etc. Selection should be made from a controlled list of terms. See D.10 Manifestation Publication Types.

For Manifestations, the Publication Event that originated the embodiment of a specific Work/Variant in a Manifestation, corresponds to criteria individuated to distinguish the boundaries between Manifestations. For this reason, conceptually, and also in practice, "publication type" overlaps the main definition of "Manifestation type," as explained in 2.1 Boundaries between Manifestations and, as such, is already described. Institutions have the option to decide whether to repeat this information or not.

- **Publication date**

Record the date on which Work/Variant or Manifestation was released or otherwise made available. Dates should be formatted according to ISO 8601 or some other recognised standard.

- **Region**

Record the country or other political or physical geographic entity where the Publication Event took place (e.g. first projection in the framework of a theatrical distribution) or made the Work/Variant or Manifestation available (e.g. distribution area).

---

204 Some institutions specifically dealing with TV material may wish to use an actual "TV Transmission Manifestation" for this data.

If known and considered of relevance, record the name of the city or smaller geographic entity where the Publication Event took place.

For the treatment of the geographical names, see *Getty Thesaurus of Geographic Names* (TGN), or some other recognised standard.

If known and considered of relevance, record the name of the event that the publication was a part of (e.g., name of a film festival, distribution channel of a broadcaster, etc.)

If known and considered of relevance, record the specific restrictions for accessing the content (e.g. press-screening only, airplanes only, etc.).

D.4.2 Award(s) or Nomination(s)[205]

The bestowal of an award relating to the Work/Variant or Manifestation. This excludes awards for Agents alone (e.g. "for lifetime achievement"), but includes awards for individual achievements within the context of a Work or Variant (e.g. "Best screenplay"). Awards will usually be associated at the level of the Work, except for cases where features of a particular Variant are explicitly mentioned (e.g. "Best audio commentary for the visually impaired") or the award relates to a particular Manifestation (such as a DVD edition).

An Award(s) or Nomination(s) Event may be associated with instances of Agent in the role of e.g. publisher, distributor, broadcaster[206], etc. See D.8 Manifestation Agent Types and D.3 Work/Variant Agent Types. If the award was given for the achievement of a specific Agent within the context of the Work/Variant or Manifestation, identify the Agent. Also used to identify Agents that have sponsored the award.

An Award(s) or Nomination(s) Event may be associated with instances of other Events during which award winners were selected (e.g. film festival).

Record all the existing relationships of a Publication Event, if the information is known and considered of relevance.

Award(s) or Nomination(s) Event information consists of the following sub-elements:

- Award(s)/Nomination(s) date
- Nomination only
- Award name
- Achievement

- **Award(s)/Nomination(s) date**

Record the date the award was bestowed on an Agent associated with the Work, Variant or Manifestation. (Dates should be formatted according to ISO 8601 or some other recognised standard.)

205 EN 15907, 6.12 Award, pp. 25-26.
206 Some institutions specifically dealing with TV material may wish to use an actual "TV Transmission Manifestation" for this data.

- **Nomination only**

Indicate if the Work, Variant or Manifestation (or a specific achievement in the creation of it) was nominated but not among the winners. This element can be realised in a system as a "flag." If there was only a nomination, this element would be set to a logical value of "true."

- **Award name**

The name of the award or trophy, possibly including a numeric designation (e.g. 2nd Prize)

- **Achievement**

A phrase describing a specific achievement for which the award was given, if not for the Work, Variant or Manifestation in total.

D.4.3 Production[207]

A distinct event in the course of production of a Work or Variant, including the main production event OR events that are separated in space and/or time from the main production event, or known with a greater amount of detail. Examples are dates and locations where castings took place; dates and locations of shootings or other recordings; or dates and locations of particular post-production activities.

May include year/date of shooting of non-professional, actuality or unedited footage.

A Production Event may be associated with instances of Agent in the role of e.g. production company, location scout, etc. Selection should be made from a controlled list of values. See D.8 Manifestation Agent Types and D.3 Work/Variant Agent Types.

Record all the existing relationships of a Publication Event, if the information is known and considered of relevance.

Production Event information consists of the following sub-elements:

- Production Event type
- Location
- Region
- Year/Date
- Event details

- **Production Event type**

Selection should be made from a controlled list of values. See D.11 Production Event Types.

- **Location**

Any geographic name(s) or address(es) of the location(s) where the event took place

207 Adapted from EN 15907 6.11 Production Event, p. 20

- **Region**

The country or other large-scale geographic entity where the event took place

- **Year/Date**

The year/date or time-span during which the event took place. Dates should be formatted according to ISO 8601 or some other recognised standard.

- **Event details**

Any further information about the event either in plain textual form, or as an instance of a data type from another schema

D.4.4 Rights/Copyright/IPR Registration[208]

These are optional, and it is for an institution to choose whether it has the resources or requirement to compile rights data. Further more detailed information on the subject of rights/copyright/IPR registration can be found in Appendix H, Rights/Copyright/IPR Registration.

A Copyright/IPR Registration Event is the act of registering copyright or intellectual property rights for a Work or Variant with an accredited agency.

A Copyright/IPR Registration Event may be associated with instances of Agent in the role of e.g. applicant, etc. Selection should be made from a controlled list of values.

Record all the existing relationships of a Copyright/IPR Registration Event, if the information is known and considered of relevance.

Copyright/IPR Registration Event information consists of the following sub-elements:

- Registration Date
- Registration Agency
- Regional scope
- Name of applicant
- Registration number

- **Registration date**

The date on which the registration was filed or the date on which registration became effective. (Dates should be formatted according to ISO 8601 or some other recognised standard.)

- **Registration agency**

Name of the agency issuing the registration certificate (e.g. "UK Intellectual Property Office," name of a legal deposit library, etc.).

208 EN 15907 6.15 IPR Registration, pp. 23-24

- **Regional scope**

The geographic region for which copyright is claimed.

- **Name of applicant**

Name of the Agent claiming copyright in the Work or Variant.

- **Registration number**

The number assigned by the registration agency.

D.4.5 Preservation[209]

A Preservation Event is associated with a new Variant, Manifestation or Items resulting from the preservation process in which the contents of one or more Items (or fragments thereof) from Manifestations of a Work were transferred with the intention of restoring or reconstructing the content as originally intended, or safeguarding it from decay.

This includes statements about past or future treatments scheduled for the item.[210] If desired and if applicable, record one or more general types of past or future treatment activities (e.g. "added leaders", "cleaned ultrasonically", "tears repair", etc.). Selection should be made from a controlled list of values.

A Preservation Event has as typical Agent(s) the institution(s) or individual professionals that make preservation decisions. Selection should be made from a controlled list of values. See D.8 Manifestation Agent Types and D.3 Work/Variant Agent Types.

A Preservation Event can be in relationship with instances of "Other" relationships (such as technical reports, documentation material, promotional material for the specific project, etc.).

Record all the existing relationships of a Publication Event, if the information is known and considered of relevance.

Preservation Event information consists of the following sub-elements:

- Preservation type
- Preservation Date

- **Preservation type**

Record the general type of the preservation activity performed, for example, duplication, transfer, etc. Selection should be made from a controlled list of terms. See D.12 Manifestation Preservation Types.

- **Preservation Date**

Record the date or time span in which the preservation activity was performed. (Dates

209 EN 15907, 6.15 Preservation event, pp. 28-29
210 YCR 6.5, 6.6

should be formatted according to ISO 8601 or some other recognised standard.)

Add in a note any information describing the preservation process in detail.

This can include:[211]

- Genesis of the project or reason why preservation was undertaken
- Significant challenges
- Relevant research (documenting sources of information related to content or production techniques)
- Technical, aesthetic or ethical decisions
- Recommendations for further work (details concerning limitations due to source material, resources, technology, etc.)

D.4.6 Decision[212]

A Decision Event is an event in which a Manifestation of a certain Work/Variant is evaluated by a censorship body or an accredited rating agency.

A Decision Event may be associated with instances of Agent, e.g. in the role of the agency performing the rating or censorship.

A Decision Event may be associated with instances of "Other" relationship(s) (e.g., the original censorship documents).

Record all the existing relationships for the Decision Event, if the information is known and considered of relevance.

Decision event information consists of the following sub-elements:

- Decision type
- Decision date
- Regional scope
- Certificate number
- Verdict
- Decision type

- **Decision type**

Record the type or status of the decision event. Usually the term adopted is "censorship" or "revision" for decisions mandated by law, "rating" for decisions under a voluntary scheme. Further types may include special forms of evaluation, e.g. for tax privileges, as long as these are distinct from awards.

Selection should be made from a controlled list of terms. See D.13 Manifestation Decision Types.

211 Based on in-house Academy Film Archive preservation documentation.
212 EN 15907, 6.13 Decision event, pp. 26-27

- **Decision date**

Record the date on which the verdict was announced or on which the verdict was declared valid. Dates should be formatted according to ISO 8601 or some other recognised standard.

- **Regional scope**

Record the geographic region for which the verdict is (was) valid.

- **Certificate number**

Record in Arabic numerals the number issued by the agency as a unique identifier of the act(s) of rating or censorship such as censorship visas or rating certificates.

- **Verdict**

Record the outcome of the act of rating or censorship.

D.4.7 Manufacture

A Manufacture Event represents a "common" event within which the embodiment of a Manifestation occurs, owing to the instances of a number of physical items that bear the same characteristics.

Therefore, the manufacture event of a moving image Manifestation corresponds to the activity within which it was fixed on a physical carrier, through particular technical processes such as film printing, telecine, video copying, digitisation, mastering, etc., or where it is saved to an "immaterial" medium, such as a digital file.

A Manufacture Event may be associated with instances of Agent, e.g. a laboratory that prints all the copies for a theatrical distribution or a studio that masters the DVDs for a home video publication.

A Manufacture Event may be associated with instances of "Other" relationship(s).

Record all the existing relationships for the Manufacture Event, if the information is known and considered of relevance.

Manufacture event information consists of the following sub-elements:

- Manufacture type
- Manufacture date
- Manufacture region

- **Manufacture type**

Record the general type of the manufacture activity performed, for example, film printing, tele-cine, video copying, etc. Selection should be made from a controlled list of terms. See D.14 Manifestation Manufacture Types.

- **Date of Manufacture**

Record the date or time span on which the Manufacture Event took place. (Dates should be formatted according to ISO 8601 or some other recognised standard.)

- **Region of Manufacture/embodiment**

Record the country or other political or physical geographic entity where the Manufacture Event took place (e.g. the region/place where the laboratory was located). (For the treatment of the geographical names, see *Getty Thesaurus of Geographic Names* (TGN), or some other recognised standard.)

If known and considered of relevance, record the name of the city or smaller geographic entity where the Manufacture Event took place.

D.4.8 Inspection

The inspection of a particular Item for the purposes of assessing and recording the condition or treatment of the Item.

An Inspection Event may be associated with instances of Agent in the role of e.g. inventory archivist, projectionist, etc.

An Inspection Event may be associated with instances of "Other" relationship(s).

Record all the existing relationships for the Inspection Event, if the information is known and considered of relevance.

Inspection Event information consists of the following sub-elements:

- Inspection type
- Inspection date
- Inspection detail

- **Inspection type**

The general type of inspection activity performed.

If desired and if applicable, record one or more general type(s) of the inspection activity performed (e.g. projection prep, inventory). Selection should be made from a controlled list of terms. This includes statements about past or future inspections scheduled for the item.[213]

- **Inspection date**

The date or time span in which the inspection activity was performed. (Dates should be formatted according to ISO 8601 or some other recognised standard.)

- **Inspection detail**

213 YCR 6.5, 6.6

Information describing the condition of the Item in greater detail.

If desired and if applicable, record information about the condition of the Item, including nature and extent of damage. Selection should be made from a controlled list of terms. (See D.16 Manifestation/Item Condition, Preservation and Restoration.)

D.4.9 Acquisition

The acquisition of a particular Item for an institution's collection.

An Acquisition Event may be associated with instances of Agent in the role of e.g. the institution or a person or set of persons in charge of acquisitions for the institution, etc.

An Acquisition Event may be associated with instances of "Other" relationship(s).

Record all the existing relationships for the Acquisition Event, if the information is known and considered of relevance.

An Acquisition Event information consists of the following sub-elements:

- Acquisition type
- Acquisition date
- Acquisition source
- Accession date
- Acquisition detail

- **Acquisition type**

Describes the means by which the Item was acquired, for example, donation, exchange, loan, etc. Select from a controlled list of terms. See, D.15 Manifestation/Item Acquisition, Accessioning and Source.

- **Acquisition date**

The date on which the Item was physically acquired. This date is distinct from an Accession date, which should be entered only once any required assessment has been completed, and the Item has been formally added to the inventory of the collection. (Dates should be formatted according to ISO 8601 or some other recognised standard.)

- **Acquisition source**

The name of the person or organisation from which the Item was obtained, indicating whether the acquisition was direct from, for example, the donor or via an intermediary or agent. Select from a controlled list of terms. See D.15 Manifestation/Item Acquisition, Accessioning and Source.

- **Accession date**

The date on which the Item was formally added to the inventory of the collection. (Dates should be formatted according to ISO 8601 or some other recognised standard.)

- **Acquisition detail**

Information describing the acquisition of the Item in greater detail.

D.5 Manifestation Types

The Manifestation types below can be used with Manifestations associated with either Works or Variants.

D.5.1 Pre-Release

A moving image Manifestation type that may be used to represent any embodiments of a moving image Work that exist before the finalisation or release of the moving image Work. Also use for partially realised projects, i.e. productions that started filming but then project ceased before completion.

It applies to production material in general, including: original shooting elements (i.e. original camera negative, working print, original video, editing file) and/or the first recording/mixing of the sound (separate original soundtracks – dialogues, sound, music, – or the first mixed soundtrack).

It may also include, censorship submission prints, working assembly prints, rushes, costume tests, lighting tests, make-up tests, etc. where an institution may need or prefer to group together all production material, i.e. an institution may usually create rushes and tests as separate individual associated records but, where these are acquired as part of a large collection of production material for one particular moving image it prefers, for practical reasons, to keep records together for ease of access or for restoration work purposes.

It may also be used for initial record creation purposes prior to material being viewed and catalogued, which may then result in separate Work/Variant records for Rushes and Tests material to which the Manifestation record will link.

Example:

Something's got to give (Rushes)

Beauty jungle: Artist Test – Shirley Ann Field

Also applied to moving image Manifestations assembled for submission to censorship/ratings bodies, or moving image Manifestations with cuts resulting from those censorship activities.

Detail on the specific nature of the Pre-Release Manifestation (e.g. censorship cuts, working assembly edit, etc.) can be added as a property of the Manifestation Type, from controlled vocabulary or free text, as preferred.

Manifestation Types can represent a unique instance (e.g. the original negative, the first recording/mixing of the sound, censorship cuts, the working assembly edit, etc.) or, more than one instance.

Examples:

Censorship submission print
Censorship cuts
Make-up tests
Costume tests
Screen tests general
Camera negative
Assembly edit
Rushes/Dailies
Sound mixes

These describe the context, not the format. For example, a censorship print may exist as multiple Items (35mm print, ProRes, MP4)

Some of these could also be achieved by creating separate Works, rather than capturing these as Manifestations of the film work.

Examples:

Il gattopardo (Luchino Visconti, 1963)
Pre-release, original camera negative – 35mm – Technirama (horizontal frame 8 perf) – Anamorphic – aspect ratio 2,55 : 1
Work: Il gattopardo (Italy, 1963, Luchino Visconti)
Variant "first cut": 206' – first projection – 1963/03/28 (date of first projection) – Rome, Italy
Manifestation 1: Pre-release (original camera negative) – Film – 35mm – 2,55: 1 Anamorphic – Technirama (horizontal frame 8 perf) – Colour Technicolor

La voce del silenzio (Georg Wilhelm Pabst, 1953)
Pre-release, Censorship cuts – 35mm – sound positive – 1,37: 1 – black and white

Work: La voce del silenzio (Italy, 1953, Georg Wilhelm Pabst)
Manifestation1: Pre-release (censorship cuts) – Film – 35mm – sound positive – 1,37:1 – black and white

D.5.2 Theatrical distribution

A moving image Manifestation type representing Manifestations distributed and exhibited in cinema theatres. The classic examples are 35mm positive prints, or the DCP (Digital Cinema Package).

These Manifestation types can be more than one instance, created at the same time or in a different moment, from the same "reproduction" masters.

Example:

L'aigle à deux têtes (France, 1948, Jean Cocteau)

Manifestation 1 : Theatrical distribution (France – 1948 – 22/09/1948 – first projection) – 35mm French – Les Films Ariane (producer, distributor)
Manifestation 2 : Home Video Publication (France – 2010) – TF1 Vidéo (Boulogne-Billancourt)[214] (publisher)

Dubbed Variant
Manifestation 1: Theatrical distribution (Italy – 1949 – censorship visa) – 35mm – Italian (dubbed) – title "L'aquila a due teste" – Italfrancofilm (distributor)
Manifestation 2: Home Video Publication (Italy – 2009 – 25/09/2009) - DVD – French and dubbed Italian (spoken languages), Italian subtitles – Gruppo Editoriale Minerva Raro Video (publisher) – DVD edition by Gabrielle Lucantonio.

D.5.2.1 Theatrical distribution (country of origin)

Refers to a public theatrical screening of the film in the country where the film was (primarily) made. For multi-national co-productions, the country of origin is the country where the primary production company is based.

Example:

Mujeres al borde de un ataque de nervios (Spain, 1988-03-23)

D.5.2.2 Theatrical distribution (outside country of origin)

Refers to a public theatrical screening of a manifestation outside the country where it was made. In many cases in BFI cataloguing this will refer to the first documented UK screening of a non-UK film.

Example:

Women on the Verge of a Nervous Breakdown (UK, 1989-06-16)

D.5.2.3 Theatrical distribution (country unknown)

Refers to a known public theatrical release, where the country cannot be ascertained.

Example:

Kiss Me Kate (1953, country unknown)

214 http://cinema.encyclopedie.films.bifi.fr/index.php?pk=47676&_ga=1.256088331.1431169682.1413365901

D.5.3 Non-theatrical distribution

A moving image Manifestation screened or exhibited outside the public theatrical context. For example, industrial film, training film, medical film, where screening often takes place within a private institutional context; film club screenings; educational screenings.

Example:

The Queen (United Kingdom, 2006, Stephen Frears)[215]
Variant: Censored for airplanes (UK and USA?)
Manifestation: Non-theatrical distribution (USA – Delta Airlines).[216]

Che cos'è la geografia (Italy, 1953) (genre: Educational Film)
Manifestation 1: Non-theatrical distribution – 16mm- silent with Italian intertitles –b/n – 20'

United Nations peacekeeping: situation report, USA, 1978 (United Nations Film) (genre: Educational film)
Manifestation 1: Non-theatrical distribution – 16mm- sound– colour

Stevie Wonder salutes Nelson Mandela, USA, 1985 (United Nations Film) (genre: educational film)
Manifestation 1: Non-theatrical distribution– 16mm- sound– color – 8'

D.5.4 Not for release

Any moving image Manifestation where the viewing activity was private, due to the nature of the work or the nature of the viewing. For example, amateur film / home movies, where screening usually takes place in a private familial context only; or an uncut manifestation of a feature film screened for crew only.

Example:

Albert Einstein at country home, Caputh, near Berlin, May 1931. (genre: home movie)
Manifestation 1: Not for release– film – 16mm [217]

Incontro con Paolo e Vittorio Taviani, Italy, 2004 (genre: event record)
Manifestation 1 (Original): Not for release – MiniDV – 2004 – Italy –CSC-Cineteca Nazionale

Viaggio in Congo (Italy, 1912, Guido Piacenza) shots not edited)
Augmented / Preservation Variant – (ordering of the shots and addition of explaining intertitles based on the personal diary records of the director) (ordering and editing, including new explaining intertitles, based on personal diary records of the director)

215 http://the-numbers.com/movies/2006/QUEEN.php/
216 Cornick, Michael. (2008). *Modern Film Censorship: Television, Airlines, and Home Entertainment*. p. 44
217 See FIAF Rules 1992 complete record: Example 29.

Manifestation 1: Not for release (archival access) – film 35mm – b/n – silent

D.5.5 Unreleased

Refers to Manifestations which do not represent a release/distribution event, but where the work was intended for release (therefore, distinct from "Not for release", see above), e.g. the film was made, completed and intended for release, but was not then released due to censorship or political impediments, or other reason.

Examples:

Robinson Warszawksi (Poland, 1948, Jerzy Zarzycki)
Film was never released. It ran into censorship problems for portraying the heroism of non-Communist underground movement that also fought against the Nazis. Film was re-edited with major plot changes and released as Miasto Nieujarzmione in 1950.

Primavera (Italy, ca. 1920, Licurgo Tioli) (Italian silent film, which is not included in the censorship records and according to the sources, was never released/distributed, but it exists as a nitrate tinted 35mm print at the CSC-Cineteca Nazionale in Rome).

D.5.6 Home viewing publication

A published Manifestation for viewing in the home or similar small-scale private context, of any type of work. For example, a Blu-ray release of a feature film, for viewing in the home; or a DVD compilation release of a set of non-fiction film works.

Example:

A day in the life. Four portraits of post-war Britain (UK, DVD/Blu-ray, 2010)

The most used formats are VHS, DVD, and Laserdisc, but this definition can also include 9.5mm Pathé Baby or 8mm packages in use from the 1950s-1980s (e.g.. the 1977 *Star Wars* home video in 8mm).

NOTE: When the *production* process involves changes related to the publication, marketing, etc. (e.g., a change in publisher, a repackaging, a new distributor and so on), the resulting product may be considered a new *Manifestation* as well (see 2.1 Boundaries between Manifestations).

Example:

Fellini Satyricon (Italy, 1963, Federico Fellini)
Manifestation 1: Home Video Publication – VHS (Italy – 1987 – De Laurentiis/ Ricordi Video (publisher)

The Queen (United Kingdom, 2006, Stephen Frears)[218]
Manifestation 1: Theatrical distribution (UK – 2006 – first projection) – 35mm – English
Manifestation 2: TV Broadcast (UK 2007-09-02)
Manifestation 3: Home video – DVD (UK distribution – 2007-03-12)
Manifestation 4: Home video – DVD Blue Ray (USA – 2007-04-24)

D.5.7 Broadcast

A moving image Manifestation type for TV transmission. It encompasses professional video and digital formats, i.e. Digital Betacam, HDCam, etc.

Example:

The Queen (United Kingdom, 2006, Stephen Frears)
Manifestation 2: TV Broadcast (UK 2007-09-02)

It happened one night (USA, 1934, Frank Capra)
Manifestation 1: Theatrical distribution (USA, 1934): 35mm – black and white – 105 minutes – Columbia Pictures Corp. (producer, distributor) –
Manifestation 2: Broadcast (broadcast on Turner Classic Movies – 2013-11-01, 08:00) black and white – mono – 105 minutes.

Lazarus rising, (in the series Supernatural), Season 4 Episode 1 (USA, 2008, Kim Manners)
Manifestation 1: TV Broadcast (USA 2008-09-18, 21:00-21:55, The CW) colour – stereo – 55 minutes (slot); 40 minutes (actual running time)
Manifestation 2: TV Broadcast (UK, 2009-01-25, 21:00-22:00, ITV2) colour – stereo – 60 minutes (slot); 40 minutes (actual running time)

D.5.8 Internet

A moving image Manifestation distributed on the Internet (stream or download) for works of any type, those conceived as Internet works or those conceived in other type but subsequently distributed on the internet (for free or pay).

Example:

Amor pedestre (Italy, 1914, Marcel Fabre)
Manifestation 1: Theatrical distribution – Italian intertitles – film – 35mm – silent – tinted – 1914 – Italy
Manifestation 2: Internet – digital file – [201-?] – Cineteca Italiana (internet publisher) (http://cinestore.cinetecamilano.it/index.php?option=com_content&view=article&id=21:amor-pedestre&catid=30&Itemid=104&lang=it- – 4')

A film Johnnie (USA, 1914, George Nichols)
Translated Variant: Danish intertitles -35mm silent – tinted – Denmark 191[?] -Ti-

218 http://the-numbers.com/movies/2006/QUEEN.php/

tle: Chaplin fridsstöraren
Preservation Variant: (of Translated Variant)
Manifestation 1: Internet – digital file – [201-?] – European Film Gateway (internet publisher)
http://www.europeanfilmgateway.eu/it/node/33/detail/A+film+Johnnie/video:MTU4Yzg1OWUtZGJhZC00ZGUxLTg2MWYtZDEyM2Y0YTA3ODQ0X1VtVndiM05wZEc5eWVWTmxjblpwWTJWU1pYTnZkWEpqWlhNdlVtVndiM05wZEc5eWVWTmxjblpwWTJWU1pYTnZkWEpqWlZSNWNHVT06OmF2Q3JlYXRpb24uZGZpLmRrL0RGSV9hdkNyZWF0aW9uXzQwNjM0/paging:dmlkZW8tMS00LWltYWdlLTEtNC1zb3VuZC0xLTQtcGVyc29uLTEtNC10ZXh0LTEtNA== 13')

Brennende Grenze (Germany, 1926-27, Erich Waschneck)
Manifestation 1: Internet –digital file – [200-?] –Deutsches Filminstitut – DIF (internet publisher)
http://www.filmportal.de/node/42289/video/1219949 – 2h 26' 18''

Hollywood Stadium mystery (USA 1938, David Howard)
Manifestation 1: Theatrical distribution – English (spoken language) – film – 35mm b/n – 1938 -USA
Manifestation 2: Internet – digital file – 619.3 MB – [200-?] – USA – archive.org (internet publisher) – https://archive.org/details/Hollywood_Stadium_Mystery_1938
Manifestation: Internet – digital file – 512Kb MPEG4 – [200-?] – USA – archive.org (internet publisher) – https://archive.org/details/Hollywood_Stadium_Mystery_1938

Cat-Women of the Moon (USA, 1953, Arthur Hilton)
Manifestation 1 : Theatrical distribution: English (spoken language) – film – 35 mm – b/n – 1953 – USA
Manifestation 2: Internet – English (spoken language) digital file – DivX – [200-?] – USA -https://archive.org/details/Cat_Women_of_the_Moon; – 442.1 MB
Manifestation 3: Internet – English (spoken language) – digital file – 512Kb MPEG4 – [200-?] – USA – https://archive.org/details/Cat_Women_of_the_Moon – 259.6 MB

A Syrian love story (United Kingdom, Sweden, Denmark, 2015, Sean McAllister)
Manifestation 1: Theatrical distribution: Arabic, English, French (spoken language); English subtitles – Digital – Digital Cinema Package (DCP) – colour – 2015-09-18 – United Kingdom
Manifestation 2: Internet: Arabic, English, French (spoken language); English subtitles – digital file

D.5.9 Preservation/Restoration

Refers to manifestations which represent the outcome(s) of restoration events/activities, usually involving selection and aggregation of materials from diverse source elements to replicate an 'original' or 'ideal' manifestation. Some institutions may use this to refer to restorations undertaken by the institution (not to be confused with the Variant, resulting from reconstruction made by aggregating different sources, see 1.1.2 Boundaries between Works and Variants/Manifestations.

Example:

The great white silence (2010) (United Kingdom, Herbert Pointing, 1924) (DVD –Dual Format Edition – BFI)

Metropolis (Germany, Fritz Lang, 1927)
The Complete Metropolis – Blu Ray – (2010 restoration – Kino International, USA, 2010)[219]

Nosferatu. Eine Symphonie des Grauens (Germany, 1922, Friedrich Wilhelm Murnau) Blu-Ray of the preservation/Restoration Variant: 2005-2006 restoration – Murnau Stiftung/Transit Classics – Deluxe Edition – 2014 – EAN 888430505797[220]

D.5.10 Unknown

Use only when there is insufficient contextual information to enable informed use of any specific Manifestation type from the list above. For example, to be used when undertaking data cleaning of obsolete legacy Manifestations, when no information is available and it is not practical to examine the primary source to establish context.

D.6 Language Usage Types

- Dialogue language(s)
    - Spoken language
    - Sung language
    - Signed language
    - No dialogue
- Written languages
    - Subtitles
    - Captions
    - Intertitles
- Language(s) of summaries on containers
- Language(s) of accompanying material

D.7 Manifestation/Item Physical Description

Many of the physical description elements are considered specific to Manifestations and are inherited properties of the Items associated with the Manifestations. This approach is recommended where possible so that the data only need be captured once in order to eliminate redundancies. However, it is understood that many elements may be repeated at the Item level due to systems designs. Therefore, the list of elements below indicates those that can be conceivably recorded at the Manifestation level only, at the Manifestation or Item level, and at the Item level only.

D.7.1 Manifestation/Item General Carrier Type

Film

219 http://www.silentera.com/video/metropolisHV.html.
220 http://www.murnau-stiftung.de/movie/674 and http://www.schnittberichte.com/news.php?ID=7433

Video Tape
Video Disc
Digital Tape
Digital Disc
Digital File

D.7.2 Manifestation/Item Specific Carrier Type

Institutions should develop standard lists of terms to indicate the specific carrier type or refer to authoritative existing lists.

For optical media, only add commercially produced media here. If the optical media is "writable" and is being used to store a digital file, put the digital file format in the General Carrrier Type, and the optical storage media in Specific.

Examples include, but are not limited to:

YEE (http://myee.bol.ucla.edu/catrul.doc 5.3.3 (physical carriers)
AMIM2 5D, pp. 18-19 (for gauges/width values)
AMIM2 5B7, pp. 10-11 (including both "tape" and "disc" based video formats).
RDA 3.20; YEE (http://myee.bol.ucla.edu/catrul.doc 5.3.14 (for encoding formats).
PBCore instantiationPhysical (http://metadataregistry.org/concept/list/vocabulary_id/145.html) (for physical carriers)
PBCore instantiationDigital (http://pbcore.org/pbcoreinstantiation/instantiation-digital/) (for broad digital formats)

Additional sources of information include several SMPTE standards, engineering guidelines, and recommended practices. These are some of the most common terms, but not a complete or definitive list.

Film Gauge	Video	Audio	Optical	Digital File	Digital File Encoding
35mm	1-inch C Format	2" audioreel	CD	DPX	MPEG-4
16mm	Digital Betacam	1" audioreel	DVD	MOV	Quicktime
Super 16mm	Betacam SP	½" audioreel	Blu-Ray	MP4	Real video
8mm	2-inch Quadruplex	¼" audioreel	Laser Disc	MXF	SVCD
Super8mm	HDCAM SR	audiocassette		AVI	VCD
9.5mm	D1	35mm magnetic track			Windows Media
17.5mm	D5	16mm magnetic track			
70mm	DVCPRO HD				

For digital files, list the physical carrier on which the file is stored. For all other materials, use this element to provide more specific information on the physical carrier.

Institutions should develop standard lists of terms to indicate the specific carrier type or refer to authoritative existing lists.

These are some of the most common terms, but not a complete or definitive list.

LTO5
LTO6
T10000D
HDD (abbreviated for "external hard drive")
DVD-R
Blu-Ray

D.7.3 Item Preservation/Access status

Master
Viewing
Accessioned
On Loan
Status pending
Removed

D.7.4 Manifestation/Item Sound Type

Sound
Silent
Mute
Combined
Combined as Mute
Combined as Sound
Mixed
Temporary

D.7.5 Manifestation/Item Sound Fixation Type

Needle sound
Optical
Magnetic
Analogue sound
Digital

D.7.6 Manifestation Unit Types

Reel
Roll

Cassette
Cartridge
Loop
Disc
File
Digital tape

D.7.7 Item Base – Film or Video

Acetate
Acrylic
CTA
Diacetate
Mainly safety
Mainly nitrate
Mixed
Mylar
Nitrate
Polyester
PVC
Safety
Video
Vinyl

D.7.8 Item Element Type

Colour Positive
Colour Negative
Copper Toned Positive
Cyan Matrix
Direct BW Positive
Original negative
Duplicate negative
Positive
Original positive (reversal film)
Duplicate positive
Lavender
Image negative
Sound negative
DCP

D.7.9 Item File Size – Digital

GB (Gigabyte)
KB

D.7.10 Item Codec type

See also:
PBCore essenceTrackEncoding (http://metadataregistry.org/concept/list/vocabulary_id/156.html)
EBUVideoCompressionCode (https://www.ebu.ch/metadata/cs/web/ebu_VideoCompressionCodeCS_p.xml.htm

VIDEO

AVC
D10
NIL ProRes 422 (HQ)
S10
JPEG2000
MPEG-4 H264/AVC Main Profile

AUDIO

AIFF
WAV

D.7.11 Manifestation/Item Colour Type

Colour
Colour + Black & White
Tinted
Black and white
Black and white (tinted)
Black and white (toned)
Black and white (tinted and toned)
Sepia

D.7.12 Manifestation/Item Colour Standard

Pathécolor
Technicolor
Kinemacolor
Anscocolor
Ferraniacolor
Fujicolor
Kodachrome

Eastmancolor
RGB
YUV

D.7.13 Item Sound System

Dolby SR
Dolby Digital
Mute
Combined Magnetic Sound
Combined Optical Sound
VA RCA Duplex

D.7.14 Aspect Ratio

Examples of "aspect ratio" value lists include, but are not limited to the *Technical Glossary of Common Audiovisual Terms* (National Film and Sound Archive Australia) and the PBCore essenceTrackAspect Ratio http://metadataregistry.org/concept/list/vocabulary_id/129.html

2.34:1
2.39:1
2.52:1
2.7:1
4:3

D.7.15 Aperture

Academy 1.33:1
Full Height
Full Screen
Flat
Anamorphic
3D
Pan and scan
Pillarbox (bars added at the sides)
Letterbox/Widescreen (bars added at the top and bottom)
Windowbox (bars added at the side and the top and bottom)

D.7.16 Item Stock

This is a preliminary list, and not exhaustive.

FILM

Eastman Kodak
Fuji
Agfa

VIDEO

3M

Agfa
Agfa Gavaert
Akai
Ampex
Ansco
BASF
Brifco
Fuji
Sony

<u>AUDIO</u>

Ampex
Scotch
3M
Shamrock

<u>OPTICAL</u>

Maxell
Memorex
Philips
Verbatim

<u>DIGITAL TAPE</u>

Fuji
HP
Oracle
Sony

HARD DRIVES

Hitachi
Seagate
Toshiba
Western Digital

D.7.17 Item Bit Depth

10
16
24
32

D.7.18 Item Frame Rate/Transfer Speed

16fps

23.98 fps
24fps
25fps
30fps
48fps
Variable

D.7.19 Item Resolution

Standard Definition
High Definition
2k
4k
6k
8k

D.7.20 Item Source Device

Examples of hardware required to play the source item.

DVSI
VT20
HDCAM SRW5500/2

D.7.21 Item Line Standard

405
525
625
720
1080

D.8 Manifestation Agent Types

D.8.1 Distributor (theatrical)

Agent responsible for the theatrical distribution of a Manifestation

D.8.2 Distributor (non-theatrical)

Agent responsible for the non-theatrical distribution

D.8.3 Broadcaster

Agent responsible for the broadcasting of a Manifestation, namely the network or station on which it aired or the network which makes it available on demand

D.8.4 Publisher

Agent responsible for the home video publication or for the web publication of a moving image Manifestation: i.e. the publishing company, which often is the same as the distribution company

D.8.5 Manufacturer

(Optionally, this information can be specified directly at the Item level)

Agent responsible for the activities of manufacturing a Manifestation: i.e. a laboratory.

D.8.6 Agent responsible for preservation

Agent responsible for the preservation of a Manifestation: namely the rights-owner(s), the distributor(s) or an archive.

D.8.7 Agent responsible for reproduction or transfer

(Optionally, this information can be specified directly at the Item level)

Agent responsible for the activities of duplication/reproduction/transfer (dupes and masters): namely the rights-owner(s), the distributor(s) or an archive. (name: personal, corporate).

D.8.8 Agent responsible for the archival availability

(Optionally, this information can be specified directly at the Item level)

The institution responsible for the availability of a moving image Manifestation intended for consultation or exploitation for cultural "fair" use, on the premises or through the activities of the institution

D.8.9 Agent responsible for the mere availability

(Optionally, this information can be specified directly at the Item level)

Agent responsible for making available a Manifestation not intended for public release (distribution, publication or broadcasting) in private environments

D.8.10 Agent unclear or undetermined

(Optionally, this information can be specified directly at the Item level)

Indicate if the Agent is unclear or undetermined, i.e. has not yet been determined. Also, if the Agent could be one of two or more possibilities then name them and qualify that there is uncertainty as to which is correct.

D.8.11 Agent not identified

(Optionally, this information can be specified directly at the Item level)

Indicate if the Agent cannot be identified, i.e. not identified after extensive research to determine the Agent.

D.9 Work/Variant Publication Types

These are not pertinent as both Works and Variants have Manifestations and it is the latter that are published.

D.10 Manifestation Publication Types

Release
Publication
Distribution
Broadcast
Online Transmission (e.g. Internet, Intranet)
Pre-Release
Theatrical distribution
Non-theatrical distribution
Not for release
Home video publication
Broadcast
Unknown

D.11 Production Event Types

Casting
Outdoor shooting
Indoor shooting
Post-Production

D.12 Manifestation Preservation Types

Duplication
Transfer
Reproduction
Digitisation

D.13 Manifestation Decision Types

Censorship
Revision
Rating

D.14 Manifestation Manufacture Types

Film printing
Telecine
Video copying
Scanning
Mastering
Uploading

D.15 Manifestation/Item Acquisition, Accessioning and Source

D.15.1 Item Acquisition type

Donation
Exchange
Loan
Purchase
Off-air recording

D.15.2 Item Acquisition source type

Donor
Agent
Intermediary

D.16 Manifestation/Item Condition, Preservation and Restoration

D.16.1 Item Copy Condition Base/Emulsion – Film and Video

Brittle
Buckled
Light Scratches
Heavy Scratches
Tears
Warped
Hydrolysis

D.16.2 Item Copy Condition Perforations – Film

Foil Patches
Torn
Pulled
Missing

D.16.3 Item Surface Deposit – Film and Video

Mould
Rust
Oil deposits
Dirt
Drying marks

D.16.4 Item Image – Film and Video

For film, this relates to the inherent qualities of the Emulsion rather than the physical condition of the Emulsion.

For video, refer to AV Artifact Atlas for guidance on terms.

http://avaa.bavc.org/artifactatlas/index.php/A/V_Artifact_Atlas

Discolouration
Magenta Bias
Faded
Print through in mould
Drop-outs

D.16.5 Item Decomposition – Film and Video

Powder
Sticky
Sticky at head

D.16.6 Item Shrinkage - Film

Description of the level of any shrinkage that has occurred to the Item, ideally in percentages.

1-1.5%
1.5-2%
2-2.5%

D.17 Other Relationships for Works, Variants, Manifestations, Items

D.17.1 Work/Variant Other Relationship Types

Work/Variant Other Relationship Types	Term list
"Is based on"	Adaptation from novels, plays, etc.
"Is a performance of"	Recording of live stage presentations of music, plays, dance, etc.
"Contains"	Compilation, series/serial, (see Appendix E, Aggregates).
"Is Contained in"/ "is part of"	Episode, number, part, extra (see Appendix E, Aggregates).
"Has a sequential relationship with"	Sequel, prequel, serial/series (see Appendix E, Aggregates).
"Has a relationship to promotional material "	Trailer, promo, banner, press-kit, poster, etc.
"Has a relationship to an "object" (a non-moving image resource)"	Book, photos, drawings, paintings, etc.
"Has a relationship to an archival document"	Script, production papers, author/agent personal papers, etc.
"Has a relationship to a Work "about" the Work/ Variant in question"	Review, study, article, commentary, "making of" documentary, restoration report, etc.

D.17.2 Manifestation Other Relationship Types

Other Relationship Types (strictly pertaining to the Manifestation)	**Term list**
"is part of"	part
"Has a relationship to promotional material "	trailer, promo, banner, press-kit, poster, etc.
"Has relationship to an "object" (a non-moving image resource)"	Accompanying booklet, image (i.e. photo of the cover), poster, a metadata set (i.e. for a digital file), etc.
"Has a relationship to an archival document"	Censorship visa, release/distribution agreement, laboratory technical paper, author/agent personal paper, etc.
"Has a relationship to a Work "about" the Manifestation in question" (not only moving image Works)	Review, study, article, commentary, restoration report, etc.
"Has a relationship to a pre-release Manifestation"	Censorship cuts, Make-up tests, Costume tests, Screen tests general, Camera negative Assembly edit Rushes/Dailies Sound mixes

D.17.3 Item Other Relationship Types

Item Other Relationship Types	**Term list**
"Has a relationship to another Item"	
"Contains"	Compilation (unintentional – mere use of the same carrier: see Appendix E, Aggregates)
"Is Contained in"/ "is part of"	Episode, number, part, etc. included in an unintentional/ convenient compilation (see Appendix E, Aggregates).
"Associated separation negative"	Different colour elements held on separate Items whereby each Item would be needed to create a whole new print of the moving image, e.g. Yellow, Cyan and Magenta Separation Negatives, each of which have to be combined in Technicolor Three Colour Strip Process to make a new colour print.

"Associated Sound/Associated image"	Where sound and image components are held on separate Item, and would both be needed to create a whole new print e.g. On DPX and Wav, 35mm Mute Pos and Magnetic track
"Preservation clone of/Has preservation clone"	Reflecting association of 2 identical master digital copies, as per best practice for digital collections
"Access copy of/Has Access copy"	E.g. an MP4 viewing access copy created from a preservation of a master DPX
"Source of/Has Source"	In-house copying of held Items creating new Items, e.g. to create a viewing copy, copy on a different format, copy Nitrate to Safety etc.
"Has a relationship to an "object" (a non-moving image resource)"	Can/container and label (description of, photo of, etc); punch tapes FCC (frames count cue) found in the can/container
"Has a relationship to an archival document"	Censorship visa, laboratory report, projection instructions (in general papers in the can/container or related to the specific item and held in separate archive), acquisition contract, DCP key
"Has a relationship to a Work "about" the Item in question"	Inspection report, restoration report, etc. (in general papers in the can or related to the specific item and held in separate archive)

D.18 List of form terms for Supplied/Devised titles[221]

FORM TERM	USE	EXAMPLES
announcement(s) **TV announcement(s)** **Theatre announcement(s)**	Television or theatrical announcements (short, non-commercial content shown to theatre audiences for various purposes, including requesting the audience not to smoke, talk, etc.) Does not include Public Service Announcements. Archives may use the general term "announcements" or more specific description such as "TV announcement." For announcements clearly designed to be aired during a particular programme or for a particular moving image work, create a partially supplied/devised Title.	• Announcements. NBC • Announcements. AMC Theatres • Theatre announcements. Animated no smoking announcements • Theatre announcements. Burnley Collection • Forever Amber. Theater announcement • The Adventures of Ozzie and Harriet. Announcement. Special message. Salesman greetings
blooper(s)/gag reel(s)	Also known as blow-ups. For blooper(s)/gag reel(s) associated to a particular program or for a particular moving image work, create a partially supplied/devised Title.	• Bloopers. CBS • McCabe & Mrs. Miller. Bloopers • International House. Gag reel. W.C. Fields earthquake sequence Burn Notice. Bloopers. Season 1

221 Adapted from UCLA Film & Television Archive, Cataloging Procedure Manual—Voyager, Section 5, Filmographic Record – Body of the Description, http://old.cinema.ucla.edu/CPM%20Voyager/CPMV05.html#5.2

<table>
<tr><td>commercial(s)
TV commercial(s)
Internet commercial(s)</td><td>When possible, add:
- name of the product;
- kind of the product (if not clear from the name of the product);
- name of the company (if not clear from the name of the product).
At the moving image work level include additional information, if available:
- the year it was broadcast or released;
-actors, actresses or other prominent people who appear;
-whether the commercial is animated or is a singing commercial (i.e. includes a jingle);
- whether the item catalogued is a demo reel or part of a demo reel (a sample of the commercials made by a particular agency, for example).</td><td>• Commercials. Ajax
• Commercials. Alka-Seltzer. Spanish
• Commercials. Animated. United World Films
• Commercials. Bel Air and Raleigh cigarettes. 1962
• Commercials. Box no. 16
• Commercials. Carnation evaporated milk. Burns and Allen
• Commercials. Cigarettes
• Commercials. Classic TV commercials
• Commercials. Colgate toothpaste. If you had a million
• Commercials. IBA Awards, 21st. Animated
• Commercials. Kellogg's cereals. Beverly Hillbillies cast</td></tr>
<tr><td></td><td>For commercials designed to be aired during a particular television or Internet programme, create a partially supplied/devised Title.</td><td>• The Burns and Allen Show. Commercials
• Naught For Hire. Internet commercials</td></tr>
<tr><td>debate(s)</td><td>For a formal debate between two people; do not use for, e.g. 'U.N. Cypress debates'.
For fully supplied/devised titles only.</td><td>• Debates. California gubernatorial. Jerry Brown-Evelle Younger, no. 1
• Debates. California's gubernatorial. Minority candidates, no. 1
• Debates. Democratic presidential candidates. 1984-04-05
• Debates. Presidential candidates. Gerald R. Ford and Jimmy Carter, no. 1</td></tr>
</table>

electronic press kit(s)	Use fully supplied/devised titles for unidentifiable videos. For electronic press kits created for a particular moving image (theatrical, television or Internet programme).	• Unidentified electronic press kit. • A League of Their Own. Electronic Press Kit • 61st Annual Academy Awards Show. Electronic Press Kit
excerpt(s)	For moving image content identified as being sequence(s), segment(s), clip(s), or fragment(s) (except, for "newsclip(s)," and "study fragment(s)," see below). Not for content that is simply incomplete. For excerpts clearly associated to a particular moving image work, create a partially supplied/devised Title.	• Unidentified Rudolph Maté fragments • Unidentified television programme. Segment. Interview with Evans Frankenheimer • Gone With the Wind. Excerpt • King of Jazz. Excerpts. Dancing sequences • Toast of the town. Excerpt. Imogene Coca segment • Unfaithfully yours. Excerpts • Dark half. Excerpts. Review clips
fight(s)	For an official fight between two or more people; do not use for, e.g. Ultimate Fighting Championship fights. For fully supplied/devised titles only.	• Fights. Dempsey vs. Levinsky • Fights. Moore vs. Martinez. Archie Moore, Martinez fight, Buenos Aires, Argentina.

home movies/personal record(s)/domestic record(s)	Do not use merely for footage shot by an amateur; amateur-shot factual footage should be treated as 'unedited footage' (see Unedited footage below). "Home movies" should be used only for moving images recording personal or family events, usually filmed or recorded by an amateur (FIAF Glossary). For fully supplied/devised titles only.	• Home movies. Brisson, Kryssing • Home movies. Robert A. Taft, Sr.
infomercial(s)	For a commercial presentation that combines advertising with information, and is very similar in appearance to a news programme, talk show, or other non-advertising programme content. Generally is much longer than a commercial. Common on cable networks. When possible, add: - name of the product; - kind of the product; - name of the company, in that order of preference. For fully supplied/devised titles only.	• Infomercial. Household products • Infomercial. Eggies System. Hassle-free hard boiled eggs. • Infomercial. Happy Nappers. Play pillows.
interview(s)	For an interview related to a particular moving image (theatrical, television or Internet programme), create a partially supplied/devised title.	• Interview. Paul Coates interviews John F. Kennedy • Interview. Walt Disney • George Stevens: A Filmmaker's Journey. Interviews. Ann Del Valle, John Del Valle, Rouben Mamoulian

music	For soundtracks or scores associated with a particular moving image; includes supplementary music such as overtures, intermission music and exit music.	• Olimpiada en Mexico. Overture • Broken Blossoms. Music
music cuts	Use only for fully supplied/ devised titles (see "trims" for partially supplied/devised Titles).	• Music cuts. Big band • Music cuts. Lyn Murray Orchestra • Music cuts. Themes for sports announcements • Music cuts. Unidentified orchestra
music video(s)	For video shorts, such as those shown on MTV, designed to exhibit a musical work. Includes videos related to moving image works, (i.e. a song from a soundtrack and having images of the moving image work). Use fully supplied/devised titles for unidentifiable music videos.	• Dancing in the Street. Music video. • Wild Wild West. (1999). Music video. • Unidentified music video.
newsclip(s)	Use for edited news segments from newsreels and/or television broadcasts (FIAF 1.5.2.2.) For clips from a particular news programme, use a partially supplied/devised title.	• Newsclips from various newsreels. No. 5 • Newsclips. CBS News. No. 5 • Newsclips. Kinograms • Newsclip. WRC-TV News. Cagney, James • CBS News. Newsclips. 2011 U.S. recession
outtakes	For content identified as being cuts or outtakes from a particular moving image.	• Casablanca. Outtakes
pilot	For television or Internet programmes.	• The Brady bunch. Pilot
political programme(s)	For fully supplied/devised titles only.	• Political programme. Illinois gubernatorial campaign, 1990. Steven Baer for Governor

political spot(s)	For fully supplied/devised titles only.	• Political spots. California gubernatorial campaign, 1966. Ronald Reagan and Edmund G. Brown • Political spots. California State Assembly campaign, 1973. Bill Lockyear for 14th Assembly • Political spots. Kennedy presidential campaign. Adlai Stevenson for Kennedy
press conference(s)	For fully supplied/devised titles only.	• Press conference. Kennedy presidential campaign. Los Angeles, Ambassador Hotel • Press conference. President Richard Nixon
promotional(s) **promotional film (s)** **promotional video (s)**	Also known as Demo reel(s)/demo tape(s) for advertisements and convention films prepared for exhibitors, industry people, etc. rather than audiences. For content publicising a particular moving image, including 1) a compilation of scenes from a moving image, used to sell the idea of making the moving image to potential backers, or prepared for exhibitors, industry people, etc., rather than audiences, or, 2) promotional content that is too long to be considered a trailer, e.g. a featurette or behind-the-scenes film or profile of the actor(s) or director(s).	• The arrangement. Promotional film • Frenzy. Promotional film. Rushes • Thelma & Louise. Promotional video for DVD release • Promotional film. Cinemascope. Demo reel • Promotional film. NBC (a film about NBC for exhibitors)

publicity	For information disseminated in order to attract public notice, promoting a network or collection of programmes; separate from theatrical or TV trailers, announcements, or promotionals. For information disseminated in order to attract public notice in relationship with a particular moving image, use a partially supplied/devised title; separate from theatrical or TV trailers, announcements, or promotionals. Includes short publicity spots designed for television that promotes a particular, upcoming television show.	• Promos • Promos. CBS (advertisements for the network itself) • Promos. NBC programs (a collection of promos for NBC programs) • The Three Musketeers. (1993). Publicity • 62nd Annual Academy Awards Show. TV publicity
public service announcement(s)	For television or theatrical PSAs. For PSAs designed to be aired during a particular television or Internet programme or theatrical screening, use a partially supplied/devised title.	• Public service announcements • Public service announcements. Army. Join the people who've joined the Army • Public service announcements. Community and church groups • Public service announcements. Filmex • Public service announcements. Handicapped children • Public service announcements. March of Dimes theatrical spot • The Snake Pit. Public service announcement. Statement by Department of Public Health, Province of Saskatchewan

rehearsal(s)	For content showing rehearsals of a particular moving image. Use fully supplied/devised titles for unidentifiable rehearsals.	• The adventures of Ellery Queen. Prescription for Treason. Rehearsal • Unidentified television programme. Rehearsal
rushes	For content identified as being the first print made of a day's filming for a particular moving image.	• An act of murder. Rushes
sound effects	For sound effects related to a particular moving image. Use fully supplied/devised titles for sound effects where the moving image work is not known, or for unedited sound effects.	• Das Boot. Sound effects. • Unidentified feature film. Sound effects. • Unidentified sound effects. Compilation
speech(es)	For fully supplied/devised titles only.	• Speech. Kennedy presidential campaign. A time for greatness • Speech. Kennedy presidential campaign. Louisville, Ky • Speech. Kennedy presidential campaign. United Auto Workers
study fragment(s)	For excerpted content from a particular moving image to be used for the purposes of teaching.	• Some Like It Hot. Study fragment
test(s)	For content identified as being screentests, wardrobe tests, prop tests, etc., for a particular moving image, create a partially supplied/devised title.	• Tests. Buzz Henry screen test • Tests. UCLA acting, directing, camera tests • Gone With the Wind. Color test. • À bout de souffle. Screen test. Jean-Paul Belmondo.
theatre advertising		• Theater advertising. Bennett and Bedell advertisement

<table>
<tr><td>trailer(s)

theatrical trailer(s)

TV trailer(s)

Internet trailer(s)</td><td>For an advertisement for a particular moving image, to be screened in theatres, on television or streamed on the Web; includes teaser trailers.

Archives may use the general term "trailers" or more specific description such as "TV trailer."

For multi-part Manifestations/ items formed by more than one trailers.

For trailers connected to a particular moving image work, create a partially supplied/ devised Title.

Do not confuse with public service announcements, theatre advertising, announcements, political spots, etc.</td><td>• Trailers. Republic titles

• La Haine. Trailer
• Three on a match. Theatrical trailer
• Dai-Nihonjin. TV trailer</td></tr>
<tr><td>trims</td><td>For portions of a moving image scene or soundtrack (e.g. music cuts) left over after the selected section has been used in final cutting.</td><td>• The Exorcist. Trims
• Directed by William Wyler. Interview trims.</td></tr>
<tr><td>unedited footage</td><td>For unedited footage shot for a particular moving image programme, or series.</td><td>• 60 minutes. 1969-01-07. Unedited footage. Smothers Brothers reading. Newhart, airport controller</td></tr>
<tr><td>unedited newsfilm</td><td>For unedited footage shot for a news programme or news series; includes television and newsreels.</td><td>• Movietone News. Lowell Thomas Remembers. Unedited newsfilm.</td></tr>
<tr><td>unedited sound track</td><td>For unedited sound track recorded for a particular moving image.</td><td>• Stargate: The Ark of Truth. Unedited sound track</td></tr>
</table>

Appendix E, Aggregates (Compilations, Multi-component productions)

E.1 Definition

A moving image aggregate is a Manifestation embodying two or more distinct Works/ Variants.[222]

It is not necessary to create an actual Manifestation Type of "Aggregate Manifestation" in existing Manifestation Type lists.

Defining an aggregate is an intellectual process followed in order to identify and select the particular structure best suited for dealing with the nature and content of such entities in cataloguing.

E.2 Identifying Aggregates

E.2.1 Aggregate or Carrier

It is important to distinguish between actual intended compilation or multi-component moving images, e.g. *Victorian cinema no. 8* (containing various short films from the 1890s edited together onto a new reel for a particular theatrical showing or publication), and an unintentional compilation, reflecting simple use of a single carrier, i.e. two short Charlie Chaplin films that happen to be acquired on one reel or transferred onto one tape for storage convenience.

Editing and creative assembly decisions were taken to create the first example, and it constitutes a Collection Aggregate (see E.3.1 Collection Aggregates). The second was just incidental or convenient assembly and is not an aggregate, and so would not have an aggregate Manifestation. The two Chaplin films would each have their own Work, Manifestation, and Item records, but those Items would have the same location/package number.

Any aggregate will have an element of intention, whether simple or complex. Assessments will need to be made, where possible, as to whether the intention was for creative/ intellectual or convenient purposes, and then represented accordingly.

222 Adapted from Working Group on Aggregates definition for a moving image context . Final Report of the Working Group on Aggregates, September 12, 2011, http://www.ifla.org/files/assets/cataloguing/frbrrg/AggregatesFinalReport.pdf

E.2.2 "Hybrid" Aggregates and multi-component moving images (e.g. Anthology/Portmanteau films or TV programmes)

Multi-component Works are ones conceived and created from their inception to consist of multiple individual components that make up a whole, for example anthologies, portmanteau films and television programmes (e.g., *Dead of night, Quartet, From beyond the grave*).

These should be treated as straightforward Monographic Works. (See 1. Moving Image Works and Variants).

The different sections making up the whole were **not** independently created Works/ Variants with an existence in their own right outside the film. It was one film intentionally structured as a series of different stories, sometimes linked together by scenes and characters, into one continual whole.

This is not the same as a later editing together of separate individual independent Works/Variants with their own earlier individual Manifestations, e.g.

> Portrait of a miner (Great Britain, 2002; BFI 2 disc DVD of various individual National Coal Board short films).

Other multi-component moving images often have a common theme, and usually comprise different shorts or elements made by different directors specifically as part of that Work, e.g.,

> Chacun son cinéma ou ce petit coup au cœur quand la lumière s'éteint et que le film commence. (France, 2007): Compilation film of 33 three-minute films by various directors for the Cannes Film Festival's 60th anniversary.
>
> 1'09"01 September 11 (France, Egypt, Great Britain, Mexico, USA, 2002): 11 short films in which different directors give their impressions of the themes and events of the date September 11 2001 and the attacks on the World Trade Centre and the Pentagon.
>
> Ro.Go.Pa.G. (Italy, France, 1963): 4 episodes by 4 different directors, no common theme: R. Rossellini (Illibatezza), J.L. Godard (Il mondo nuovo), P. Pasolini (La ricotta), U. Gregoretti (Il pollo ruspante).
>
> New York stories (1989): 3 episodes by 3 different directors, common theme. Directors Woody Allen (Oedipus Wrecks), Francis Ford Coppol (Life without Zoe), Martin Scorsese (Life lessons).
>
> Tre passi nel delirio / Histoires extraordinaires (Italy-France, 1968): 3 episodes by 3 directors, common theme: L. Malle, (William Wilson), F. Fellini (Toby Dammit), R. Vadim (Metzengerstein),

With these there was no original intention for the components to be independent[223], and there should **always** be a single Monographic Work record with a single Manifestation for them. The different component titles may be added as alternative titles to the Work record to assist in retrieval or access, and/or details of individual component titles and content given in the synopsis field on the Work. For example:

> Aria (USA, UK, 1987)
>
> Ten directors interpret various operatic arias:
>
> On-screen titles [and sources] for segments (which are not numbered on-screen) are:
>
> [1] Un ballo in maschera Nicolas Roeg/Un ballo in maschera [extracts from "Un ballo in maschera" by Giuseppe Verdi]
>
> [2] La vergine degli angeli Charles Sturridge/La forza del destino ["La vergine degli angeli" from "La forza del destino" by Giuseppe Verdi]
>
> [3] Armide Jean-Luc Godard/Armide [«Enfin il est en ma puissance» and other extracts from «Armide» by Jean-Baptiste Lully]
>
> [4] Rigoletto Julien Temple/Rigoletto ["La donna è mobile" and other extracts from "Rigoletto" by Giuseppe Verdi]....

Credits (i.e., Agents) for all the components should be attached to this single Work record, following on-screen credits as far as possible but also including an indication of which component they belong to where the on-screen credits may not be clear on this. For example:

- **Title**

  Aria (Original)

  Credits

Directed by: Nicolas Roeg Un ballo in maschera, Charles Sturridge La vergine degli angeli
'Images': Jean-Luc Godard Armide, Julien Temple Rigoletto, Bruce Beresford Die tote Stadt
Directed by: Robert Altman Les Boréades, Franc Roddam Liebestod, Ken Russell, Derek Jarman Depuis le jour, Bill Bryden I Pagliacci
©: LightYear Entertainment, Virgin Vision
Produced... by: Boyd's Company
Presents: RSV Productions, Virgin Vision
A Don Boyd production: Don Boyd, Jim Mervis, RVP Productions, Tom Kuhn, Charles Mitchell
Produced by: Don Boyd

223 Although where these are made by both different directors and production companies there may have been dual consideration of potential future independent release

Co-producer (for Virgin Vision): Al Clark, Mike Watts
Co-ordinating Associate Producer: David Barber
Co-ordinating Associate Producer: Michael Hamlyn
Co-ordinating Associate Producer: Paul Spencer, Richard Bell Un ballo in maschera, Luc Roeg Un ballo in maschera, Paul Spencer La vergine degli angeli, Nessun Dorma, I Pagliacci, François Hamel Armide, Amanda Pirie Rigoletto, Iain Brown Die tote Stadt, Scott Bushnell Les Boréades, Joni Sighvatsson Liebestod, James Mackay Depuis le jour
Associate Producer: Michael Hamlyn I Pagliacci
Associate Producer: Kevan Pegley I Pagliacci
Executive in Charge of Production: Arnold J. Holland, Joan Aceste
European Production Co-ordinator: Gabrielle Tana
US Production Co-ordinator: Elizabeth Moyer
Written by: Nicolas Roeg Un ballo in maschera, Charles Sturridge La vergine degli angeli, Julien Temple Rigoletto, Bruce Beresford Die tote Stadt, Robert Altman Les Boréades, Franc Roddam Liebestod, Ken Russell Nessun Dorma, Derek Jarman Depuis le jour, Bill Bryden I Pagliacci, Don Boyd I Pagliacci
Director of Photography: Harvey Harrison Un ballo in maschera, Gale Tattersall La vergine degli angeli, Caroline Champetier Armide, Oliver Stapleton Rigoletto, Dante Spinotti Die tote Stadt, Pierre Mignot Les Boréades, Frederick Elmes Liebestod, Gabriel Beristáin Nessun Dorma, I Pagliacci, Mike Southon Depuis le jour, Christopher Hughes Depuis le jour
Special Stills Photographer: Snowdon Un ballo in maschera, John Swannell La vergine degli angeli, Jonathan Lennard Armide, Greg Gorman Rigoletto, Bob Carlos Clarke Die tote Stadt, David Bailey Les Boréades, Annie Leibovitz Liebestod, Terry O'Neill Nessun Dorma, Angus McBean Depuis le jour, Koo Stark I Pagliacci
Supervising Co-ordinating Editor: Marie-Thérèse Boiché

Each component title should not usually be created as a new Work, as this is not how the content was conceived (i.e., it was designed to be packaged and viewed together and is not separable) and none of them would then have any Manifestation record as an individual Work. Those institutions that have the ability or desire to separate them out to tie separate descriptions (e.g., credits) to each component part (i.e. representing the parent-child relationship), may represent them as Analytic Works (see D.1 Work/Variant Description Types).

Should an institution acquire some or all of the components on different physical Items, then these should be linked to the Manifestation for the whole. In such cases it is simply a matter of a partial/incomplete acquisition, in the same way that only 2 reels of a 3 reel feature film might be acquired.

Intellectually these multi-component films are "hybrid" aggregates – they consist of semi-independently created Works, i.e. each can be very different and made by different directors and/or production companies – but they were always envisaged as forming a whole with the other components; although some or even all may sometimes subsequently also be released as individual shorts.

To use a music analogy they are rather like a concept album, which is made up of individual songs/tracks that may even have one or two released as singles, but they were created originally as part of a larger concept or unfolding story to be listened to and appreciated as a whole; and which is different in nature to a "Best of.." or "Greatest Hits ..." compilation album.

Where an individual component does have a subsequent independent release, that component should then also be created as a new Work/Variant in its own right, with its own relevant Manifestation, and linked to the original multi-component Work in an associative "contains/contained in" relationship.

> Toby Dammit, (episode by F. Fellini part of Tre passi nel delirio / Histoires extraordinaires, Italy-France, 1968): 2008 restored version on 35mm of the individual episode, with its own new Italian titles.

Where such individual releases of components have occurred, and a physical Item for a component is acquired, assessment would then be needed to establish whether it was a partial acquisition Item of the whole original Manifestation or an acquisition of the Item of the later individual component Manifestation.

E.2.3 Excerpt titles

Similarly, films that heavily utilise footage or excerpts from other films are not aggregates, e.g., *Dead men don't wear plaid*, or *Zelig*, although these may have an associative relationship with the original Works/Variants from which the footage was taken should an institution wish. They are using **partial** footage combined with new and different footage shot for a new and different film entirely, rather than editing together whole individual Works into an aggregate.

E.2.4 Other compilations

The nature of some compilations means that creating Works for each component is neither relevant nor practical, i.e. compilation reels of unidentified or untitled content (not usual in the bibliographic world but common in moving image archives).

There may not always be the immediate available knowledge as to whether something is an intentional compilation (in which case it would be an aggregate) or simply a convenient carrier. Where there is doubt then create a single Aggregate Manifestation and Aggregating Work[224].

Later research and cataloguing may then establish whether this aggregate record is retained and added to, or deleted after being used as a temporary working tool for initial record creation of acquisitions.

224 It is easier for the Cataloguer to default to treating as an Aggregate initially and create a single Work, Manifestation, and Item, rather than potentially create multiple skeletal "unidentified" Works, Manifestations and Items that then have to be deleted subsequently if it is discovered the entity is an Aggregate.

E.3 Types of moving image Aggregates

E.3.1 Collection Aggregates

Sets of multiple independently created Works/Variants, which are "published"[225] together in a single manifestation.

Examples:

Universal Cinema Classics' Going my way (1944)/Holiday Inn (1942).

Both works were republished in one volume on DVD by Universal Studios in 2001. The two works are complete and were not changed in any noticeable way. Although both films were produced by the same studio and are both musicals, there is no other significant relationship between them. The story lines are quite different and they don't share any common characters.

The aggregate also contains two additional works: the trailers for both features.

The following two examples have production companies or time period themes in common:

Walt Disney treasures: Silly symphonies – The historic musical animated classics DVD, Buena Vista Home Entertainment, 2001, 2 discs (31 cartoons)

I film dal vero di produzione estera. 1895-1907 (Collection of 32 titles Lumière, Edison and Mutoscope) English; Italian ; Accompanying the book: Aldo Bernardini, I film dal vero di produzione estera 1895-1907- La Cineteca del Friuli (publisher), 2008, ISBN 978-88-86155-24-3

E.3.2 Augmentation Aggregates

A Collection Aggregate with further additional material, i.e. interviews, out-takes, additional scenes, documentary about the making of the film, etc. on the same Manifestation. The vast majority of commercial DVD editions now contain "extras" and so are Augmentation Aggregates.

Example:

2003 Warner Home Video publication of Casablanca (1943).

The Collection aspects of the aggregate include the theatrically released motion picture; documentaries "You must remember this" and "Bacall on Bogart"; the Looney Tunes homage "Carrotblanca"; premier episode from

225 Published within the context of moving image means released or broadcast, and may also include in-house aggregate creation

the "Casablanca" TV series; and, original and reissue theatrical trailers.

The Augmentation aspects of the aggregate include an introduction by Lauren Bacall; nearly 10 minutes of newly found deleted scenes and outtakes; "Screen Guild Players Radio Production" with the three stars, plus rare scoring session outtakes; production history gallery (includes photos, press materials, studio correspondence, memorabilia, musical outtakes); and, two separate feature-length audio commentaries by Roger Ebert and Rudy Behlmer.

E.3.3 Parallel Aggregates

Identical moving image Works/Variants but in different languages released on one Manifestation.

Example:

Le declin de l'empire American/The decline of the American Empire (1986)

A publication in 2004 by Seville Films contains three language versions; French dialogue, English dubbed dialogue, English subtitles. There is complete parallelism between the English and French Variants; each is equal in duration and, except for the language, appear to be equivalent.

For Aggregate Manifestations record the length/duration of the whole, i.e. the total of all the units/running times that constitute the Aggregate. In addition there is the option to qualify this with details of the duration of each individual unit in either a Notes field, or in multiple occurrences of the duration fields, depending on what systems used permit or an institution decides. (See 2.3.5.2.1 Physical extent of an Aggregate Manifestation and 2.3.5.3.1 Duration of an Aggregate Manifestation)

E.4 Titling of Aggregates

The title of the aggregating Work should reflect that of the Manifestation. The component titles may additionally be added to the aggregating Work as alternative title types (see A.2.4 Alternative). They may also be added to any Items as alternative title types.

Titling of aggregates follows the same principles as that of other types of entities (see Appendix A, Titles and Title Types).

The title of the aggregate Manifestation forms the basis, but that title may be a "title proper" or a fully or partially devised/supplied title. (See A.2.2 Title Proper orA.2.5 Supplied/Devised Titles).

Aggregates may be formed by an archive or institution itself for in-house or other event purposes. In these instances the title type should indicate it is a devised/supplied title in both the aggregate Manifestation and aggregating Work, as well as the Item.

E.5 Modelling Aggregates

An aggregate is a Manifestation, but "the process of aggregating the Works/Variants itself is an intellectual or artistic effort and therefore meets the criteria for a Work. In the process of creating an aggregate Manifestation, an aggregating Work is produced. This effort may be relatively minor or represent a major effort resulting in an aggregate that is significantly more than a sum of its parts. . . The aggregating Work may or may not be deemed important enough to be recorded.[226]"

An institution may therefore be able to choose whether to create a new aggregating Work or not, although this flexibility may be restricted by other factors.

In practical terms creating aggregates and how they are modelled, will be determined by structures and capabilities of an institution's database or other systems.

Under FRBR and CEN an aggregate Manifestation is allowed to have a many-to-many relationship with Works/Variants, i.e., it can have a "part of" relationship with more than one Work/Variant.

However, many database systems are structured in a way that does not allow this and will only permit links or relationships between Manifestation records and a single Work/ Variant record at all times, i.e., a one-to-many Work/Variant-Manifestation relationship.

There are also potential implications for those organisations using international identifiers or registration numbers, e.g., ISAN gives a number to what they define "compilation": "a compilation work is a collection of two or more separate works (each identified with its own ISAN) in a single distribution package"[227].

This may have a bearing and impact on decisions relating to whether to produce an aggregating Work or not.

The model of creating an aggregating Work is recommended. With systems that only allow for a one-to-many Work/Variant-Manifestation relationship, then an aggregating Work should **always** exist (for Collection, Augmented and Parallel Aggregates), and the aggregate Manifestation linked as "part of" it.

In addition, the multiple independently created moving image Works/Variants of the aggregate should also ideally be created as separate individual Works/Variants, and then linked in an associative relationship using "contains/contained in" terms with the aggregating Work.

It is recognised that the ability to do this may be dependent on sufficient information and details about the individual Works/Variants being available to create such individual records. Where this is insufficient the titles of the individual Works/Variants making up the aggregate may be added as alternative title types to the aggregating Work. This will assist in accessibility and identification.

---

226 Working Group on Aggregates. Final Report of the Working Group on Aggregates, September 12, 2011, http://www.ifla.org/files/assets/cataloguing/frbrrg/AggregatesFinalReport.pdf
227 Definition of "Compilation" in http://www.isan.org/resources/glossary.html#index_A (ISAN Glossary of Terms)

For how aggregate records may be structured in a 1-level hierarchy system see I.7 Example 7. Aggregate DVD Television Serial and Episode records in 1-level Hierarchy Models. Whilst this relates to a television example the same principles can be applied in the case of film collection and augmented collection aggregates.

E.5.1 Collection Aggregates Modelling

Many collection aggregates have their own new title, e.g., *The Audrey Hepburn collection* (consisting of *Breakfast at Tiffany's, Funny face* and *Sabrina*); *Heroes of the sky* (consisting of *Angels one five, The Dambusters, Aces high*); *Portrait of a miner* (consisting of various *Mining review* shorts). These should be the titles of the aggregate Manifestation, and also any new aggregating Work record.

The individual component titles may also be added as alternative title types to the aggregating Work.

Some collection aggregates do not have their own new title, e.g., in 2008, Odeon Entertainment released a DVD double-bill of classic British thrillers, *Bond of fear* (1956) and *Blackout* (1950), with no collection title.

The treatment of the aggregate title may differ from institution to institution, especially in cases where multiple Works are contained in the collection aggregate and recording all titles in a single title field would be unwieldy. There is the option of an institution using a devised/supplied title (see A.2.5 Supplied/Devised Titles).

Examples

Bond of fear ; Blackout
Bond of fear; [other segment]
[Odeon Entertainment double feature: Bond of fear and
Blackout [DVD double feature]]

E.5.1.1 Model: Collection Aggregate Manifestation within one-to-many Works/Variants-Manifestations

This model involves creation of a new aggregating Work record. Works link together in associative relationship "contains/contained in" and aggregate Manifestation links to aggregating Work in "part of" relationship.

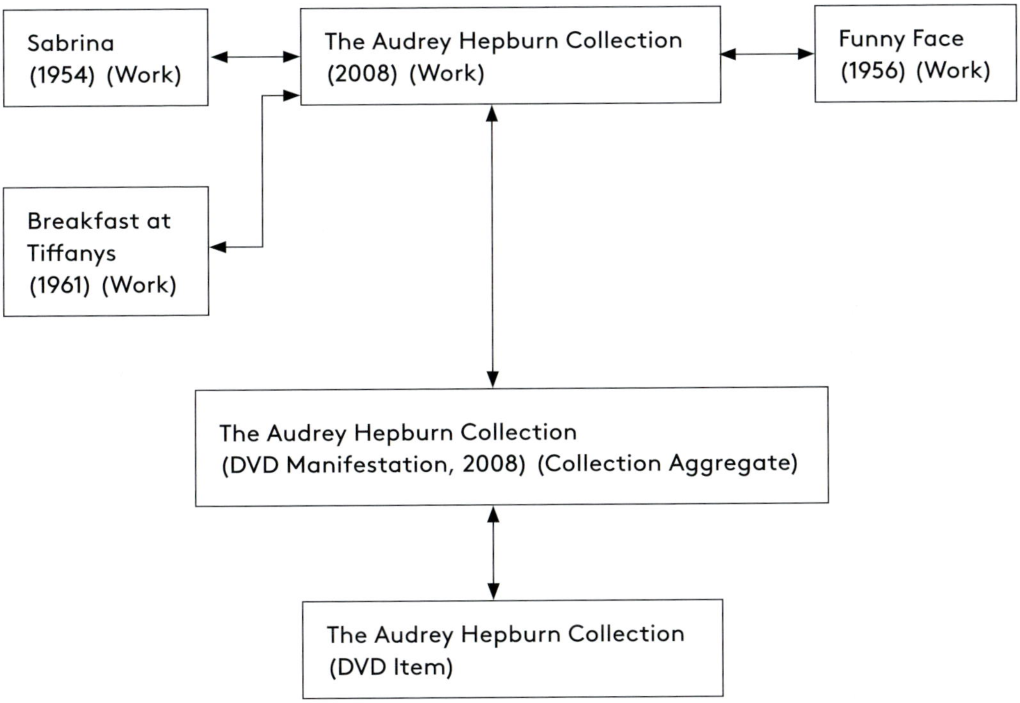

E.5.1.2 Model: Collection Aggregate Manifestation within many-to-many Works/Variants-Manifestation

A single Aggregate Manifestation links to the many individual Works/Variants in "part of" relationship.

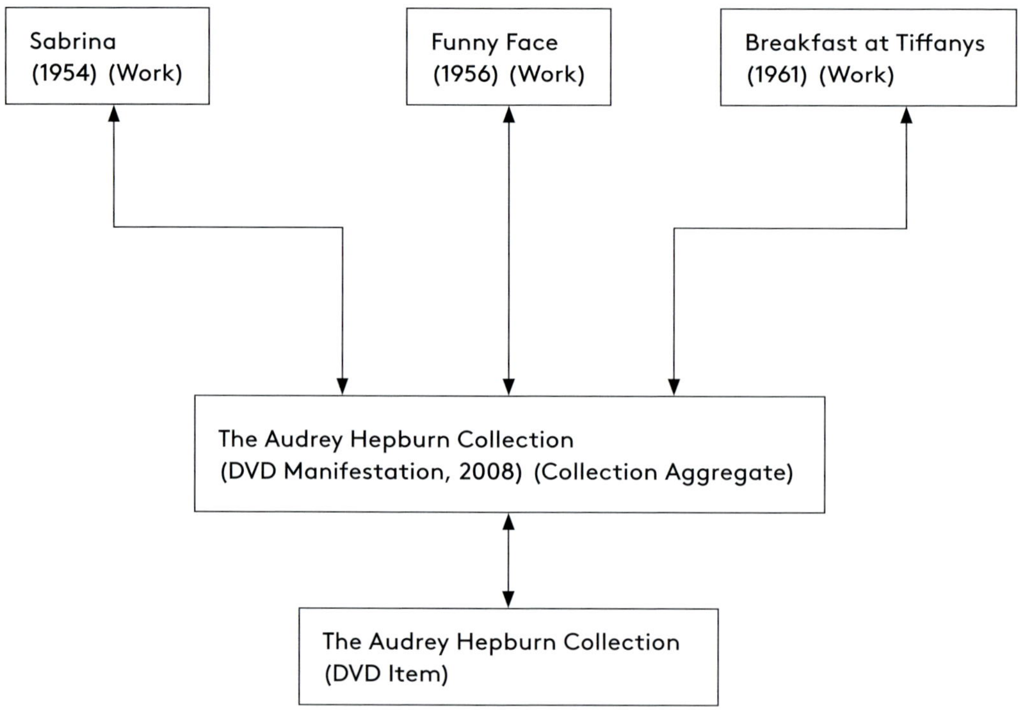

E.5.1.3 Model: Collection Aggregate Manifestation with no aggregated Item, only unaggregated individual Items

This model involves creation of a new aggregating Work record.

The original individual Works and aggregating Work link together in associative relationship "contains/contained in" and aggregate Manifestation links to aggregating Work in "part of" relationship, with individual Items rather than one aggregated Item linking to aggregate Manifestation in "part of" relationship.

This model may occur particularly with internet broadcasts and digital files, whereby an aggregate Internet Manifestation is available as an Internet broadcast, but is streamed in from individual digital files (i.e. individual Items) seamlessly and consecutively, not from a single aggregated digital file, i.e. a thematic compilation of three short films of the late 19th century is devised and entitled "Victorian Cinema 3"[228]. The internet user views the whole aggregate Manifestation as one entity, but it is streamed from separate digital Items streamed seamlessly one after the other.

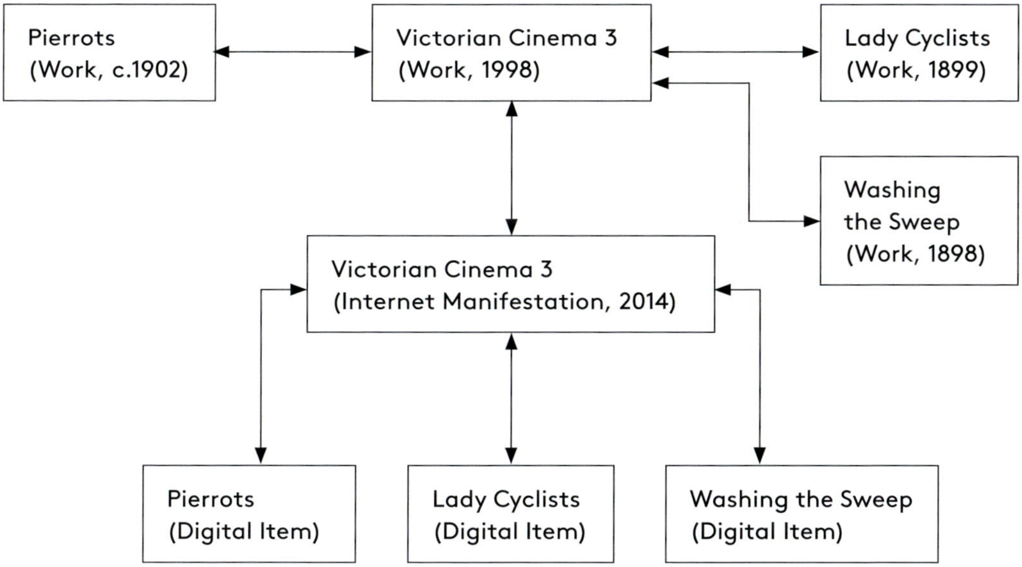

228 Example Victorian Cinema 3 is an illustrative example only, and not yet streamed in this way

In the above scenario each of the Items could be given the same location/package number and each could have the alternative title of "Victorian Cinema 3". Similarly, the individual titles could also be added as alternative titles to the aggregating Work if an institution wishes, to aid searchability and access.

E.5.2 Augmented Collection Aggregate

Augmented Collections can vary considerably from simple augmentations, e.g., the Work(s) plus a selection of special features such as bonus scenes and a photo gallery with some commentary; or, more complex augmentations.

Modelling for Augmented Collection Aggregates follows the same principles as those for Collection Aggregates.

E.5.2.1 Model: Augmented Aggregate Manifestation with one-to-many Work/Variants-Manifestations

This involves creation of a new aggregating Work record. Works link together in associative relationship "contains/contained in" and aggregate Manifestation links to aggregating Work in "part of" relationship.

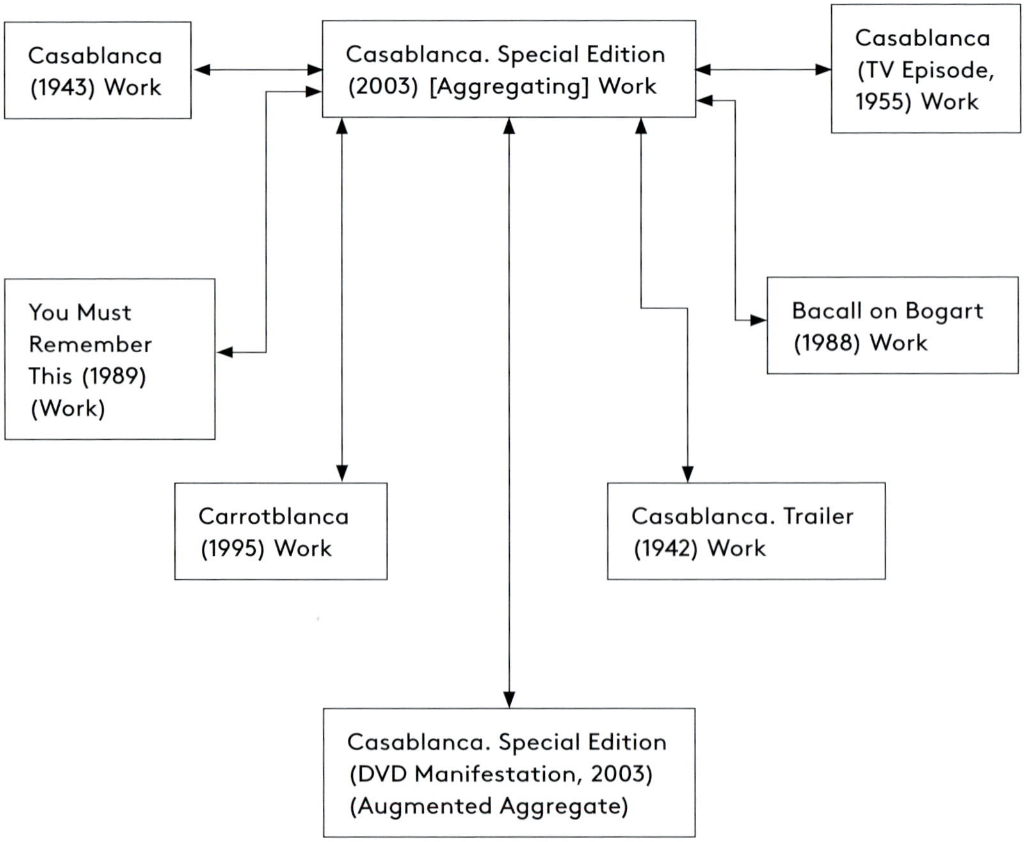

E.5.2.2 Model: Augmented Aggregate Manifestation for many-to-many Work/Variants-Manifestations

Single Aggregate Manifestation links to all individual Works/Variants in "part of" relationship.

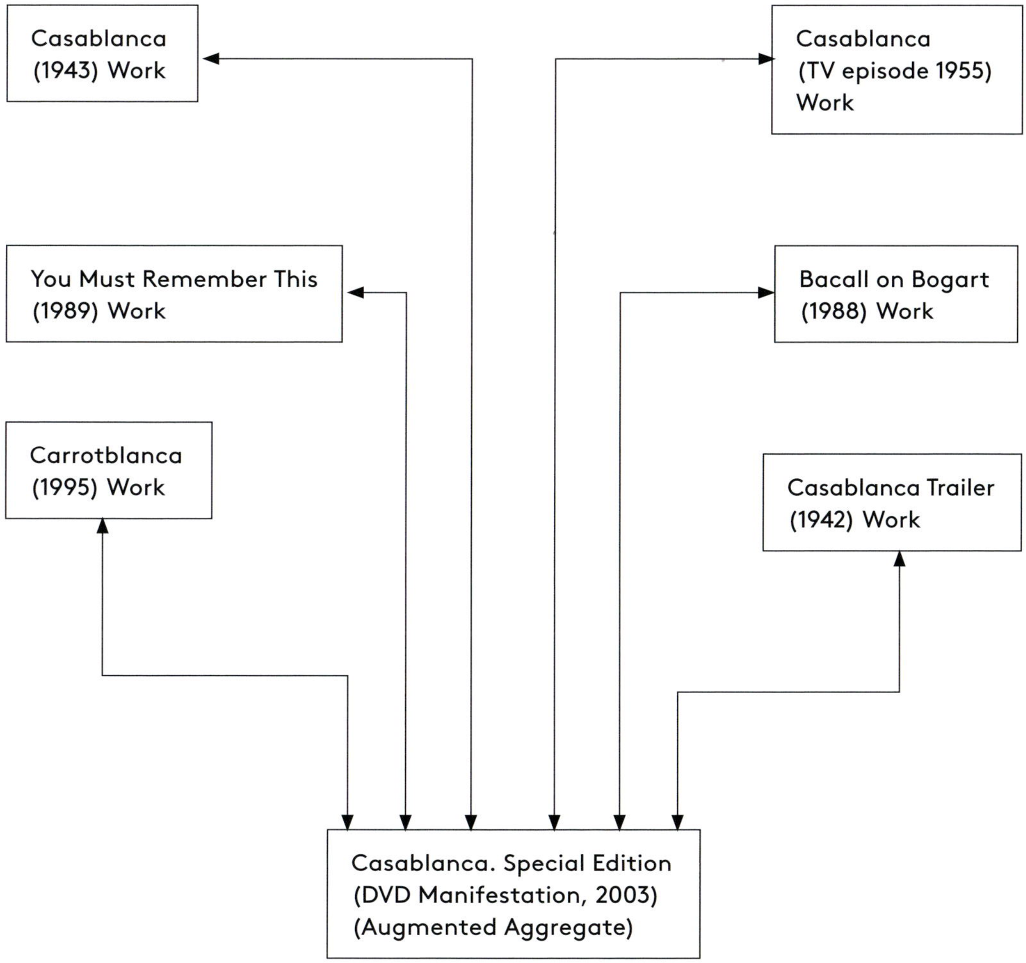

An institution can choose whether to create all components of the Augmented aggregate Manifestation as Works, or selected ones.

However, in cases of Augmented Aggregates it is recommended to always create a corresponding aggregating Work, as the Work record will contain relevant fields for extra data such as new credits pertaining just to the aggregate. Similarly synopsis or notes fields can then be utilised to give full description of contents.

More importantly, it is not always practical or feasible for many cataloguing systems to deal with creating records for non-moving image materials such as booklets, or text.

Example:

> Charlie Chaplin. The Mutual films. Volume 1.
> Contains: 6 short Chaplin Mutual films – Behind the screen, The immigrant, Easy Street, The rink, The cure, The adventurer. Plus DVD extras: Topical Budget newsreel footage of Chaplin on voyage and visit back to Britain; filmed interview with Carl Davis [who did music soundtrack for the aggregate]; on-screen text biographies of Edna Purviance and Eric Campbell. Plus sleeve notes by Frank Scheide.

An aggregating Work record for the above enables adding of credits, for example, the music composer for the soundtrack on the aggregate, the interviewees, etc.; associative "contains/contained in" relationship links to any individual films or newsreel works; and then any other remaining details of the Work that cannot be linked in associative relationships may be added as free text in synopsis or notes fields.

E.6 Credits (i.e. Agents) for Aggregates

An institution may choose only to add the credits relating to the aggregating Work itself, especially where associative "contains/contained in" relationship links exist, and credits can be found on those associated individual records. Alternatively, it may choose to add the credits for all the component Works and the aggregating Work to the aggregating Work record.

E.7 Series, Serials and Newsreels

All the above examples and modelling of aggregates have purposefully not included newsreels or film or TV series/serials. This is because these do not actually constitute aggregates under the Aggregates definition.

FRBR includes the terms "serials" and "series" within examples of Collection Aggregates. However, these are in relation to bibliographic materials, and moving image series/serials are not the equivalent of articles written for a periodical, but different in nature.

E.7.1 Film/Video or TV series/serials

On the surface these would seem to be aggregates as it could be argued they are made up of different components (episodes) brought together to make a "whole" (series/serial). However, it is not logical under the definitions of aggregates to structure and view TV or film/video serial/series as aggregating Works.

The starting point of an aggregate is the Manifestation "embodying two or more Works/Variants." Each episode of a film/video or TV series/serial has its own unique individual release/broadcast Manifestation, not a single aggregate one. There was never the original intention for all the episodes (independent individual Works/Variants) to be released/broadcast in one single Manifestation.

A later subsequent DVD publication or digital file production may occur, warranting an aggregate Manifestation, but this does not happen with all series/serials.

Where an institution's cataloguing system has Work Series-Work Monographic hierarchy structure then the aggregate Manifestation of a DVD release/boxed set of the series/serial, or multiple episodes from that series, could be linked as "part of" the Work Series record.

There could then be a clarifying note on the Manifestation where necessary, i.e. to clarify which episodes are included if the series continued with more episodes not on the particular aggregate Manifestation, or the aggregate Manifestation pertained to one particular series/season within the Series.

See example below for *The thick of it* DVD boxed set:

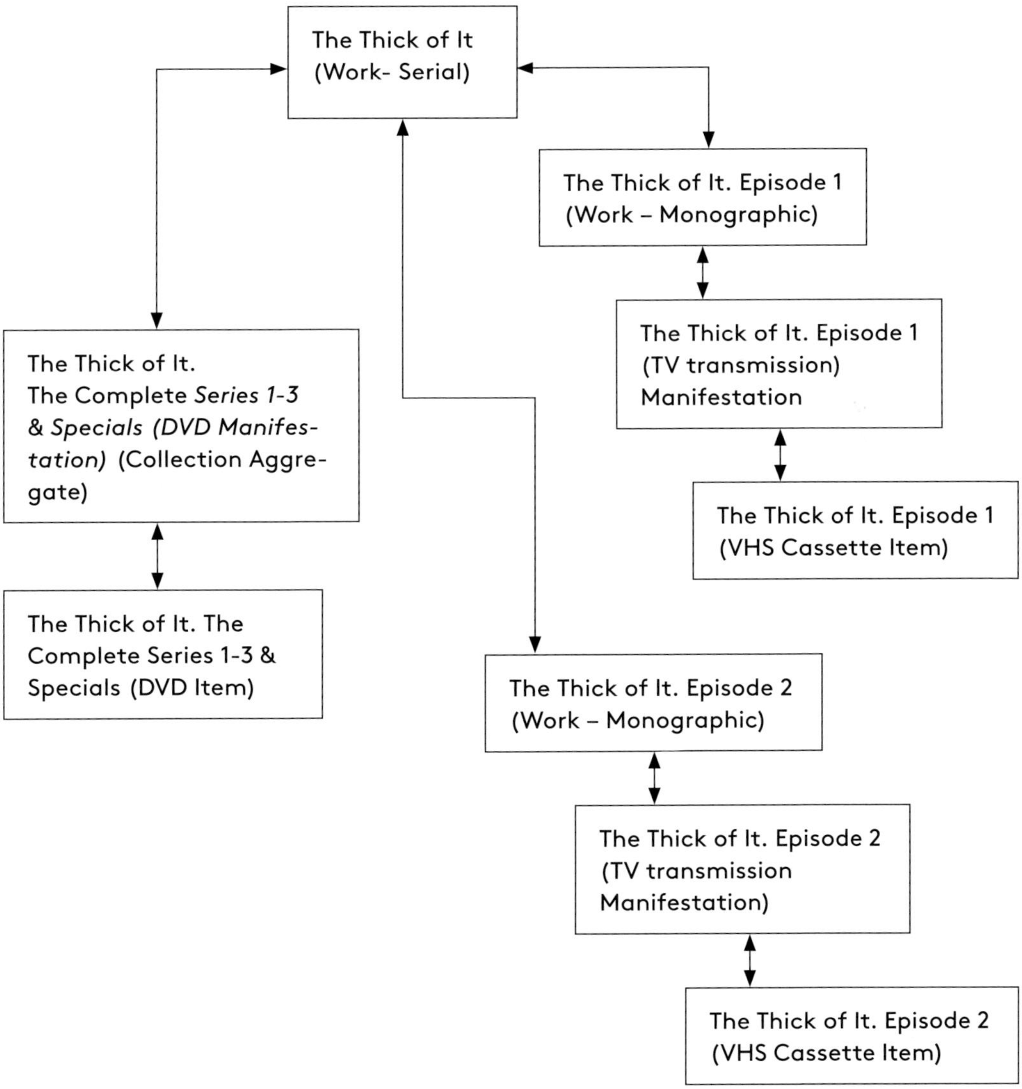

Alternatively, a model similar to E.5.1.2 Model: Collection Aggregate Manifestation within many-to-many Works/Variants-Manifestation can be used, whereby a single Aggregate Manifestation links to the many individual Works/Variants in "part of" relationship:

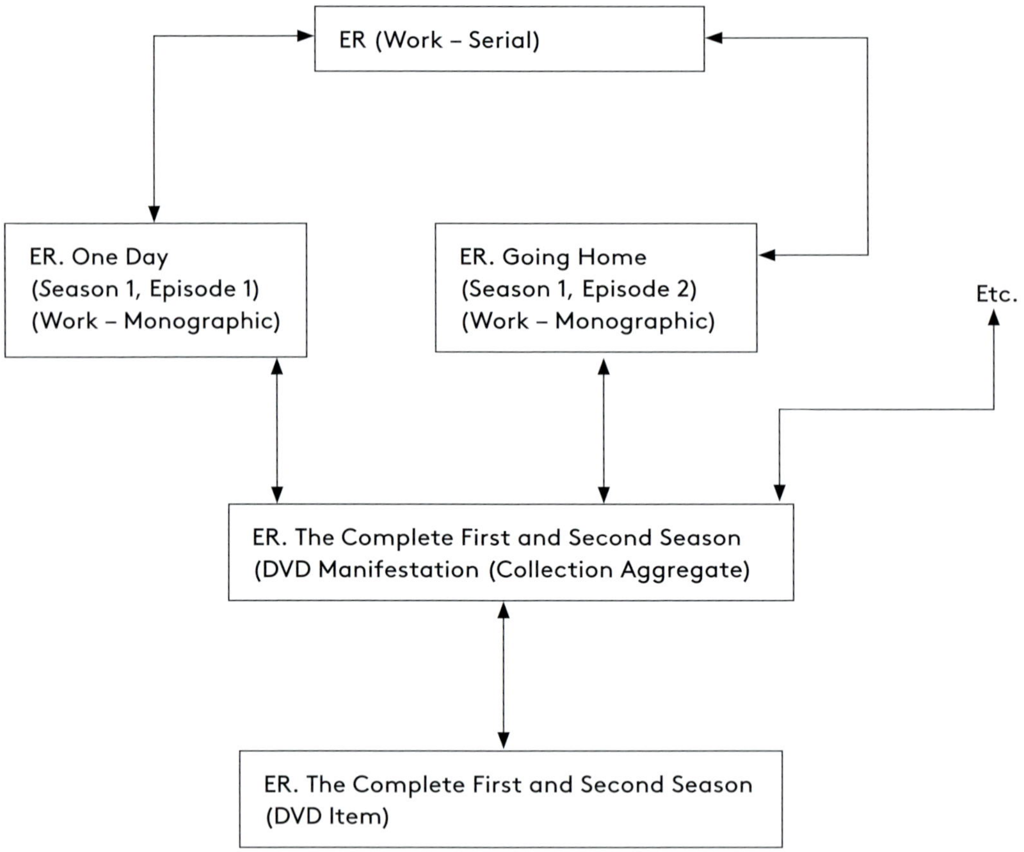

Where this Serial Work–Monographic Work hierarchy structure does not exist, then a new aggregating Work may be created and linked via an associated contains/contained in relationship in line with models for any other Collection Aggregate.

Example:

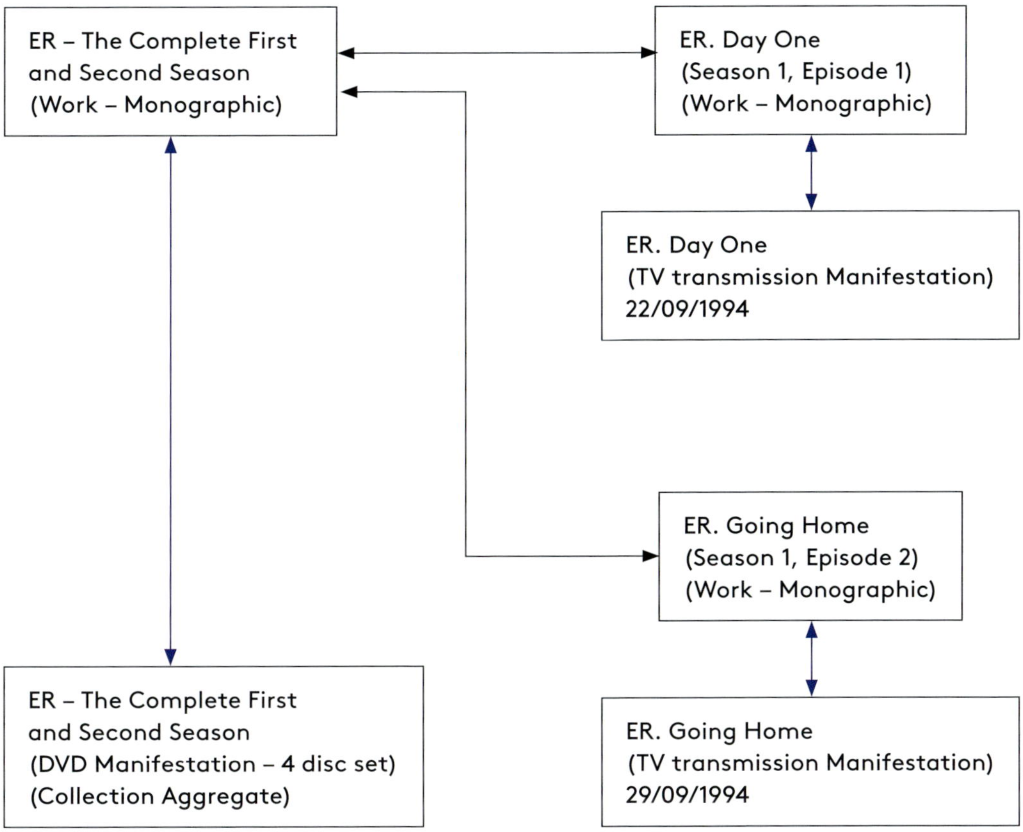

For how this might be modelled in a flat or single hierarchy system see I.7 Example 7. Aggregate DVD Television Serial and Episode records in 1-level Hierarchy Models

It is also possible for particular individual episodes from different moving image series/serials to be taken and formed together into a Collection or Augmentation Aggregate, in which case they would then follow the same pattern of structure as any other such aggregate, i.e. with an aggregate Manifestation and aggregating Work record, and associative relationship links to any existing individual Work/Variant episode records.

E.7.2 Newsreels and TV news/current affairs programmes

These also do not constitute aggregates.

The nature of news/newsreels is that the different stories do not constitute "independently created Works/Variants" and are more akin to multi-component moving images (see Section E.2.2), in that each component is meant to create the whole via filmed links that are an integral planned part and structure of an original single Work concept.

The process of creation of these is with one whole programme in mind made up of different filmed elements – the same as planned different location shooting (and crews) of different scenes in a feature film that are then edited together to create the whole. It is never envisaged that the individual news stories would ever have an independent individual release/broadcast on their own.

The same principles hold true for film newsreels.

Similarly, many early current affairs TV programmes were designed as "magazine" programmes featuring a balanced mix of stories (often serious and light mix). These stories also are not "independently created Works/Variants" but filmed by regular crews and personnel associated with a particular current affairs programme, with an overall editorial creative decision and intent of them being one component of a whole individual Work. The "whole" would then have a Transmission Manifestation. The component parts do not.

It is possible that only individual components of newsreels/news programmes may be acquired by an institution. In such cases it is simply a matter of a partial/incomplete acquisition, in the same way that only 2 reels of a 3 reel feature film might be acquired. The acquisition Item record would be linked as "part of" the whole Manifestation (link to existing newsreel example in Titling section re. this).

Appendix F, Additional background on the manual update

When FIAF established its Cataloguing Commission in 1968 (which merged with the Documentation Commission in 1997 and is now called the Cataloguing and Documentation Commission), the new Commission set, as its first task, the creation of a compendium of advice on practical cataloguing. The result of this work was the *Film Cataloguing* manual (New York: Burt Franklin & Co.) published in 1979.

Having completed this background work, the Commission turned, in 1980, to the next task – that of providing an international standard set of rules for the style, content, and format of cataloguing records. The Commission relied upon the *International Standard for Bibliographic Description for non-Book Materials* (ISBD (NBM)) (London: IFLA, 1977, rev. 1987) from the related discipline of librarianship, which had already achieved recognition among library professionals worldwide. Because the ISBD (NBM) rules were directed to generalised collections of widely available audio-visual materials, they did not solve the technical, preservation and scholarly information needs inherent to archival moving images. The ISBD (NBM) could nonetheless serve as a model for FIAF by providing a framework into which the Commission could place its basic principles of archival moving image cataloguing and upon which it then built these principles into a complete set of cataloguing rules, *The FIAF Cataloguing Rules for Film Archives* (1991).

The resulting manual divided archival moving image cataloguing information into seven areas of description along the lines of *ISBD (NBM)*, but with some differences in the areas of description and their order to address the particular needs of moving image materials.

In 2004, the Commission recognised the need to revise and update a manual conceived for a non-computerized and "analogue" world. It designed and disseminated the Survey of Moving Image Cataloguing Practice in Film Archives (2005-2006). The survey responses revealed specific areas the community wanted revised and issues particular to moving image archives that the new approach should consider (see Appendix F.1 for a listing of these areas and issues).

In 2008, the Commission met in Paris to set goals and a plan of action for new guidelines (see Appendix F.2 for listing of goals).

The authors of this revision compared the 1991 FIAF Rules with the most recent FRBR-based cataloguing documents, publications and standards related to moving images, in order to evaluate and take aspects of them into account. These documents, publications and standards included:

- *RDA: Resource Description and Access* (RDA)
- The thought papers of the Online Audiovisual Catalogers (OLAC) Cataloging Policy Committee (CAPC) Moving Image Work-Level Records Task Force
- The work done by Martha Yee (Cataloging Supervisor at the UCLA Film & Television Archive): *Cataloging Rules* (2008) and *Moving image cataloging: how to*

create and how to use a moving image catalog (2007)

- The European Standards Committee (CEN) Cinematographic Works Standard (CWS) (EN 15744 and EN 15907).

F.1 Survey of Moving Image Cataloguing Practice in Film Archives (2005-2006)

Specific areas the community wanted revised:[229]

- Expand and improve physical description, including complete information about physical conditions and restoration procedures. Implement the description of digital objects.
- Improve the Copyright area.
- Streamline and re-structure the Notes Area, currently too extensive and containing too many heterogeneous pieces of information.
- Adopt or suggest consistent criteria for the content description, especially for non-fiction moving images.
- Introduce a Standard Number Area (i.e. to include the ISAN -International Standard Audiovisual Number – or national standards).
- Introduce a Terms of Availability / Access Area.

To address issues particular to moving image archives, the revision should also consider:

- the history of the document in hand before and after the acquisition in the archive
- the description of the collection to which it belongs, according to the specific archival standard rules (i.e. ISAD)
- links with moving image-related materials associated with moving image items, such as papers, censorship visas, booklets, laboratory reports, archive notes, etc.

F.2 2008 Paris meetings goals and a plan of action

- Represent a corpus of contextualized suggestions, rather than a set of authoritative directions, so that they will easily integrate with institutions' existing procedures.
- Be accessible on the Internet.
- Reflect a consistent terminology outlined in a glossary.
- Be compatible with existing metadata and data communication structures

229 These areas are a further example of how the functions of a catalogue for moving image archives are different than for those of a library, paper-based archives, or museum.

such as Dublin Core, MARC, and the CEN CWS.

- Use the FRBR conceptual model, especially since RDA and the CEN CWS are heavily based on the model.

F.3 Relationship of *FIAF Cataloguing Rules* to *Functional Requirements of Bibliographic Records* (FRBR), *Resource Description and Access* (RDA) and The European Standards Committee (CEN) Cinematographic Works Standard EN 15907

Like the 1991 *FIAF Cataloguing Rules*, the authors of this manual have chosen to adopt current standards and practices, such as those outlined in FRBR, RDA, and EN15907, while expanding them to be more specific and granular regarding the particular needs of moving image cataloguing. Listed below are some of the key attributes of these standards and their relationship to recommendations in the new *FIAF Cataloguing Manual*.

F.3.1 Entities

Functional Requirements for Bibliographic Records (FRBR) was published in 1998 by the International Federation of Libraries Association. It is based on the entity-attribute-relationship model of analysis, and has been incorporated into the structure of both RDA and EN 15907.

FRBR identifies and defines three groups of entities:[230]

- Group 1 (products of intellectual or artistic endeavor)
  - Work
  - Expression
  - Manifestation
  - Item

- Group 2 (responsible for content, production, or custodianship of Group 1 entities)
  - Person
  - Corporate Body

- Group 3 (may serve as subjects of Group 1 entities)
  - Group 1 and 2 entities
  - Concept
  - Object
  - Event
  - Place

230 FRBR Final Report, pp. 12-16; Taylor, p. 4.

This manual focuses almost exclusively on the Group 1 entities, their attributes and relationships. Although it also briefly provides guidelines for the description of the Group 2 and Group 3 entities, we recommend the use of other manuals and appropriate existing national or international standards for more detail in these areas.

F.3.1.1 Existing standards for describing Entities

Existing standards for describing Entities include:

- RDA
  - Section 3: Person, Family, & Corporate Body (Chapters 8-11)
  - Section 4: Concept, Object, Event & Place (Chapters 12-16)
  - Appendix F: Additional Instructions on Names of Persons

- ISAAR (CPF): International Standard Archival Authority Record for Corporate Bodies, Persons and Families, 2nd Edition (http://www.ica.org/10203/standards/isaar-cpf-international-standard-archival-authority-record-for-corporate-bodies-persons-and-families-2nd-edition.html) - International Council of Archives);

- EFG Metadata Schema & Vocabularies – 3.6 Agent (http://www.efgproject.eu/guidelines_and_standards.php)

Authority files

- VIAF (The Virtual International Authority File)
- ISNI (International Standard Name Identifier (ISO 27729) – (http://www.isni.org/)
- IdREf (Identifiants et Référentiels) – (http://www.icacds.org.uk/eng/ISAAR(CPF)2ed.pdf)
- Library of Congress Subject Headings (LCSH) and the Library of Congress Genre-Form Thesaurus (LCGFT)

F.3.1.2 Definitions of the "Work" and "Variant" Entities

The FIAF Cataloguing and Documentation Commission has chosen to model this manual on definitions of "Work" and "Variant" adopted by the European Standards Committee, rather than the FRBR and RDA definitions of "Work" and "Expression," to make these concepts more practical for describing moving images. FRBR and RDA consider "works" and "expressions" to be abstract entities that only acquire physical characteristics at the "manifestation or "item" level. However, moving image "works" are more easily conceptualized as concrete entities. This is because a moving image work only becomes such through a complex process involving multiple contributors. This process results in a "fixed" or "expressed" object (whether analogue or digital) that typically combines a visual part (the moving image), and a textual part (the soundtrack or intertitles).[231] There-

231 Yee. "The Concept of *Work* for Moving Image Materials, p. 33.

fore, the concept of a moving image work comprises both the content and the process of realisation in a moving image medium.[232]

Further, this manual continues to follow the precepts already outlined in *Film Cataloguing* and *FIAF Cataloguing Rules for Film Archives* by including the concept of "original." The *FIAF Cataloguing Rules for Film Archives* recommend using the "original release title or broadcast title in the country of origin, i.e., the country of the principal offices of the production company or individual by whom the moving image work was made"[233] to identify a Work. "Owing to the complex interrelationships of persons and corporate bodies in the creation of a moving image work, the original release or broadcast title is chosen as the single element which can provide the level of consistency and standardisation requisite for any national and international networking or sharing of cataloguing data."[234]

Likewise, the "original" defined here contains characteristics that persist across any variation or output of a moving image work and that reflect the original intentions of its realisation, including: circumstances of the creation process such as date(s) and place(s) of production, most contributions by agents such as directors, screenwriters, production companies and cast members, as well as certain statements about the contents.[235]

In this way, a moving image work as a concept is closer to a combining of FRBR and RDA's work and expression entities. This definition also aligns closely with the concept of "work primary expression" formulated by the Online Audiovisual Catalogers (OLAC) Cataloging Policy Committee (CAPC) Moving Image Work-Level Records Task Force and the CEN's EN 15907. A primary difference here is that EN 15907 specifies for the concept of "original" to be expressed in association with an instance of a Manifestation that embodies the original Work.

The use of the term "variant" is not a mere substitute for the term "expression." In the context of moving images, variants and expressions cannot be considered equivalent concepts because moving image works are already their own expressions.[236] As explained above, a moving image work has by definition taken a form (been expressed) and contains specific attributes that correspond to the concept of an "original" or "primary expression." The variants correspond to all other "expressions." For example, a colorized version of *The asphalt jungle* (1950) does not express the original work; it contains a variation from the original idea conceived by John Huston and put into form. If there is no variation from the work as originally conceived, there is no "variant," but under FRBR there would always be an "expression." This exemplifies why these concepts are not equal: that is, there may not always be a variant but there must always be an expression.[237]

---

232 EN 15907, 4.1.1, p. 8.
233 FIAF, 1991, p. xiii
234 FIAF, 1991, p. xiii
235 Adapted from the definition of a Cinematographic Work in EN 15907, 4.1.1, p.8.
236 Journal of Digital Media Management Vol. 2, 3, 00–00 © Henry Stewart Publications 2047- 1300 (2013) The EN 15907 moving image metadata schema standard and its role in a digital asset management infrastructure, by Detlev Balzar, Stephen McConnachie, Thelma Ross.
237 Laurent Bismuth (personal communication, May 08, 2011)

F.3.1.3 Definitions of the Manifestation and Item Entities

A Manifestation is the embodiment of a Work/Variant and includes all the analogue or digital forms that are derived from a Work/Variant and bear common characteristics with respect to shared intellectual content and physical format. It may be whole or incomplete or a fragment.

An Item is the physical product of a Manifestation of a Work or Variant, i.e. the physical copy of a Work or Variant. It may be whole or incomplete or a fragment. In the case of purely digital media, an Item is defined as the availability of the computer file, irrespective of the number of backup copies that may exist[238].

F.3.1.4. Boundaries between entities

The traditional practice within moving image archives of incorporating variation information into a record enabled this one record to carry within it all the details relative to the differing components of a whole.[239] Within the framework of the FRBR and RDA models, and the EN 15907 schema, the work record represents this "one record," incorporating certain descriptive details, but the placement of the variation information changes. Different editions, versions, or variations are represented by the variant and manifestation entities, and the differences are recorded at the appropriate level or on the particular entity record, or designated in some way as belonging to the specific entity. The treatment of an "information resource" by using the four-tier hierarchy to express the concept allows it to be described and viewed at each of the four levels: for example, a documentary is, simultaneously, a particular copy or component pieces (item(s)), a particular publication (manifestation), a particular edition (variant), and a particular piece of work (work).

It remains essential to users of archival moving image material that information describing the original work and information describing the item in hand are presented in a manner that clearly delineates this relationship. The relationship in library terms is described as the concept of "edition" and it includes any changes in content or changes in carrier. Separate editions of printed library material are catalogued separately, and usually no attempt is made to determine whether edition statements always indicate major changes in content.[240] "Publication," in the context of a moving image archive, is used interchangeably with "distribution" and means "making the resource available."[241] For moving image materials, the terms most analogous to this concept of edition are

238 Digital medium definition taken from CEN's "Film Identification – enhancing interoperability of metadata. Element sets and structures. FprEN 15907:2010 (E)

239 FIAF, 1991, p. xii

240 FIAF, 1991, p. xii

241 Andrea Leigh, (drawn from personal communication, May 05, 2011)

"versions with major changes" and "variations with minor changes."[242] (see http://www.fiafnet.org/images/tinyUpload/E-Resources/Commission-And-PIP-Resources/CDC-resources/FIAF_Cat_Rules.pdf)

In moving image archives, both the occurrence of a change in the content and the extent of the change are important. In most cases, for moving image materials, the changes in content are a function of some form of editing.

The treatment of the concepts of "versions with major changes" and "variations with minor changes" in this revision shift to a focus on changes in content and changes to carrier and correlate to the boundaries between the variants (changes in content) of a work and its manifestations (changes in carrier). This does not replace the need to create a version with major changes as a new Work where this is necessary and appropriate 1.1.2 Boundaries between Works and Variants/Manifestations.

F.3.2 Attributes

This manual provides a granular nomenclature for describing the attributes of the moving image entities, Work, Variant, Manifestation and Item (WVMI). The guidelines do not specify the attributes for entities related to the WVMI entities, for example, Agents (i.e., Persons, Families, Corporate Bodies, etc.). For recording the attributes of Agents (e.g. first name, last name, nationality, etc.), refer to authoritative sources such as *Functional requirements for authority data: a conceptual model* or tools such as the Library of Congress Name Authority File.[243]

F.3.3 User Tasks

FRBR and RDA have defined and adopted the following tasks reflecting the traditional core functions of the catalogue:[244]

find—i.e., to find resources that correspond to the user's stated search criteria

identify—i.e., to confirm that the resource described corresponds to the resource sought, or to distinguish between two or more resources with similar characteristics

select—i.e., to select a resource that is appropriate to the user's needs

---

242 FIAF, 1991, p. xii-xiii. They are defined as following in the 1991 rules:
Versions with major changes. If the cataloging agency has determined that the item in hand differs significantly from the original work, i.e., major editing has been done, the item is described in a separate cataloging record. The item in hand is designated a version of the original work with major changes, e.g., short version, classroom version, etc., and the distribution information for the separate version is recorded. The relationship to the original work is indicated in the edition/version statement, and, in most instances, in a note. Distribution information relating to the original work may also be indicated in a note.
Variations with minor changes. When the cataloging agency determines that an item, although designated as being re-edited, e.g., a "new edition," has not indeed been changed significantly, it may express this relationship by recording the statement of responsibility for the original in area one, the variation and statement of responsibility for the variation in area two, and the production, distribution information for both the original and variation copies in area three. Multiple edition/version/variation statements may be given when cataloging multiple variations with minor changes.

243 Patton, Glenn E. 2009. *Functional requirements for authority data: a conceptual model.* München: K.G. Saur.

244 FRBR Final Report, p. 82; RDA, 0.0, Purpose and Scope

obtain—i.e., to acquire or access the resource described.

RDA added an additional set of user tasks based on those defined in IFLA's Working Group on Functional Requirements and Numbering of Authority Records (FRANAR), and describe an entity associated with a resource:

find—i.e., to find information on that entity and on resources associated with the entity

identify—i.e., to confirm that the entity described corresponds to the entity sought, or to distinguish between two or more entities with similar names, etc.

clarify—i.e., to clarify the relationship between two or more such entities, or to clarify the relationship between the entity described and a name by which that entity is known

understand—i.e., to understand why a particular name or title, or form of name or title, has been chosen as the preferred name or title for the entity.

These user tasks are listed because they are pertinent to moving image cataloguing and can be adapted to cover many of the search and discovery needs of those who might seek moving images. For example, Martha Yee (2007) provides one adaptation of the functions of the library catalogue for moving images:

To find, identify, select, and acquire: [245]

- All the *versions* (*Variants*) of a sought *Work* (for example the various "director's cuts" of *Blade runner* as well as the original release version), specified by its title, or by its title in conjunction with the name of one of its creators or by date, that are held by your collection or to which you license access.
- All the *copies* (*Manifestations* or *Items*) of a particular version (*Variant)* of a *Work* (for example, all the copies you hold of the studio's director's cut) that are held by your collection or to which you license access.
- All the *Works* of a particular person (for example, director, actor, costume designer) or corporate body (for example, studio) that are held by your collection or to which you license access.
- All the *Works* on a subject (for example, the Vietnam War) that are held by your collection or to which you license access.
- All the *Works* in a particular form or genre (for example, animation, gangster films) that are held by your collection or to which you license access.

Representation (or, principle of transcription)

The basic principle of transcription is an area in which archival moving image cataloguing frequently deviates from traditional library cataloguing. Whereas traditional library cataloguers typically transcribe descriptive data directly from the physical item, this is not always the case in archival moving image cataloguing. Because of this, earlier moving image cataloguing rules and standards (FIAF, AMIM) have suggested the term

245 Yee, 2007, p. 16.

"preferred" rather than "chief" source of filmographic information for representing moving images. The importance of reflecting the original details of a moving image work is a primary principle of organisation for moving image archives. This underlies another practice of moving image cataloguing, which was also recommended in the 1991 FIAF Rules, namely choosing the original release title in country of origin as the preferred title for a work. Other titles (e.g., translated titles, re-release or reissue titles, titles on the item or accompanying material, etc.), are recorded at the appropriate entity level, or designated as belonging to the appropriate entity, and linking mechanisms from other titles to the original release title should be utilised.

Because, however, it is not always possible for a cataloguer to determine an original release title, guidelines are also provided for choice of the preferred title of the work when either: 1) the concept of original release title is not applicable (as in the case of unedited footage), or when 2) a cataloguer is unable, through research, to determine the original release title.

Rights Information

Because national and international rights regulations for moving image materials govern not only the copying of materials for subsequent use, but also the screening and/or viewing of such materials, information concerning rights is considered of paramount importance to most moving image archives. These guidelines include a separate area for the recording of information about the rights status of moving image materials for the entities that make up a moving image resource. The guidelines include provisions for recording both original and current rights information, as well as for indicating when the cataloguer has not been able to find any information. Since rights issues are complex legal matters, some moving image archives prefer to maintain separate legal files, or sometimes even to leave the resolution of rights issues entirely to the responsibility of the user or client. For these reasons, the recording of rights information has been designated "optional." For a more extensive and expanded further exploration of rights and potential rights data to capture, see Appendix H, Rights/Copyright/IPR Registration.

Appendix G, Elements of Description comparison

1991 FIAF Cataloguing Rules (ISBD based), EN 15907 and FIAF Moving Image Cataloguing Manual

Moving Image Work / Variant

FIAF Moving Image Cataloguing Manual	EN 15907	1991 FIAF Cataloguing Rules (ISBD based)
Attributes of the entity	**Attributes**	
Description Type • Analytic • Monographic	DescriptionLevel • Analytic • Monographic	
• Serial • Collection	• Serial • Collection	Series Area
• Variant type Censored Dubbed Subtitled Abridged/Condensed Augmented	VariantType	Version/variation area
Elements (including main attributes)	**Elements**	
• Identifier	Identifier (number)	
• Title Title type Identifying Preferred Other title information Alternative Supplied/Devised	Identifying title (human readable)	Title area
• Country of reference	Country of reference	Production/distribution area
• Year/Date	Year of reference	Production/distribution area
• Language(s)	Language	Production/distribution area
• Content description	Content description	Notes area
• Notes		Notes area
• History		Notes area

Relationships (including main attributes)	Allowed relationships	
• Agents Agent type (e.g. cast/credits)	HasAgent	Production/distribution area
• Events Event type Publication Award(s) or Nomination(s) Production Rights/Copyright/IPR Registration Preservation (Variant) Decision (Variant)	HasEvent	Production/distribution area Notes area
• Subject terms	HasSubject	Notes area
• Other relationships	HasOtherRelation	Notes area
• Manifestations	HasManifestation	Production/distribution area Physical description area

Moving Image Manifestation

FIAF Moving Image Cataloguing Manual	EN 15907	1991 FIAF Cataloguing Rules (ISBD based)
Attributes of the entity	**Attributes**	
• Manifestation Type Pre-release Theatrical distribution Non-theatrical distribution Not for release Unreleased Home viewing publication Broadcast Internet Preservation/Restoration Unknown	ManifestationType	Production/distribution area

Elements (including main attributes)	Elements	
• Identifier	Identifier	
• Title Title type Proper Other title information Alternative Supplied/Devised	Title	Title area
• Language	Language	Physical description area
• Format	Format	Physical description area
• Extent	Extent	Physical description area
Relationships (including main attributes)	**Allowed relationships**	
• Agents Agent type Distributor (theatrical) Distributor (non-theatrical) Broadcaster Publisher Manufacturer Agent responsible for preservation Agent responsible for reproduction or transfer Agent responsible for archival availability Agent responsible for the mere availability Agent unclear or undetermined Agent not identified	HasAgent	Production/distribution area Notes area
• Events Event type Publication Award(s) or Nomination(s) Licensing Preservation Decision Manufacture	HasEvent	Production/distribution area Physical Description area Notes area
• Other relationships	HasOtherRelation	Notes area
• Item	HasItem	Physical Description area

Moving Image Item

FIAF Moving Image Cataloguing Manual	EN 15907	1991 FIAF Cataloguing Rules (ISBD based)
Elements (including main attributes)	**Elements**	
• Identifier	ManifestationType	Production/distribution area
• Title Title type Proper Other title information Alternative Supplied/Devised	Title	Title area
• Holding institution		Notes area
• Item Material type	MaterialType	Physical description area
• Item-specifics	ItemSpecifics	Physical description area Notes area
• Access conditions		Physical description area
• Notes for moving image Items		Notes area
Relationships (including main attributes)	**Allowed relationships**	
• Agent(s) (e.g., preservation technician, donor, etc.)	HasAgent	Notes area
• Events Event type Licensing Preservation Inspection Acquisition	HasEvent	Notes area
• Other Relationships	HasOtherRelation	Notes area

Appendix H, Rights/Copyright/IPR Registration

H.1 Rights in a moving image Work

The intellectual property rights in a moving image work are known by various terms such as Copyright, Ayant droit, Droit d'Auteur, IP or simply Rights. These IP rights are complex entities, reflecting the complexity of a moving image work's creation; and they vary across legal frameworks and across historical periods. It is therefore impractical to define a minimum cataloguing requirement which is compliant across all territories and periods. In addition, it should be noted that legal frameworks can change across time, so data which is not useful today can become useful if the legal definition changes – for example the definitions of author outlined below.

With that context in mind, the following attempts to define a good practice set of properties which the moving image cataloguer should consider, both in reference to their specific legal framework, and in reference to potentially useful data over the lifecycle of the archive's activity. In short: capturing more of the core rights data now will safeguard future archival activity better than capturing less of that rights data now.

It is important to note that intellectual property rights in a moving image work are created automatically, regardless of any requirement for formal registration by the creators of the work. In addition, it is worth noting that in some legal territories, unlike literary, dramatic, musical or artistic works, moving image works do not have to meet the criterion of 'original' to be protected with intellectual property rights. Finally, it is worth noting that unpublished works are often treated differently under law to published works, so it is recommended that the cataloguer capture a statement where it is known that a work is unpublished (for example, home movies).

The recommended properties below are preceded by some background information.

H.1.1 Background information

H.1.1.2 Source of data

Regarding the source of intellectual property data, it is recommended to obtain the relevant information from onscreen text, taken from the first official manifestation in the primary country of origin. Historically this has been a theatrical release in the primary country of production, but as that model changes to include simultaneous online publication of moving image works across multiple territories, this recommendation should accommodate this fluidity: capture the data from the best available manifestation source representing the arguable 'first fixation' of the work, and document that source in your work record. Alternatively, use information given by the production companies or rights holders, or from other authoritative secondary sources.

H.1.1.3 Authors of a moving image Work

The Authors of a moving image work are the first owners of the intellectual property rights. As the defined authors of the moving image work differ substantially across territories, the following examples illustrate these differences, and emphasise the usefulness of a broad data capture policy.

UK: The Producer and the Principal Director are the Authors of the work, and therefore the first copyright holders.

Producer: this can be either a person (natural person) or a company (legal person). The producer is defined as 'the person by whom the arrangements necessary for the making of the film are undertaken'. The notion of the 'producer' presupposes that at the core of the production process there is a person or company which co-ordinates, controls and organises the production. For this reason, the recommendation below is to capture both Production Company and named individual Producer.

Principal Director: as credited onscreen.

France: distinct from the UK model, in France it is those natural persons (not legal persons) who make a creative contribution to the film that are considered authors, so production company / producer are not authors.

Director

Author of the script

Author of the adaptation (if different)

Author of the dialogue (if different)

Author of musical composition written for the film

(plus 'assimilated' authors of pre-existing protected works e.g. author of an original novel, or playwright)

Germany: The German model is very similar to the French, again focusing on the creative contributions made by natural persons, but the list can be extended to include a broader set of persons – e.g. cameramen as author – as German Law does not specify the persons deemed as authors.

USA: The US model has a number of categories of authors who make creative contributions (rather like Germany), but the law does not define the 'authors', and in any case most individuals will be contracted under 'work for hire' provisions which means that the producer is the owner of the intellectual property rights.

These first owners of the intellectual property rights (or their heirs, in the event of their death) retain these rights until one of two events takes place:

1. They (or their heirs) actively sell, assign or otherwise transfer the rights

2. The rights expire, according to specific legal framework(s)

Again, the definitions of what makes a work 'out of copyright' differ across territories and periods, so it is impractical to offer a universally compliant cataloguing approach. However, in many contexts, the lapse occurs at a stated period after the death of the last of the Authors (or the 'connected persons' in the UK). For example, in the UK framework, the work is out of copyright at 70 years following the last death of these 'connected persons': Director, Screenplay author, Dialogue author, Music composer.

In the US, where a moving image Work is often a Work of corporate ownership, the current copyright term for a published Work expires 95 years after initial publication or 120 years after creation, whichever expires first. However, between 1923-2002 there were periods where other formalities needed to be followed in order to retain copyright: during some periods, a Item required "notice" (a copyright symbol or statement) on the work; in other periods, the Work had to be renewed in the 28th year after initial publication.[246]

As intellectual property rights can be transferred, and can lapse, it is recommended that cataloguers capture statements about the rights' status: current / previous / out of copyright, and the dates of transfer / lapse, as described below. In addition, as death dates are so critical in establishing the status of *out of copyright*, it is recommended that cataloguers capture the death dates of key contributors where known (and where feasible, that person records for key 'authors' are associated with equivalent entities in an official registry of persons, such as VIAF, ISNI or other).

H.1.1.4 Layers of protection for the 'work' as abstraction, and the 'fixation' or 'recording' of the work in a concrete form

The complexity and variation in the intellectual property rights surrounding a moving image work also extends to multiple layers of protection, in some legal frameworks. Bluntly described, these multiple layers protect the 'work' as an abstraction (with the rights held by the 'authors', as defined above) and, separately, the 'fixation' or 'recording' of the work as a film. This second layer is often called Related Rights or Neighbouring Rights, and often these rights are owned by the Producer.

This layered approach is not always present in law, for example in the UK it is the fixation (the recording) that is protected by copyright. But some prominent examples of this layered approach are the USA, where a film is protected as an original work of expression as distinct from the recording; and France and Germany, which both have separate protection for the work and the recording.

Given the territorial variation, once again, rather than recommend different data properties for the different countries, instead it is recommended to capture a core set of rights data properties, which should provide information sufficient for all possibilities

246 For guidance on copyright terms in the US, see Peter Hirtle's chart "Copyright terms and the public domain in the United States," updated annually. http://copyright.cornell.edu/resources/publicdomain.cfm

within the different frameworks.

H.1.1.5 Orphan works

Orphan works are defined as those works which are 'still protected by copyright but whose authors or other rightholders are not known or cannot be located.' (from the OHIM Orphan Works Database website at https://oami.europa.eu/ohimportal/en/web/observatory/orphan-works-database). The absence of information about ownership has prevented archives from exploiting their collections in revenue-generating or access-driving initiatives: for example, online display of digitised collections.

Multiple formal schemes are emerging to register so-called 'orphan works' works in certified, searchable databases. These schemes require the registering organisation to undertake 'diligent search' (e.g., the OWLS guidelines here: https://www.gov.uk/government/publications/orphan-works-diligent-search-guidance-for-applicants) with minimum requirements, and the registration then allows the organisation to exploit the work within parametres defined in legal frameworks.

Three prominent examples (which offer slightly different exploitation rights as outcomes of registration) are the European Union Orphan Works Database (https://oami.europa.eu/orphanworks/); the UK version, called Orphan Works Licensing Scheme, or OWLS, (https://www.gov.uk/copyright-orphan-works); and the Canadian version, called Unlocatable Copyright Owners (http://www.cb-cda.gc.ca/unlocatable-introuvables/brochure1-e.html). The United States has not yet passed legislation on orphan works, but the Regsiter of Copyrights is actively seeking to change the laws.[247]

The cataloguer within a moving image archive that is undertaking such registration should add data derived from that registration activity, for example unique identifier for the registration, URL to online database record, link to certificate on PDF, etc.

H.1.1.6 Rights-protected works that may be used within, or created during, a film production

These are the types of protected works which are often contained within a new moving image work, or indeed created by the making of a moving image work, and which are often referred to as 'underlying rights' or "third-party rights." When establishing Manifestation rights (see below), these underlying rights must be investigated and cleared as required.

Literary Works – such as a pre-existing novel or play used as the basis for the film screenplay

Dramatic Works – Script(s)

Musical Works – pre-existing music; commissioned music

Artistic Works – such as décor, costumes

247 Priorities and special projects of the United States Copyright Office (October 2011), http://copyright.gov/docs/priorities.pdf

Performances – actors' performances, musical performances of pre-existing music, musical performances in commissioned music

Sound Recordings – if commissioned for pre-existing music

Films – such as archival footage; special effect footage

H.1.2 Recommended properties to capture in describing the rights context of a moving image Work

1. Copyright holder and Copyright Date, as displayed on screen (often associated with a © symbol)

2. Status of intellectual property rights holder:

    a. Current

    b. Previous (where rights are known to have transferred), with date of transfer if known

3. Producer and Production Companies

4. Director(s), with death dates if known

5. Screenplay author(s), with death dates if known

6. Dialogue author(s) (if different), with death dates if known

7. Author(s) of underlying literary work (book, play, etc) if relevant, with death dates if known

8. Music composer(s), with death dates if known (note that this refers to the composer of any music commissioned for and used in the film, rather than any pre-existing music used within the film – see 10)

9. Full cast if feasible, or main billed cast at a minimum, with death dates if known

10. Detail of any pre-existing works (moving or still image, dramatic, literary or musical works) contained within the moving image work, with provenance and ownership captured as fully as possible. (This set of contained works is often referred to as 'underlying rights', alongside the Performers' rights of the cast).

    a. title

    b. creator

    c. creation date

    d. rightsholder if known

    e. dates of rights transfer if relevant and if known

11. Production Date: capture a Start Date and End Date if possible, capturing the full known period of production.

12. Release Date (taken from first published manifestation, historically the theatrical release in primary country of production, but now with more fluid criteria)

13. Unpublished status (because often under law unpublished works are treated

differently to published works)

14. Orphan Works registration scheme. The suggested data to capture is:
    a. name of scheme e.g. OHIM (EU), OWLS (UK)
    b. unique identifier for the work in the scheme's database
    c. URL for online record in the scheme's database / website
    d. filename / link to digital version of 'orphan work' registration document
    e. name of member of archive staff responsible for registration
    f. date of registration
    g. date of expiry of licence granted by registration scheme

H.2 Rights in a Manifestation

The rights in a Manifestation are typically licences, contracts or agreements between the Work's copyright owner / intellectual property rights owner, and a third party, enabling that third party to exploit the work legally by copying it, distributing, broadcasting or publishing it, extracting from it, incorporating it in another work, etc.

Typically, a Work's owner can offer multiple licences to multiple parties to exploit the work in different publication territories, publication formats, publication platforms; and typically the licence can be exclusive or non-exclusive (in other words, multiple parties can be granted similar exploitation rights to the same work at the same time). Finally, the licence typically states a date range within which the exploitation can take place, with the extreme (and rare) example being 'in perpetuity', enabling the licensee to exploit the work within the terms without an end date.

Examples of publication modes or platforms and other exploitation models which are often used in moving image Manifestation licences: Theatrical, Home Video, Television, VOD (Video on Demand), DTO (Download to Own), Educational, B2B (Business to Business) footage sales, Plane/Ship/Hotel.(see D.5 Manifestation Types).

Often an exploitation of a moving image Work in a particular Manifestation requires the licensee to obtain additional clearances from third parties, as these 'underlying rights' (eg music, performers, stills) exist in parallel to the core intellectual property rights in the moving image Work. Depending on the context, and the importance of this information for the institution, the cataloguer may consider capturing the clearance of these underlying rights, as previously described in H.1.1.6.

Finally, where an archive holds copyright / intellectual property rights in a work, that archive may itself grant licences to third parties to exploit the work. This situation, where the archive supplies permission or licence to another party to exploit a work, is often referred to as 'rights out' or sales – the opposite of 'rights in' or acquisitions, meaning the archive obtains an exploitation licence from the owner. In that case, the cataloguer should document not only rights in but also rights out: name and contact details for licensee, territories, platforms, date ranges, exclusive or non-exclusive.

Given the context above, it may be useful for an archive to capture whether it is an acquirer of the manifestation rights being documented, a granter of the rights, or simply a documenter of the rights.

H.2.1 Recommended properties to capture in describing the rights context of a Manifestation

1. Relationship to rights being documented:

    a. Rights Out / Sales (where the archive is the granter of rights to an external party)

    b. Rights In / Acquisitions (where the archive is the obtainer of rights from an external party)

    c. Documenter only (where the archive is neither the granter or obtainer, but simply an observer)

2. Licensee organisation's or individual's name, with contact details if required

3. Licensing organisation's or individual's name, with contact details if required

4. Platforms or modes permitted within the license, using controlled value list. Suggested terms include: Theatrical, Home Video, Television, VOD (Video on Demand), DTO (Download to Own), Educational, B2B (Business to Business) footage sales, Plane/Ship/Hotel.

5. Geographical territories permitted within the license, using controlled value list representing the relevant territories

6. Date range of license, preferably entered separately as Start Date and End Date, to enable system queries against end date

7. Exclusive or non-Exclusive, where known

8. Filename of agreement: Capture the filename of an electronic version of any agreement pertaining to the manifestation's licence, or where possible a link to the file in a persistent, available directory within the organisation's infrastructure.

H.3 Rights in an Item

The rights in a moving image Item typically refer to the ownership (or transfer of ownership) of an object, either on a physical / analogue carrier such as a 35mm film print, or a digital file such as a DCP / DCDM or ProRes. The transfer of ownership (sometimes referred to in legal terms as 'transfer of title') is important for an archive to document, as it establishes legal ownership of the collection.

Typically, the transfer involves a contract, deed or agreement signed by both parties to certify that ownership of the object is transferred to the archive, and often this is a complex legal document. It is recommended therefore that the cataloguer capture the essential metadata elements below, and where feasible they should associate the catalogue record with an electronic version of the contract, by capturing filename / link to that document.

It should be understood that ownership of the Item does not imply any rights to exploit the Work, as outlined in the Manifestation section (for example, to digitise the object and display online, or distribute to cinemas); and it certainly does not imply any change in the intellectual property rights in the work itself. However, often during acquisition decision-making, an archive will undertake research into the broader rights context: is the work in or out of copyright?; if it is, who owns that copyright?; if they are unknown can it be considered an orphan work?; has it been registered as such?; if it is not an orphan work?, who owns the exploitation rights in the relevant territories, platforms? Cataloguers should therefore consider capturing details of this rights check activity when documenting the transfer of ownership of the item.

Particular acquisition agreements between object owner and archive may enforce restrictions on the archive, preventing them from undertaking certain activities on the item (for example, preventing them from digitising the item for preservation, or preventing them from exhibiting the item in internal cinema). Any such restrictions should be captured in a 'Provisos of acquisition', 'Conditions of access' or 'Conditions of reproduction' set of fields, as outlined below. In addition, the acquisition agreement may enforce a protocol for disposal of any objects which are not ultimately accessioned into the archive's permanent collection: for example, disposal may require approval by acquisition source.

However, it is important to note that any acquisition agreement or contract must not undermine the archive's rights under law. For example, in the UK, under recent legislative changes (Copyright Exceptions) a moving image archive has the right to 'copy works for archiving and preservation reasons if they are part of a permanent collection and it is not reasonably practicable to purchase a replacement' (from https://www.gov.uk/government/uploads/system/uploads/attachment_data/file/375956/Libraries_Archives_and_Museums.pdf). Therefore a specific acquisition agreement could not attempt to prevent that right to copy for preservation.

In the United States, an archive's right to copy for access and preservation is covered under Section 108. However, this section only applies to archives and libraries with specific qualifications.[248] The current Register of Copyrights has set revising Section 108 as one of her priorities.[249]

In Italy, since 2004, the Cineteca Nazionale can legally use the copies acquired by legal deposit (3 years after the deposit), or by copying/printing for cultural and non-profit purposes by way of derogation from copyright law.

Below, a set of properties are recommended for describing the rights around the Acquisition, and separately around the Loan, of moving image items.

248 http://www.copyright.gov/title17/92chap1.html#108
249 http://search.copyright.gov/search?utf8=%E2%9C%93&affiliate=copyright&query=section+108

H.3.1 Recommended properties to capture in describing the rights context of a moving image Item

H.3.1.2 Acquisition

See also D.4.9 Acquisition

This section is drawn from BFI policies.

1. Internal staff contact name: Captures the name of the staff member responsible for progressing and completing the agreement.
2. Agreement status: Captures the current stage in the completion of the agreement.
    a. In progress
    b. Hardcopy agreement sent
    c. Signed hardcopy agreement received
    d. Completed
3. Agreement completion date: Captures the date from which the agreement is considered as having legally come into effect e.g. the latest date recorded on a signed hardcopy of an Acquisition agreement.
4. Acquisition method: Denotes the form of acquisition represented by the record, e.g. a donation, a bequest left in the will of a benefactor, or an internally produced off-air recording.
    a. Bequest
    b. Commission
    c. Donation
    d. Off-air recording
    e. Purchase
    f. Unknown
5. Acquisition source: Represents the person or institution through which the BFI is receiving the acquisition. Where possible, this should take the form of a link to a record within the archive's Persons and Institutions authority dataset.
6. Acquisition source type: Qualifies the relationship between the Acquisition and the Acquisition source – i.e. is the acquisition source the legal owner of the item, or are they the authorised agent of the owner acting on their behalf such as in the case of a bequest or purchase through auction.
    a. Item Owner
    b. Agent
7. Acquisition source contact details: Captures the contact details of the acquisition source, primarily their postal address. Alternatively, where possible, this could be captured in the associated Person and Institution record.

8. Acquisition purchase price: Captures the price paid for the purchase of the complete acquisition as a integer.

9. Acquisition funding source: Captures the source of acquisition funding. This could represent funding secured through an external organisation, benefactor, or an internal budget.

10. Acquisition purchase currency: Qualifies the content of the Acquisition purchase price field with the currency of the purchase. Suggest using 3-character ISO 4217 codes.

11. Initial rights check status: Indicates the status of initial rights checks required as part of the acquisition process.

a. Rights holder(s) recorded in Work record

b. Rights holder is Acquisition source

c. Rights holder could not be identified

12. Acquisition date: Captures the date on which the agreement was signed – this is the date on which the agreement becomes legally binding. In some context, instead of this signature date, archives capture the date on which the Item physically entered the premises / infrastructure of the archive. Using this 'entry date' can be problematic, as items can arrive onsite before agreement is signed, or can arrive without any form of signature or indeed knowledge that it is in transit i.e. receipt of an unsolicited deposit. Therefore it is recommended to use the signature date.

13. Accession date: Captures the date on which the Item formally entered the collection of the archive. Often this definition is dependent on formal documentation within the archive's collections management system, with a unique accession reference / identifier assigned.

14. Acquisition rationale: Text field or controlled field allowing the staff responsible for the acquisition to capture the rationale behind the acquisition in relation to the archive's published collecting policy or other formal governance model.

15. Acquisition authoriser: Captures the name of the senior member of staff who approves the acquisition in question.

16. Acquisition authorisation date: Captures the date that the acquisition was approved by a senior member of staff.

17. Acquisition provisos: Captures any provisos or clauses agreed with the acquisition source e.g any form of access/publication embargo. Note that this should not undermine the archive's rights under law. This may be captured using a text field, or it may be controlled. And if required, it may be broken out into specific proviso areas as in 18 and 19 below.

18. Conditions governing reproduction: Text field or controlled field to capture specific restrictions on the archive's ability to copy the item in the analogue or digital domain, for preservation or other purposes. Note that this should not undermine the archive's rights under law.

19. Conditions governing access: Text field or controlled field to capture specific restrictions on the archive's ability to offer internal or external access to the item,

for research or commercial purposes. Note that this should not undermine the archive's rights under law.

20. Provisos expiry date: Captures the date upon which the associated proviso expires, if at all – e.g. the end of a publication embargo.

21. Item reproduction requested: Captures whether the supply of a duplicate copy to the acquisition source is one of the terms of acquisition agreed with the acquisition source.

22. Item reproduction terms: Captures the terms under which reproduction of the acquired material will be supplied to the Acquisition source.

a. Reproduction at Acquisition source expense

b. Reproduction at mutually agreed expense

c. Reproduction at archive's expense

23. Item reproduction notes: Field to allow the terms of reproduction to be further qualified, e.g. the exact division of mutually agreed expense for reproduction.

24. Terms of disposal for unaccessioned items: Records the agreed method of disposal for material not being accessioned into the archive's permanent collections, as authorised by the Acquisition source.

a. Return to acquisition source

b. Transfer to another institution

c. Archive authorised to dispose

25. Filename of agreement: Capture the filename of an electronic version of the Acquisition agreement, or where possible a link to the file in a persistent, available directory within the organisation's infrastructure.

H.3.1.3 Loan

1. This section outlines the properties that are specific to Loan agreements, distinct from Acquisitions

2. Lender: Represents the person or institution from which the archive is receiving the loan. Where possible, this should take the form of a link to a record within the archive's Persons and Institutions authority dataset.

3. Lender type: Qualifies the relationship between the Lender and the Acquisition source – i.e. is the lender the legal owner of the item, or are they the authorised agent of the owner acting on their behalf.

a. Item Owner

b. Agent

4. Lender contact details: Captures the contact details of the lender, primarily their postal address. Alternatively, where possible, this could be captured in the associated Person and Institution record.

5. Loan start date: Captures the agreed date from which the loan commences.

6. Loan end date: Captures the end date of the loan, as defined prior to the commencement of the loan.

7. Item reproduction requested: Captures whether the supply of a duplicate copy to the lender is one of the terms of loan agreed with the lender.

8. Item reproduction terms: Captures the terms under which reproduction of the loaned material will be supplied to the lender.

   a. Reproduction at Lender expense

   b. Reproduction at mutually agreed expense

   c. Reproduction at archive's expense

9. Item reproduction notes: Field to allow the terms of reproduction to be further qualified, e.g. the exact division of mutually agreed expense for reproduction.

10. Filename of agreement: Capture the filename of an electronic version of the Loan agreement, or where possible a link to the file in a persistent, available directory within the organisation's infrastructure.

Appendix I, Examples of records containing core elements in the different levels of hierarchy

These include examples of feature films, a documentary, a short fiction film, a home movie, a television series and episode, and an aggregate television DVD and episode. It is recognised that field names in different institutions' systems will not necessarily use identical terms to those of the core concepts or this manual (see 0.2 Core elements of description). Some may also have multiple occurrences and multiple fields connected with each element, whilst others may use few or no field names. Some institutions may also have additional fields and data for in-house needs. The following examples reflect some of these possible differences.

I.1 Example 1. Feature film in 3-level, 2-level and 1-level hierarchies

Example 1 depicts 3-level, 2-level and 1 level model hierarchies (see 0.2.1 Elements of description across Works, Variants, Manifestations, and Items) for the same film.

In this first example, as an initial illustration, the corresponding data of the core concepts has the same matching colours as used in the list below, and the core concept term is also given in italics and square brackets alongside the most equivalent field name.

Fields and data in black are additional elements and data, that also mainly correspond with the wider Attributes, Elements and Relationships stipulated in CEN EN15907 and found at 1. Moving Image Works and Variants, 2. Moving Image Manifestations, and 3. Moving Image Items.

Core concepts (0.2 Core elements of description)

Title
Series/Serial
Cast
Credits
Country of reference
Original format
Original Length
Original duration
Language
Year of reference
Identifier
Subject/genre/form
Content description

3-Level Hierarchy Model

WORK

Title *[Title]*	Title type
The Ladykillers	Original
The Lady killers	Help search

Work type: Film | Filmographic level: Monographic

Production country *[Country of reference]* : United Kingdom

Date(s) *[Year of reference]*	Date type
1955	Copyright
1955-12	Release

Category *[Form]*: Fiction | Genre *[Subject/Genre]*: Comedy, Crime

Synopsis: A gang of train robbers hide out at the lodgings of one of them, posing as an amateur string quartet. The innocent and upright elderly lady who owns the house is used by them, and is an inadvertent catalyst for their plans unravelling and the gang turning on each other.

On-screen credit	Name *[Credits]*
Directed by	Mackendrick, Alexander
Production Company	Ealing Studios
A Production by	Balcon, Michael
Associate Producer	Holt, Seth
Unite Production Manager	Peers, David
Production Supervisor	Mason, Hal
Assistant Director	Pevsner, Tom
[Assistant Director (2nd)]	Meadows, John
[Assistant Director (3rd)]	Birkett, Michael
Continuity	Manheim, Felicia
Story and Screenplay by	Rose, William
Director of Photography	Heller, Otto
Technicolor Colour Consultant	Bridge, Joan
Camera Operator	Waterson, Chic (as Waterson, Chick)
[Focus Puller]	Parslow, Ray
[Clapper Loader]	Bryce, Alan
[Stills]	Hanscomb, Harold
Special Effects	Pearson, Syd (as Pearson, Sydney)
Editor	Harris, Jack
Assistant Editor	Aldous, Harry
[Assistant Editor (2nd)]	Clark, Jim
[Assistant Editor (2nd)]	Clark, Robin

Art Director	Morahan, Jim
[Assistant Art Director]	Davey, Bert
[Draughtsman]	Shampan, Jack
Scenic Artist	Robinson, W. Simpson
Costume Designer	Mendleson, Anthony
Make-up	Garfath, Alec (as Garfath, Alex)
Hairstyles	Martin, Daphne
Music Composed by	Cary, Tristram
Played by	The Sinfonia of London
Conducted by	Mathieson, Dock
Recordist	Wilkins, Leo
Sound Supervisor	Dalby, Stephen (as Dalby, Steven)
[Sound Assistant]	Fairbairn, Harry
[Boom Operator]	Wortham, Don
Sound Editor	Stone, Gordon
Character	Name *[Cast]*
Professor Marcus	Guinness, Alec
Major Courtney	Parker, Cecil
Louis Harvey	Lom, Herbert
Harry Robinson	Sellers, Peter
One-Round Lawson	Green, Danny
police superintendent	Warner, Jack
Mrs. Louisa Wilberforce	Johnson, Katie
police sergeant	Stainton, Philip
barrow boy	Howerd, Frankie
[pavement artist]	Sharp, Len
[left luggage clerk]	Goodwin, Harold
[cab driver]	Connor, Kenneth
[junkman]	Griffiths, Fred
[Amelia]	Kerry, Evelyn
[Hypatia]	Burls, Hélène
[old lady]	Hodgson, Phoebe
[Lettice]	Martin, Edie
[Scotland Yard man]	Melford, Jack
[constable]	Moore, Robert
[nervous man]	Rudling, John
[large lady]	Brindley, Madge
[Miss Pringle]	Griffiths, Lucy
[second cab driver]	Kydd, Sam
[policeman]	Wilson, Neil

[constable in station]	Roberts, Ewan
[burglar]	Corcoran, Michael
[cast]	Roberts, Lynne
[cast]	John, Anthony
[cast]	Robb, Sandra
[cast]	Johns, Stratford
[cast]	Ayres, Janet
[cast]	Evans, Peter
[cast]	Green, Kevin
[cast]	Hart, Janet
cast]	Pike, Colin

[Identifier] Identification number W-35195
[Identifier] EIDR identifier 10.5240/1C59-EFCF-AAF0-F735-71AB-H

Event: Production – Date: 1955 Location(s): Frederica Street, Islington, London N7
Cheney Road, Kings Cross, London NW1

Relationships:
Parts title

M-34312 The Ladykillers

MANIFESTATION

[Identifier] Identification number: M-34312

Title *[Title]*	Title type
The Ladykillers	Original

Manifestation type: Theatrical (main country of origin)

Language *[Language]*	Usage
English	Dialogue (original)

[Original format] General Format: Film Specific Format: 35mm
Colour Colour system: Technicolor Sound
[Original duration] Running time – 97 minutes *[Original length]* Length: 8142 feet
Event: Release - Release Country: United Kingdom Date: 1955-12

Distributor: Rank

Relationships:

Part of title	Parts title
35195 The Ladykillers	C-88339 The Ladykillers

↓

<u>ITEM</u>

Title	Title type
The Lady killers	Original

Physical Description: Colour Positive Status: Master
Item type: Film Base: Safety Gauge: 35mm Colour Colour system: Technicolor
Sound Sound system: VA Bilateral Stock: Kodak

Language: English Usage: Dialogue

Number of cans/cassettes: 5 Number of Reels: 10 Total footage: 7981 feet

Institution record identification number: C-88339
Can identification number: 61470E

Access conditions: Restricted access to preserved film
Emulsion condition: New
Observations: No sound on main and end titles; scratches on first 20 ft of reel 5
Current location: XYZ203040 Home location: BKS102030

Event type: Inspection Movement number: 3 Reason: Perforation inspection
Date: 1968-10-02

Event type: Preservation Treatment: Damaged perforations on reels 2 and 7 repaired
Treatment date: 1968-10-05 Technician: Joe Bloggs

Event type: Acquisition Donor: FIAF Acquisition Date: 1959-09-03

Relationships:
Part of title
M-34312 The Ladykillers

2-Level Hierarchy model

WORK

Title *[Title]*	Title type
The Ladykillers	Original
The Lady killers	Help search

Work type: Film — Filmographic level: Monographic

Production country *[Country of reference]*: United Kingdom

Date(s) *[Year of reference]*	Date type
1955	Copyright
1955-12	Release

Category *[Form]*: Fiction — Genre *[Subject/Genre]*: Comedy, Crime

Synopsis *[Content Description]*: A gang of train robbers hide out at the lodgings of one of them, posing as an amateur string quartet. The innocent and upright elderly lady who owns the house is used by them, and is an inadvertent catalyst for their plans unravelling and the gang turning on each other.

On-screen credit	Name *[Credits]*
Directed by	Mackendrick, Alexander
Production Company	Ealing Studios
A Production by	Balcon, Michael
Associate Producer	Holt, Seth
Unit Production Manager	Peers, David
Production Supervisor	Mason, Hal
Assistant Director	Pevsner, Tom
[Assistant Director (2nd)]	Meadows, John
[Assistant Director (3rd)]	Birkett, Michael
Continuity	Manheim, Felicia
Story and Screenplay by	Rose, William
Director of Photography	Heller, Otto
Technicolor Colour Consultant	Bridge, Joan
Camera Operator	Waterson, Chic (as Waterson, Chick)
[Focus Puller]	Parslow, Ray
[Clapper Loader]	Bryce, Alan
[Stills]	Hanscomb, Harold
Special Effects	Pearson, Syd (as Pearson, Sydney)
Editor	Harris, Jack
Assistant Editor	Aldous, Harry

[Assistant Editor (2nd)]	Clark, Jim
[Assistant Editor (2nd)]	Clark, Robin
Art Director	Morahan, Jim
[Assistant Art Director]	Davey, Bert
[Draughtsman]	Shampan, Jack
Scenic Artist	Robinson, W. Simpson
Costume Designer	Mendleson, Anthony
Make-up	Garfath, Alec (as Garfath, Alex)
Hairstyles	Martin, Daphne
Music Composed by	Cary, Tristram
Played by	The Sinfonia of London
Conducted by	Mathieson, Dock
Recordist	Wilkins, Leo
Sound Supervisor	Dalby, Stephen (as Dalby, Steven)
[Sound Assistant]	Fairbairn, Harry
[Boom Operator]	Wortham, Don
Sound Editor	Stone, Gordon
Character	Name *[Cast]*
Professor Marcus	Guinness, Alec
Major Courtney	Parker, Cecil
Louis Harvey	Lom, Herbert
Harry Robinson	Sellers, Peter
One-Round Lawson	Green, Danny
police superintendent	Warner, Jack
Mrs. Louisa Wilberforce	Johnson, Katie
police sergeant	Stainton, Philip
barrow boy	Howerd, Frankie
[pavement artist]	Sharp, Len
[left luggage clerk]	Goodwin, Harold
[cab driver]	Connor, Kenneth
[junkman]	Griffiths, Fred
[Amelia]	Kerry, Evelyn
[Hypatia]	Burls, Hélène
[old lady]	Hodgson, Phoebe
[Lettice]	Martin, Edie
[Scotland Yard man]	Melford, Jack
[constable]	Moore, Robert
[nervous man]	Rudling, John
[large lady]	Brindley, Madge

[Miss Pringle]	Griffiths, Lucy
[second cab driver]	Kydd, Sam
[policeman]	Wilson, Neil
[constable in station]	Roberts, Ewan
[burglar]	Corcoran, Michael
[cast]	Roberts, Lynne
[cast]	John, Anthony
[cast]	Robb, Sandra
[cast]	Johns, Stratford
[cast]	Ayres, Janet
[cast]	Evans, Peter
[cast]	Green, Kevin
[cast]	Hart, Janet
[cast]	Pike, Colin
[Identifier] Identification number	W-35195
[Identifier] EIDR identifier	10.5240/1C59-EFCF-AAF0-F735-71AB-H
Event: Production – Date: 1955	Location(s): Frederica Street, Islington, London N7 Cheney Road, Kings Cross, London NW1
Relationships:	
Parts title	C-88339 The Ladykillers

MANIFESTATION/ITEM

Institution record identification number: C-88339
Can identification number: 61470E

Title	Title type
The Ladykillers	Original
The Lady killers	Help search

Manifestation type: Theatrical (main country of origin)

Event: Release - Release Country: United Kingdom Date: 1955-12
Distributor: Rank

Language *[Language]*	Usage

English Dialogue (original)
[Original duration] Running time – 97 minutes *[Original length]* Length: 8142 feet

Number of cans/cassettes: 5 Number of Reels: 10 Total footage: 7981 feet

Physical Description: Colour Positive Status Master
Item type: Film *[Original format]* Base: Safety Gauge: 35mm Colour
Colour system: Technicolor Sound Sound system: VA Bilateral Stock: Kodak

Access conditions: Restricted access to preserved film
Emulsion: New
Observations: No sound on main and end titles; scratches on first 20 ft of reel 5
Current location: XYZ203040 Home location: BKS102030

Event type: Inspection Movement number: 3 Reason: Perforation inspection Date: 1968-10-02

Event type: Preservation Treatment: Damaged perforations on reels 2 and 7 repaired
Treatment date: 1968-10-05 Technician: Joe Bloggs
Event type: Acquisition Donor: FIAF Acquisition Date: 1959-09-03

Relationships:
Part of title
W-35195 The Ladykillers

1-Level Hierarchy model

Title *[Title]*	Title type
The Ladykillers	Original
The Lady killers	Help search

Work type: Film

Filmographic level: Monographic

Production country *[Country of reference]*: United Kingdom

Date(s) *[Year of reference]*	Date type
1955	Copyright
1955-12	Release

Category *[Form]*: Fiction

Genre *[Subject/Genre]*: Comedy, Crime

Synopsis *[Content description]*: A gang of train robbers hide out at the lodgings of one of them, posing as an amateur string quartet. The innocent and upright elderly lady who owns the house is used by them, and is an inadvertent catalyst for their plans unravelling and the gang turning on each other.

On-screen credit	Name *[Credits]*
Directed by	Mackendrick, Alexander
Production Company	Ealing Studios
A Production by	Balcon, Michael
Associate Producer	Holt, Seth
Unit Production Manager	Peers, David
Production Supervisor	Mason, Hal
Assistant Director	Pevsner, Tom
[Assistant Director (2nd)]	Meadows, John
[Assistant Director (3rd)]	Birkett, Michael
Continuity	Manheim, Felicia
Story and Screenplay by	Rose, William
Director of Photography	Heller, Otto
Technicolor Colour Consultant	Bridge, Joan
Camera Operator	Waterson, Chic (as Waterson, Chick)
[Focus Puller]	Parslow, Ray
[Clapper Loader]	Bryce, Alan
[Stills]	Hanscomb, Harold
Special Effects	Pearson, Syd (as Pearson, Sydney)
Editor	Harris, Jack
Assistant Editor	Aldous, Harry
[Assistant Editor (2nd)]	Clark, Jim
[Assistant Editor (2nd)]	Clark, Robin

Art Director	Morahan, Jim
[Assistant Art Director]	Davey, Bert
[Draughtsman]	Shampan, Jack
Scenic Artist	Robinson, W. Simpson
Costume Designer	Mendleson, Anthony
Make-up	Garfath, Alec (as Garfath, Alex)
Hairstyles	Martin, Daphne
Music Composed by	Cary, Tristram
Played by	The Sinfonia of London
Conducted by	Mathieson, Dock
Recordist	Wilkins, Leo
Sound Supervisor	Dalby, Stephen (as Dalby, Steven)
[Sound Assistant]	Fairbairn, Harry
[Boom Operator]	Wortham, Don
Sound Editor	Stone, Gordon
Character	Name *[Cast]*
Professor Marcus	Guinness, Alec
Major Courtney	Parker, Cecil
Louis Harvey	Lom, Herbert
Harry Robinson	Sellers, Peter
One-Round Lawson	Green, Danny
police superintendent	Warner, Jack
Mrs. Louisa Wilberforce	Johnson, Katie
police sergeant	Stainton, Philip
barrow boy	Howerd, Frankie
[pavement artist]	Sharp, Len
[left luggage clerk]	Goodwin, Harold
[cab driver]	Connor, Kenneth
[junkman]	Griffiths, Fred
[Amelia]	Kerry, Evelyn
[Hypatia]	Burls, Hélène
[old lady]	Hodgson, Phoebe
[Lettice]	Martin, Edie
[Scotland Yard man]	Melford, Jack
[constable]	Moore, Robert
[nervous man]	Rudling, John
[large lady]	Brindley, Madge
[Miss Pringle]	Griffiths, Lucy
[second cab driver]	Kydd, Sam

[policeman]	Wilson, Neil
[constable in station]	Roberts, Ewan
[burglar]	Corcoran, Michael
[cast]	Roberts, Lynne
[cast]	John, Anthony
[cast]	Robb, Sandra
[cast]	Johns, Stratford
[cast]	Ayres, Janet
[cast]	Evans, Peter
[cast]	Green, Kevin
[cast]	Hart, Janet
[cast]	Pike, Colin

[Identifier] EIDR identifier 10.5240/1C59-EFCF-AAF0-F735-71AB-H
[Identifier] Institution record identification number: C-88339
[Identifier] Can identification number: 61470E

Event: Production – Date: 1955 Location(s): Frederica Street, Islington, London N7
Cheney Road, Kings Cross, London NW1

Release Country: United Kingdom Release Date: 1955-12
Theatrical release (in country of origin)
[Original duration] Running time – 97 minutes *[Original length]* Length (original footage): 8142 feet
Number of cans/cassettes: 5 Number of Reels: 10 Total footage: 7981 feet

Physical Description: Colour Positive Status: Master
Item type: Film *[Original format]* Base: Safety Gauge: 35mm Colour
Colour system: Technicolor Sound Sound system: VA Bilateral Stock: Kodak

Language *[Language]*: English Usage: Dialogue (original)

Access conditions: Restricted access to preserved film
Emulsion condition: New
Observations: No sound on main and end titles; scratches on first 20 ft of reel 5
Current location: XYZ203040 Home location: BKS102030

Event type: Inspection Movement number: 3 Reason: Perforation inspection
Date: 1968-10-02

Event type: Preservation Treatment: Damaged perforations on reels 2 and 7 repaired
Treatment date: 1968-10-05 Technician: Joe Bloggs

Event type: Acquisition Donor: FIAF Acquisition Date: 1959-09-03

I.2 Example 2. Documentary film in 4-level hierarchy

In this second example, the corresponding data of the core concepts also has the same illustrative matching colours as used in the Core Elements list in Example 1 (see below), and there are also links to the relevant sections of the manual relating to those elements.

Core concepts (0.2 Core elements of description)

Title
Series/Serial
Cast
Credits
Country of reference
Original format
Original Length
Original duration
Language
Year of reference
Identifier
Subject/genre/form
Content description

WORK			
1.2 Attributes of a Moving Image Work/Variant			
1.2.1 Work/Variant Description Type	D.1 Work/Variant Description Types	**monographic**	**monografická**
1.3 Elements of a Work/Variant			
1.3.1 Work/Variant Identifier		urn:nbn:sk:sfu-ko1ugsb	urn:nbn:sk:sfu-ko1ugsb
1.3.1.1 Identifier Type		URN:NBN	URN:NBN
1.3.1 Work/Variant Identifier		SFD000163	SFD000163
1.3.1.1 Identifier Type		SFÚ identifier [local]	identifikátor SFÚ [lokálny]
1.3.2 Title		Obrazy starého sveta	Obrazy starého sveta
1.3.2.1 Title Type	A.2 Title Types	A.2.0 Preferred [original: slo]	preferovaný [originálny: slo]
1.3.2 Title		Pictures of the old world	Pictures of the old world

1.3.2.1 Title Type	A.2 Title Types	A.2.4 Alternative [translated title: eng]	alternatívny [preklad názvu: eng]
1.3.2 Title		Images du vieux monde	Images du vieux monde
1.3.2.1 Title Type	A.2 Title Types	A.2.4 Alternative [translated title: fre]	alternatívny [preklad názvu: fre]
1.3.2 Title		Bilder einer alten Welt	Bilder einer alten Welt
1.3.2.1 Title Type	A.2 Title Types	A.2.4 Alternative [translated title: ger]	alternatívny [preklad názvu: ger]
1.3.2 Title		Картины старого мира	Картины старого мира
1.3.2.1 Title Type	A.2 Title Types	A.2.4 Alternative [translated title: rus]	alternatívny [preklad názvu: rus]
1.3.2 Title		Kartiny starogo mira	Kartiny starogo mira
1.3.2.1 Title Type	A.2 Title Types	A.2.4 Alternative [translated title:rus & transliterated title]	alternatívny [preklad názvu: rus a transliterácia názvu]
1.3.3 Country of reference		Slovakia [Czechoslovakia]	Slovensko [Československo]
1.3.4 Year/Date of reference		1972	1972
1.3.4.1 Date Type		year of production	rok výroby
1.3.5 Language(s)		Slovak	slovenčina
1.3.5.1 Language Term		slo	slo
1.3.5.2 Usage type	D.6 Language Usage Types	Original Language	pôvodný jazyk
1.3.5.2 Usage type	D.6 Language Usage Types	spoken language	hovorený jazyk
1.3.5.2 Usage type	D.6 Language Usage Types	sung language	spievaný jazyk
1.3.6 Content description (synopses, shotlists, etc)		Suggestive portraits of old people from the Liptov and Orava regions who are able to enjoy their individual freedom even in the times of civilisational chaos and insecurity.	Sugestívne portréty starých ľudí z Liptova a Oravy, ktorí dokážu aj v stave civilizačného chaosu a neistoty žiť vnútorne slobodní.
1.3.6.1 Content Description Type		synopsis	anotácia

1.3.7 Notes	Appendix B, Cataloguer's Notes	**Text before the opening credits: These are stories of people rooted in the soil they came from. They cannot be replanted, they would perish.**	**Pred úvodnými titulkami text: Toto sú príbehy, ľudí, ktorí ostali sami sebou. Zabudnutí a prostí, vrastení do zeme, z ktorej vyšli. Nemožno ich presadiť pretože by zahynuli.**
1.3.8.2 Censorship history		**banned film (cinema release: July 1989)**	**zakázaný film (kinodistribúcia: júl 1989)**
1.4 Relationships of a Work/Variant (links/associations with other entities/records)			
Credits			
1.4.1 Agents (e.g. Cast, Credits, Person, Organisation, etc.)		**Československý film Bratislava**	**Československý film Bratislava**
1.4.1.1 Agent Activity		**Production Company**	**Produkčná spoločnosť**
1.4.1 Agents (e.g. Cast, Credits, Person, Organisation, etc.)		**Dušan Hanák**	**Dušan Hanák**
1.4.1.1 Agent Activity		**Director**	**Réžia**
1.4.1 Agents (e.g. Cast, Credits, Person, Organisation, etc.)		**Dušan Hanák**	**Dušan Hanák**
1.4.1.1 Agent Activity		**Story and screenplay**	**Námet a scenár**
1.4.1 Agents (e.g. Cast, Credits, Person, Organisation, etc.)		**Alojz Hanúsek**	**Alojz Hanúsek**
1.4.1.1 Agent Activity		**Cinematographer**	**Kamera**
1.4.1 Agents (e.g. Cast, Credits, Person, Organisation, etc.)		**Alfréd Benčič**	**Alfréd Benčič**
1.4.1.1 Agent Activity		**Editor**	**Strih**
1.4.1 Agents (e.g. Cast, Credits, Person, Organisation, etc.)		**Ondrej Polomský**	**Ondrej Polomský**
1.4.1.1 Agent Activity		**Sound**	**Zvuk**
1.4.1 Agents (e.g. Cast, Credits, Person, Organisation, etc.)		**Martin Martinček**	**Martin Martinček**
1.4.1.1 Agent Activity		**Photographs by**	**Fotografie**

1.4.1 Agents (e.g. Cast, Credits, Person, Organisation, etc.)		Vladimír Vavrek	Vladimír Vavrek
1.4.1.1 Agent Activity		Photographs by	Fotografie
1.4.1 Agents		George Frideric Handel	George Frideric Handel
1.4.1.1 Agent Activity		Music	Hudba
1.4.1 Agents		Václav Hálek	Václav Hálek
1.4.1.1 Agent Activity		Music	Hudba
1.4.1 Agents		Jozef Malovec	Jozef Malovec
1.4.1.1 Agent Activity		Music	Hudba
1.4.1 Agents		František Belfín	František Belfín
1.4.1.1 Agent Activity		Conductor	Dirigent
1.4.1 Agents		Filmový symfonický orchestr, Praha	Filmový symfonický orchestr, Praha
1.4.1.1 Agent Activity		Music Performed by	Hudbu nahral
1.4.1 Agents		Boris Hochel	Boris Hochel
1.4.1.1 Agent Activity		Script Editor	Dramaturg
1.4.1 Agents		Juraj Král	Juraj Král
1.4.1.1 Agent Activity		Production Manager	Vedúci výroby
1.4.1 Agents		Stanislav Učník	Stanislav Učník
1.4.1.1 Agent Activity		Production Supervisor	Vedúci nakrúcania
1.4.1 Agents		Oľga Hrajnohová	Oľga Hrajnohová
1.4.1.1 Agent Activity		Script-girl	Skript
1.4.1 Agents		Štefan Kondrót	Štefan Kondrót
1.4.1.1 Agent Activity		Cooperation	Spolupráca
1.4.1 Agents		Martin Gazík	Martin Gazík
1.4.1.1 Agent Activity		Cooperation	Spolupráca
1.4.1 Agents		Ján Albrecht	Ján Albrecht
1.4.1.1 Agent Activity		Cooperation	Spolupráca
1.4.1 Agents		Jan Švankmajer	Jan Švankmajer
1.4.1.1 Agent Activity		Cooperation	Spolupráca
1.4.1 Agents		Jozef Košťál	Jozef Košťál
1.4.1.1 Agent Activity		Cooperation	Spolupráca
1.4.1 Agents		Jaroslav Rihák	Jaroslav Rihák
1.4.1.1 Agent Activity		Cooperation	Spolupráca

1.4.1 Agents		Milan Hurtig	Milan Hurtig
1.4.1.1 Agent Activity		Cooperation	Spolupráca
1.4.1 Agents		Jozef Kováčik	Jozef Kováčik
1.4.1.1 Agent Activity		Cooperation	Spolupráca
1.4.1 Agents		Ján Gašparec	Ján Gašparec
1.4.1.1 Agent Activity		Cooperation	Spolupráca
Cast/ Featuring		From the lives of those mentioned below:	Zo života:
1.4.1 Agents		Veronika Ralíková	Veronika Ralíková
1.4.1.1 Agent Activity		Herself	
1.4.1 Agents		Adam Kura	Adam Kura
1.4.1.1 Agent Activity		Himself	
1.4.1 Agents		Jozef Országh	Jozef Országh
1.4.1.1 Agent Activity		Himself	
1.4.1 Agents		Juraj Michelík	Juraj Michelík
1.4.1.1 Agent Activity		Himself	
1.4.1 Agents		Anton Miček	Anton Miček
1.4.1.1 Agent Activity		Himself	
1.4.1 Agents		Františka Ševčíková	Františka Ševčíková
1.4.1.1 Agent Activity		Herself	
1.4.1 Agents		Adam Struhárňanský	Adam Struhárňanský
1.4.1.1 Agent Activity		Himself	
1.4.1 Agents		Jozef Račko	Jozef Račko
1.4.1.1 Agent Activity		Himself	
1.4.1 Agents		Alojz Kováč	Alojz Kováč
1.4.1.1 Agent Activity		Himself	
1.4.1 Agents		Matej Dudka	Matej Dudka
1.4.1.1 Agent Activity		Himself	
1.4.1 Agents		Ladislav Chudík	Ladislav Chudík
1.4.1.1 Agent Activity		commentary spoken by	interpret komentára
1.4.2 Events (e.g., IPR registration, screenings, awards, etc.) D.4.3 Production			

• Production Event type	D.11 Production Event Types	**beginning of shooting**	**prvý filmovací deň**
• Year/Date		**1971-09-13**	**1971-09-13**
• Production Event type	D.11 Production Event Types	**completion of shooting**	**posledný filmovací de[illegible]**
• Year/Date		**1972-01-09**	**1972-01-09**
1.4.2 Events (e.g., IPR registration, screenings, awards, etc.)– D.4.2 Award(s) or Nomination(s)			
• Award(s)/Nomination(s) date		**1988**	**1988**
• Award name		**Golden Sestertius, Grand Prix (Sesterce d'Or, Grand Prix)**	**Zlatý sestercius, Grand Prix (Sesterce d'Or, Grand Prix)**
• Event		**20th International Festival of Documentary Films Nyon 1988**	**20. medzinárodný festival dokumentárnych filmov Nyon 1988**
• Award(s)/Nomination(s) date		**1989**	**1989**
• Award name		**European Film Award / European Documentary - Special Mention**	**Európska filmová cena / Európske dokumenty - Osobitné uznanie**
• Event		**2nd European Film Awards 1989 (Paris)**	**2. ročník Európskych filmových cien 1989 (Paríž)**
• Award(s)/Nomination(s) date		**1990**	**1990**
• Award name		**Los Angeles Film Critics Association Award / Best Non-Fiction Film**	**Cena asociácie losangeleských filmových kritikov / Najlepší non-fiction film**
• Event		**16th Los Angeles Film Critics Association Awards 1990**	**16. ročník Cien asociácie losangeleských filmových kritikov 1990**
1.4.3 Subject/Genre/ Form terms	genre	**documentary films**	**dokumentárne filmy**
	form	**full-length films**	**dlhometrážné filmy**
1.4.4 Other relationships	D.17.1 Work/Variant Other Relationship Types	**"Has a relationship to an "object" (a non-moving image resource)"**	Má vzťah k objektu

		Obrazy starého sveta / Dušan Hanák. – The screenplay of the film: Pictures of the old world (1972). In: 322 ; Obrazy starého sveta ; Růžové sny / Dušan Hanák. – Praha : Lika klub, 2005. – ISBN 80-86069-37-0. – p. 78-127.	Obrazy starého sveta / Dušan Hanák. – Scenár filmu: Obrazy starého sveta (1972). In: 322 ; Obrazy starého sveta ; Růžové sny / Dušan Hanák. – Praha : Lika klub, 2005. – ISBN 80-86069-37-0. – s. 78-127.
1.4.4 Other relationships	D.17.1 Work/Variant Other Relationship Types	"Has a relationship to a Work "about" the Work/Variant in question"	Má vzťah k dielu o diele
		Kinožurnál [film]. 51/1988 (1988)	Kinožurnál [film]. 51/1988 (1988)
1.4.5 Variants		"Has a relationship to a Variant"	
		199999163	199999163
VARIANT			
1.2 Attributes of a Moving Image Work/Variant			
1.2.2 Variant Type	D.2 Variant Type	subtitled	s podtitulkami
1.3 Elements of a Work/Variant			
1.3.1 Work/Variant Identifier		199999163	199999163
1.3.1.1 Identifier Type		SFÚ identifier [local]	identifikátor SFÚ [lokálny]
1.3.2 Title		Pictures of the old world	Pictures of the old world
1.3.2.1 Title Type	A.2 Title Types	A.2.4 Alternative [parallel title: eng]	alternatívny [súbežný názov: eng]
1.3.5 Language(s)		English	angličtina
1.3.5.1 Language Term		eng	eng
1.3.5.2 Usage type	D.6 Language Usage Types	subtitles	podtitulky
1.4.6 Manifestations		"Has a relationship to a Manifestation"	
		299999163	299999163
MANIFESTATION			
2.2 Attributes of a Manifestation			

2.2.1 Manifestation Type	D.5 Manifestation Types	D.5.9 Preservation/Restoration	
2.3 Elements of a Manifestation			
2.3.1 Identifier		299999163	299999163
2.3.1.1 Identifier Type		SFÚ identifier [local]	identifikátor SFÚ [lokálny]
2.3.2 Title		Pictures of the old world	Pictures of the old world
2.3.2.1 Title Type	A.2 Title Types	A.2.4 Alternative [parallel: eng]	A.2.4 Alternative [parallel: eng]
2.3.4 Format of a moving image Manifestation			
2.3.4.1 Carrier type of a Manifestation			
2.3.4.1.1 General Carrier Type	D.7.1 Manifestation/Item General Carrier Type	Film	film
2.3.4.1.2 Specific Carrier Type	D.7.2 Manifestation/Item Specific Carrier Type	35 mm	35 mm
2.3.4.2 Projection characteristics of a Manifestation			
Aspect Ratio		1:1,37	1:1,37
Aperture/Image Format		Academy	Academy
2.3.4.3 Sound characteristics of a Manifestation	D.7.4 Manifestation/Item Sound Type	sound	zvukový
2.3.4.3.1 Sound systems	D.7.13 Item Sound System	combined optical sound	kombinovaný optický zvuk
2.3.4.3.2 Sound Channel Configuration	D.7.5 Manifestation/Item Sound Fixation Type	optical mono	optický (mono)
2.3.4.4 Colour characteristics of a Manifestation	D.7.11 Manifestation/Item Colour Type	black and white	čiernobiely
2.3.5 Extent of a Manifestation			
2.3.5.1 Logical extent of a Manifestation		4 reels	4 kotúče

2.3.5.2 Physical extent of a Manifestation	metres	1827,8 m	1827,8 m
2.3.5.3 Duration of a Manifestation	HH:MM:SS	01:06:38	01:06:38
2.4 Relationships of a Manifestation			
2.4.1 Agent(s)		Slovak Film Institute	Slovenský filmový ústav
2.4.1.1 Agent Activity	D.8 Manifestation Agent Types	D.8.6 Agent responsible for preservation	D.8.6 zodpovednosť za uchovávanie
2.4.1 Agent(s)		Film Laboratory Ateliery Bonton Zlin a.s.	Filmové laboratoře Ateliéry Bonton Zlín a.s.
2.4.1.1 Agent Activity	D.8 Manifestation Agent Types	D.8.5 Manufacturer	D.8.5 Manufacturer
2.4.2 Events - D.4.5 Preservation			
• Preservation type	D.12 Manifestation Preservation Types	Film restoration	Filmová obnova
• Preservation Date		2006	2006
• Note		added English subtitles	doplnené o anglické podtitulky
2.4.4 Item(s)		"Has a relationship to an Item"	
		099967	099967
ITEM			
3.1 Elements of a moving image Item			
3.1.1 Identifier		099967	099967
3.1.1.1 Identifier Type		SFÚ identifier [local]	identifikátor SFÚ [lokálny]
3.1.1 Identifier		140-ZO-A3	140-ZO-A3
3.1.1.1 Identifier Type		archive number	archívne číslo
3.1.2 Title		Obrazy starého sveta	Obrazy starého sveta
3.1.2.1 Title Type		title on can	názov na obale
3.1.3 Holding institution		Slovak Film Institute	Slovenský filmový ústav
		SK-BrSFU [MARC Code]	SK-BrSFU [MARC]
3.1.4 Item Element type	D.7.8 Item Element Type	Positive	Pozitív

3.1.5 Item Specifics/ Extent (e.g. physical/Digital description)			
3.1.5.2 Item Status	D.7.3 Item Preservation/Access status	Viewing	Na premietanie
3.1.5.8 Extent	Metres	reel 1: 552,8 m	1. kotúč: 552,8 m
	Metres	reel 2: 570,4 m	2. kotúč: 570,4 m
	Metres	reel 3: 520,4 m	3. kotúč: 520,4 m
	Metres	reel 4: 184,2 m	4. kotúč: 184,2 m
	metres	TOTAL LENGTH: 1827,8 m	DĹŽKA SPOLU: 1827,8 m
3.1.5.11 Duration	HH:MM:SS	reel 1: 00:20:09	1. kotúč: 00:20:09
	HH:MM:SS	reel 2: 00:20:48	2. kotúč: 00:20:48
	HH:MM:SS	reel 3: 00:18:58	3. kotúč: 00:18:58
	HH:MM:SS	reel 4: 00:06:43	4. kotúč: 00:06:43
	HH:MM:SS	TOTAL DURATION: 01:06:38	DĹŽKA TRVANIA SPOLU: 01:06:38
3.1.5.13 Base	D.7.7 Item Base – Film or Video	Polyester	Polyester
3.1.5.14 Stock	D.7.16 Item Stock	Eastman Kodak	Eastman Kodak
3.1.6 Access conditions		No restrictions (film print can be requested for access).	Bez obmedzení (filmová kópia je dostupná na požiadanie).
3.1.6.1 Item condition	D.16 Manifestation/Item Condition, Preservation and Restoration		
	D.16.1 Item Copy Condition Base/ Emulsion – Film and Video	Good condition	Dobrý stav
	D.16.2 Item Copy Condition Perforations – Film	Good condition	Dobrý stav
	D.16.3 Item Surface Deposit – Film and Video	Good condition	Dobrý stav
	D.16.4 Item Image – Film and Video	Good condition	Dobrý stav
	D.16.5 Item Decomposition – Film and Video	Good condition	Dobrý stav

	D.16.6 Item Shrinkage - Film	**Good condition**	**Dobrý stav**
3.1.6.2 Item location		**FA-019-12-1-1**	**FA-019-12-1-1**
3.3 Relationships of an Item			
3.3.1 Agent(s)		**Slovak Film Institute**	**Slovenský filmový ústav**
3.3.1.1 Agent Activity		**Inspected by**	**Kontroloval**
3.3.2 Events 3.3.2 Events			
3.3.2 Events - D.4.8 Inspection			
• Inspection type		**technical inspection**	**technická kontrola**
• Inspection date		**2015-05-29**	**2015-05-29**
• Inspection detail		**see 3.1.6.1 Item condition**	**pozri 3.1.6.1 Item condition**
• • Agent		**see 3.3.1 Agent(s)**	**pozri 3.3.1 Agent(s)**
3.3.2 Events - D.4.9 Acquisition			
• Acquisition type	D.15.1 Item Acquisition type	**from laboratory**	z laboratórií
• Acquisition date		**2006-12-01**	**2006-12-01**
• Accession date		**2006-12-12**	**2006-12-12**
• Acquisition detail		**Project of the Systematic Restoration of the Audiovisual Heritage of the Slovak Republic.**	**Projekt systematickej obnovy audiovizuálneho dedičstva Slovenskej republiky.**
3 3.3.3 Other Relationships	D.17.3 Item Other Relationship Types	"Has a relationship to an archival document"	Má vzťah k archívnemu dokumentu
		Záznam o stave archívneho filmového materiálu [projection instructions]	**Záznam o stave archívneho filmového materiálu**

I.3 Example 3. Silent feature film in 3-level Hierarchy Model with multiple Manifestations and items

WORK RECORD

Work identifier	[-----]
Preferred title	катька бумажный ранет
Alternative Title – transliterated	Kat'ka bumazhnyĭ ranet
Other title information	melodrama v 6 chast͡iakh
Date – original release date	1926-12-25
Category	Fiction films; Silent films; Soviet films
Content description	A young country girl who becomes an apple seller is seduced and abandoned. She finds a protector but when he is arrested for theft she finds honest work in a factory.
Subject terms	Women -- Soviet Union -- Drama. Single mothers -- Soviet Union -- Drama. Mothers -- Soviet Union -- Drama. Criminals -- Soviet Union -- Drama. Black market -- Soviet Union -- Drama. Sexual division of labor -- Soviet Union -- Drama. Soviet Union -- Social life and customs -- 1917-1970.
Agents	S͡tsenariĭ [screenplay], Mikhaila Borisoglebskogo; rezhissery [directors], Ėduard Ioganson i Fridrikh Ėrmler; proizvodstvo leningradskoĭ fabriki Sovkino [produced by the Leningrad Studio of Sovkin]. Operator [camera], Evgeniĭ Mikhaĭlov; khudozhnik [sets], Evgeniĭ Eneĭ; assistent [assistant director], Robert Maĭman; administrator, Sem Gershtenzanl. [Cast:] Veronika Buzhinskai͡a (Kat'ka), Bella Chernova (Verka), Fëdor Nikitin (Vad'ka Zavrazhin), Valeriĭ Solov͡tsov (Sëmka Zhgut). Proizvodstvo leningradskoĭ fabriki Sovkino [produced by the Leningrad Studio of Sovkino].
Country	Soviet Union
Language	Russian
Notes	Cast information provided in intertitles as film progresses. Additional credits supplied from: Kino / Jay Leyda; Sovetskie khudozhestvennye fil'my.

MANIFESTATION RECORD 1

Manifestation type	Theatrical distribution
Identifier	[-----]
Title proper	катька бумажный ранет
Alternative title – transliterated	Kat'ka bumazhnyĭ ranet
Translated title	Katka's reinette apples
Other title information	melodrama v 6 chasti͡akh
Agents	Distributor: Goskino
Carrier type – general	Film
Carrier type – specific	35mm
Projection characteristics – Aspect ratio	1.33:1
Sound characteristics	Silent
Color characteristics	Black and white
Logical extent	6 reels
Physical extent	6576 ft.
Duration	88 minutes
Type	Release print
Language	Russian intertitles only.
Notes	Titles preceding film (cataloger's translation in brackets): Iz istorii Sovetskoĭ khudozhesvennoĭ kinematografii. T͡sikl 1. Nemoe kino -- Glavnoe upravlenie kinofikat͡sii i kinoprokata i vsesoiuznyĭ gosudarstvennyĭ fond kinofil'ma pokazyvai͡ut Katka bumazhnyĭ ranet -- Ėtot fil'm byl postavlen v 1926 godu. On i͡avilsi͡a odnim iz pervykh opytov sozdanii͡a bytovoĭ dramy na sovremennom sovetskom materiale. Istoricheskiĭ interes predstavli͡aet popytka avtorov fil'ma pokazat' zhivye chelovecheskie kharaktery. [From the history of the Soviet artistic cinema. Cycle one. Silent cinema -- The Central Bureau for Film Distribution and the All-Union Governmental Cinema Collection present: Katka's reinette apples -- This film was produced in 1926. It constitutes one of the first attempts to create on the basis of contemporary Soviet material a drama from "everyday life." The authors' attempt to show living human characters is worthy of historical interest.]

MANIFESTATION RECORD 2

Manifestation type	Unknown [Video transfer]
Identifier	[-----]
Preferred title	катька бумажный ранет
Alternative Title – transliterated	Kat'ka bumazhnyĭ ranet
Parallel Title – US release title	Katka's reinette apples
Date – video transfer	[1980?]
Carrier type – general	Video tape
Carrier type – specific	1-inch Type C
Projection characteristics – Aspect ratio	1.33:1
Sound characteristics	Silent
Color characteristics	Black and white
Logical extent	1 videoreel
Temporal extent	85 minutes
Agents	Film-to-tape transfer overseen by: Pacific Film Archive
Language	Russian intertitles only.
Notes	The negative from the print used to dub this tape is missing footage. Some scenes are truncated. The footage loss between the original footage and the print is approximately 102 feet. Titles preceding film (cataloger's translation in brackets): Iz istorii Sovetskoĭ khudozhesvennoĭ kinematografii. T͡sikl 1. Nemoe kino -- Glavnoe upravlenie kinofikat͡sii i kinoprokata i vsesoiuznyĭ gosudarstvennyĭ fond kinofil'ma pokazyvai͡ut Katka bumazhnyĭ ranet -- Ėtot fil'm byl postavlen v 1926 godu. On i͡avilsi͡a odnim iz pervykh opytov sozdanii͡a bytovoĭ dramy na sovremennom sovetskom materiale. Istoricheskiĭ interes predstavli͡aet popytka avtorov fil'ma pokazat' zhivye chelovecheskie kharaktery. [From the history of the Soviet artistic cinema. Cycle one. Silent cinema -- The Central Bureau for Film Distribution and the All-Union Governmental Cinema Collection present: Katka's reinette apples -- This film was produced in 1926. It constitutes one of the first attempts to create on the basis of contemporary Soviet material a drama from "everyday life." The authors' attempt to show living human characters is worthy of historical interest.]

MANIFESTATION RECORD 3

Manifestation type	Unknown [Video transfer]
Identifier	[-----]
Preferred title	катька бумажный ранет
Alternative Title – transliterated	Kat'ka bumazhnyĭ ranet
Parallel Title – US release title	Katka's reinette apples
Date – video transfer	[1995?]
Carrier type – general	Video tape
Carrier type – specific	½ in. VHS
Projection characteristics – Aspect ratio	1.33:1
Sound characteristics	Silent
Color characteristics	Black and white
Logical extent	1 videocassette
Duration	85 minutes
Language	Russian intertitles only.
Agents	Dub from 1 in. master tape by: Pacific Film Archive
Notes	The negative from the print used to dub this tape is missing footage. Some scenes are truncated. The footage loss between the original footage and the print is approximately 102 feet. Titles preceding film (cataloger's translation in brackets): Iz istorii Sovetskoĭ khudozhesvennoĭ kinematografii. T͡sikl 1. Nemoe kino -- Glavnoe upravlenie kinofikat͡sii i kinoprokata i vsesoiuznyĭ gosudarstvennyĭ fond kinofil'ma pokazyvai͡ut Katka bumazhnyĭ ranet -- Ėtot fil'm byl postavlen v 1926 godu. On i͡avilsi͡a odnim iz pervykh opytov sozdanii͡a bytovoĭ dramy na sovremennom sovetskom materiale. Istoricheskiĭ interes predstavli͡aet popytka avtorov fil'ma pokazat' zhivye chelovecheskie kharaktery. [From the history of the Soviet artistic cinema. Cycle one. Silent cinema -- The Central Bureau for Film Distribution and the All-Union Governmental Cinema Collection present: Katka's reinette apples -- This film was produced in 1926. It constitutes one of the first attempts to create on the basis of contemporary Soviet material a drama from "everyday life." The authors' attempt to show living human characters is worthy of historical interest.]

ITEM RECORD 1 [links to MANIFESTATION 1]

Identifier – local call number	3500-01-5762
Preferred title	катька бумажный ранет
Alternative Title – transliterated	Kat'ka bumazhnyĭ ranet
Parallel Title – US release title	Katka's reinette apples
Holding institution	University of California, Berkeley Art Museum and Pacific Film Archive
Date – print date	[unknown]
Item material type	Positive
Item status	Viewing copy; release print
Unit number	6 reels of 6
Base	triacetate
Physical extent	6474 ft.
Stock	Svema
Duration	Running time at 20 fps: 01:25:49
Note	The negative from which this print was struck is missing footage. Some scenes are truncated. The footage loss between the original footage and this print is approximately 102 feet.
Item specific note	PFA 3500-01-5762. CONDITION NOTE: Last inspected: 1994 Apr 20; splices; Excellent condition: General comments on all reels: scratches are printed on, as are some splice points from the original negative; otherwise, no scratches on the print itself; reel changeover marks are hole-punched in at the end of every reel; REEL 1 (973 ft., 6 fr.): Russian academy leader tape-spliced on at head; edge code: 182 SVEMA M3 BEZOPASNAIA; SMPTE Universal leader tape-spliced at end [...]
Item specific note	AD test 2007-03-01: all reels level 0.5
Access conditions	Pacific Film Archive collection; non-circulating.
Access conditions	Restricted: Not for research use.

ITEM RECORD 2 [links to MANIFESTATION 2]

Identifier – local call number	1 in. MASTER
Preferred title	катька бумажный ранет
Alternative Title – transliterated	Kat'ka bumazhnyĭ ranet
Parallel Title – US release title	Katka's reinette apples
Holding institution	University of California, Berkeley Art Museum and Pacific Film Archive
Date – video transfer	[1985?]
Date – log-in	1992-07-14
Item material type	Positive
Item status	Master
Unit number	1 videoreel of 1
Base	video
Stock	Ampex
Duration	Running time: 01:25:49
Note	1 in. film-to-tape transfer made at 20 fps
Access conditions	Pacific Film Archive collection; non-circulating.

ITEM RECORD 3 [links to MANIFESTATION 3]

Identifier – local call number	0500-01-7801
Preferred title	катька бумажный ранет
Alternative Title – transliterated	Kat'ka bumazhnyĭ ranet
Parallel Title – US release title	Katka's reinette apples
Holding institution	University of California, Berkeley Art Museum and Pacific Film Archive
Date – video transfer	[1995]
Date – acquisition	1995-03-07
Item material type	Positive
Item status	Viewing copy
Unit number	1 videocassette of 1
Base	video
Stock	Fuji
Duration	Running time: 01:25:49
Note	Original 1 in. film-to-tape transfer made at 20 fps
Access conditions	Pacific Film Archive collection; non-circulating.

Links to original MARC-based, flat records:

Parallel to Manifestation 1: http://oskicat.berkeley.edu/record=b10385235~S43

Parallel to Manifestation 2: http://oskicat.berkeley.edu/record=b10391010~S43

Parallel to Manifestation 3: http://oskicat.berkeley.edu/record=b10390992~S43

I.4 Example 4. Short feature film in 3-level Hierarchy Model

In examples 4-6 the field names are given in red. These do not relate to the initial illustrative colour codes used in examples 1 and 2 in any way, but are simply a means of distinguishing the field name from the rest of the data.

Identification number	F7271
Title	Title type
Day of the subgenius	Original
Day of the sub genius	Help Search
Level	**Work**
Work description type	Monographic
Form	Fiction
Country of reference	United Kingdom
Year of reference	Year of reference type
2001	Copyright
Genre	Animation
Subject	Aliens, Monsters

Content description Mix of CGI and live-action representing the Church of the Subgenius' salvation of mankind from an attack of B-movie monsters and UFOs.

Agent activity	Agent
Director	Hopewell, Chris
Production company	bolexbrothers
Executive Producer	Leighton, Andy
Written by	Williams, John
Written by	Hopewell, Chris
Adapted from 'The Brag of the Subgenius' by	Stang, Ivan
Digital Composition & Animation	Ternan, Melvyn
Digital Composition & Animation	Foley, Ben
Digital Composition & Animation	Hopewell, Chris
CGI Models & Animation	Ravenstein, Claudia "Fybs"
CGI Models & Animation	Harrington, Ryan
CGI Models & Animation	Harrington, Lewis
2D Graphic Artists	Kaos
2D Graphic Artists	Hopewell, Chris
2D Graphic Artists	Chevrier, Sandrine
2D Graphic Artists	Fell, Curtis
2D Graphic Artists	Bailey, Lynn
CGI Models & Animation	Smith, James
Sound Design	Williams, John
Sound Effects	Brandt, Peter
Sound Effects	Lea, David
Parts reference	Parts title
M7272	Day of the subgenius

Identification number	M7272
Title **Day of the subgenius**	Title type Original
Level Manifestation type	**Manifestation** Theatrical (main country of origin)
General Format Video – Analogue	Specific Format Betacam SP
Widescreen Process	Wide screen (un-specified)
Aspect ratio	16:9
Colour	Colour
Sound	Sound
Language English	Language usage type Spoken
Release Country United Kingdom	Date 2001
Running time 6 minutes 36 seconds	
Part of reference F7271	Part of title Day of the subgenius
Parts reference I7274 I8003	Parts title Day of the subgenius Day of the subgenius

Identification number	I7274	
Title	Title type	
Day of the subgenius	Original	
Level	**Item**	
Item type	Video	
Status	Usage	
Master	Restricted access to preserved videotape	
Language	Language usage type	
English	Spoken	
Colour	Colour	
Aspect ratio	*16:9*	
Item catalogue date	2001	
Base	Video	
Stock	Maxell	
Colour standard	Line standard	
PAL	625	
Video format	Betacam SP	
Video duration	06:59	
Copy number	Package number	
B-188816	0011A2B	
Number of cans/cassettes	1	
Current location	date	
BK3AD123455	2013-12-11	
Home location	Start date	Removal date
PSR54321	2013-12-11	2013-12-11
Acquisition date	2011	
Donor	FIAF	
Part of reference	Part of Title	
M7272	Day of the subgenius	

Identification number	18003	
Title	Title type	
Day of the subgenius	Original	
Level	**Item**	
Item type	Video	
Status	Usage	
Master	Restricted access to preserved videotape	
Language	Language usage type	
English	Spoken	
Colour	Colour	
Aspect ratio	16:9 (full height anamorphic)	
Item catlogue date	2001	
Base	Video	
Stock	Maxell	
Colour standard	Line standard	
PAL	625	
Video format	Digital Betacam	
Video duration	06:28	
Copy number	Package number	
B-291366	0000LZI	
Number of cans/cassettes	1	
Current location	date	
BK2AB123456	2015-02-27	
Home location	Start date	Removal date
PS123456	2015-02-26	2015-02-27
Donor	FIAF	
Part of reference	Part of Title	
M7272	Day of the subgenius	

I.5 Example 5. Home Movie in 3-level Hierarchy Model

Identification number	664643	
Title	Title type	
Shots of 1932	Acquisition	
Brown Family Film	Devised	
Level	**Work**	
Work type	Film	
Category	Non Fiction	
Country	United Kingdom	
Date	start Precision	Date type
1932	circa	Production
Production status	Completed	
Genre	Amateur film	
Subject	Family life, Christenings, Seaside holidays	
Description type	Description	
Synopsis	Important events in the life of the Brown family, taking place in 1932.	
Shotlist	RL 1: Valerie Vivienne, the daughter of Edwin and Joyce, is born. Various shots of the baby being held by Edwin and Joyce; baby's christening. Some shots of the Hendon Air Pageant. Family holiday, scenes at Little Holland (near Clacton on Sea). Back home; Jack and Tops' wedding. Return to Little Holland. RL 2: Joyce and another woman are pushing prams up a hill near the beach. Edwin poses for the camera. Shots of "Red Gable", which is possibly their holiday home, outside and inside. The women hold the babies up to the camera. The men go horse riding. Shots at the beach. Outing to Tunbridge Wells, having a stroll. More shots of the baby.	
Credit	Name	
Camera Operator	Brown, Edwin G.,	
Parts reference	Parts title	
M-438218	Shots of 1932	

Identification number	M-438218	
Title	**Title type**	
Shots of 1932	Acquisition	
Level	**Manifestation**	
Manifestation type	Not for release	
General Format	Specific Format	
Film	9.5mm Film	
Colour	Black and White	
Sound	Silent	
Release Country	Date	Precision
United Kingdom	1932	circa
Dimension	Value	Unite
Length	400	Feet
Part of reference	title	
664643	Shots of 1932	
Parts reference	Parts title	
C-1264202	Shots of 1932	

Identification number		C-1264202	
Title		Title type	
Shots of 1932		Acquisition	
Brown Family Film. Shots of 1932		Devised	
Level		**Item**	
Item type		Film	
Status		Usage	
Master		Restricted access to preserved film	
Colour		Black and white	
Base		Safety	
Gauge		9.5mm	
Description		Original Reversal BW Positive	
Sound		Silent	
Stock		Pathe	
Stock date early	Precision	Stock date late	Precision
1932	circa	1932	circa
Condition emulsion		Condition base	
Scratches		Scratches	
Copy number		Package number	
1264202-1		AB12C3D	
Reel number		Total reels	
1		2	
Number of cans/cassettes		1	
Dimensions Part	Value	Unite	Precision
Total	400	feet	Estimated
Reel 1	200	feet	
Reel 2	200	feet	
Current location		Home location	
BK1AC12344		BK1AC12344	
Acquisition date		2003-01-22	
Method		Donation	
Donor		Fiaf Brown	
Part of reference		Part of Title	
M-438218		Shots of 1932	

I.6 Example 6. Television Serial and Episode records in 3-level Hierarchy Model (with Monographic Work in "part of" relationship with Serial Work)

Identification number		772521
Title		**Title type**
Hill Street Blues		Original
Hill St Blues		Alternative
Level		**Work**
Filmographic level		**Serial**
Work type		TV
Category		Fiction
Production country		United States of America
Date start	Date end	Date type
1981-01-15	1987-05-12	Television broadcast
Genre		Police drama

Work History

Drama series following the activities of an American city police precinct and its personnel.

USA. MTM Enterprises for NBC Television.

USA, NBC, transmitted 15/01/1981-12/05/1987 [7 seasons; 146 x hour]

UK, Channel 4, transmitted 22/01/1981-

Parts reference	Parts title
193074	Politics As Usual
193075	Can World War III Be an Attitude?
193076	Dressed to Kill
193077	Film at Eleven
193078	Choice Cut
193079	Up in Arms
193080	Your Kind, My Kind, Humankind
193081	Gatorbait
Etc. etc.	

Related to

Periodical: Time Out – issue 898 4 November 1987. Pages 16-17.

Abstract: Comments on the final series and interview with James B. Sikking about his role.

Periodical: City Limits – n134 27 Apr 1984 pages 17-19. 21
Abstract: Article tracing the history of the series, and examining the reasons for its success.

Periodical: TV Guide – volume 45. issue26. June 1997. pages 10-67. Article: 100 greatest episodes of all time
Abstract: TV Guide and television experts at NICK AT NITE'S TV LAND select 100 greatest episodes from drama series and sitcoms from the 1950s to 1997.

Periodical: Playback – issue Special Collectors April 1995. Page 52
Abstract: Article about the background, production and reception of the series.

Creative Screenwriting volume 5. Issue 3, June 1998. pages 24-31
Article: Creating the prime time novel: an interview with Michael Kozoll by: Douglas Heil.
Abstract: Interview with television screenwriter Michael Kozoll who discusses Hollywood screenwriting as purely business. His work on the US television series HILL STREET BLUES and DELVECCHIO is particularly mentioned.

Written by – volume 3. issue 10. November 1999. pages 16-30
Article: Upstairs/downstairs by: Alan Waldman
Abstract: Steve Bochco, Bruce Paltrow and other writers talk about the period in the 1980s when they worked together for CBS to write classic shows such as HILL STREET BLUES and ST. ELSEWHERE.

Identification number
193075

Title	Title type
Can World War III Be an Attitude?	Original

Level	**Work**
Filmographic level	**Monographic**
Work type	TV
Category	Fiction
Production country	United States of America
Date start	Date type
1981-01-24	Television broadcast

Genre	Subject
Police drama	Corruption, Bribery, Police, Car theft, Gangs, Power cuts

Description type
Synopsis
Description
Furillo focuses on a bribery case against LaRue, while Hill and Renko arrest a thief with hidden expertise.

On-screen credit	Name
Director	Butler, Robert
Production company	MTM Productions
Teleplay	Bochco, Steven
Teleplay	Kozoll, Michael

Character	Name
Captain Frank Furillo	Travanti, Daniel J.
Sgt Phil Esterhaus	Conrad, Michael
Detective Mick Belker	Weitz, Bruce
Lt Calletano	Enríquez, René
Officer Hill	Warren, Michael
Officer Renko	Haid, Charles
Lucy	Thomas, Betty
Detective LaRue	Martin, Kiel

Part of reference	Part of reference title
772521	Hill Street Blues

Parts reference	Parts title
X-58733	Can World War III Be an Attitude?
X-58734	Can World War III Be an Attitude?

Identification number	X-58733
Title Can World War III Be an Attitude?	**Title type** Original
Level	**Manifestation**
Manifestation type	TV transmission
Date 1981-01-24	
Broadcast channel	NBC TV
Coverage	Network
Country	USA
Colour	Colour
Sound	Sound
Language English	**Usage** Dialogue (original)
Part of reference 193075	**Part of reference title** Can World War III Be an Attitude?

Identification number	X-58734
Title Can World War III Be an Attitude?	**Title type** Original
Level Manifestation type	**Manifestation** TV transmission
Date 1997-02-22	
Start time: 23:35:00 End time: 00:35:00	Duration: 60 minutes
Broadcast channel Coverage Country	Channel 4 Network United Kingdom
Colour Sound	Colour Sound
Language English	Usage Dialogue (original)
Part of reference 193075	Part of reference title Can World War III Be an Attitude?
Parts reference C- 925142 C-925117	Parts reference title Hill Street Blues [22/02/1997] Hill Street Blues [22/02/1997]

Identification number
C-925142

Title	Title type
Hill Street Blues [22/02/1997]	Original
Level	**Item**
Item type	Video
Status	Usage
Viewing	Videotape can be requested for access
Language	Usage
English	Dialogue (original)
Colour	Colour
Base	Video
Colour standard	Line standard
PAL	625
Audio standard	stereo
Video format	VHS cassette
Video duration	47.12
Number of cans/cassettes	1
Current location	date
BK2AC12345	2015-06-12
Acquisition date	1997-02-22
Method	Off-Air recording
Part of reference	Part of Title
X-58734	Can World War III Be an Attitude?

Identification number	
C-925117	
Title	Title type
Hill Street Blues [22/02/1997]	Original
Level	**Item**
Item type	Video
Status	Usage
Master	Restricted access to preserved videotape
Language	Usage
English	Dialogue (original)
Colour	Colour
Base	Video
Stock	Fuji
Colour standard	Line standard
PAL	625
Audio standard	Stereo
Video format	D3
Video duration	47.12
Number of cans/cassettes	1
Current location	date
BK2AC12346	2015-06-12
Acquisition date	1997-02-22
Method	Off-Air recording
Part of reference	Part of Title
X-58734	Can World War III Be an Attitude?

I.7 Example 7. Aggregate DVD Television Serial and Episode records in 1-level Hierarchy Models

Supernatural. The Complete Sixth Season Record number: 12345
Supernatural. Season 6
USA, 2011

Kripke Enterprises Scrap Metal & Entertainment, Wonderland Sound and Vision
©2011 Warner Bros Entertainment Inc.
Distributed by Warner Home Video.
Classification: 15 (BBFC)

Fiction, Horror, Fantasy

Supernatural, Angels, Demons, Souls, Ghosts, Vampires, Shapeshifters, Alternative Realities, Fairies, Monsters, Purgatory, Hell, Heaven, Fate, Death, Possession, Time travel, Free will, Conflict, Brothers, Betrayal

Regular cast: Jared Padelecki – Sam Winchester, Jensen Ackles – Dean Winchester, Misha Collins - Castiel

Guest stars: Jim Beaver - Bobby Singer, Mark A. Sheppard – Crowley, Mitch Pileggi - Samuel Campbell, Cindy Sampson - Lisa Braeden, Sebastian Roché – Balthazar, Nicholas Elia - Ben Braeden, Jessica Heafey - Gwen Campbell, Corin Nemec - Christian Campbell, Julia Maxwell – Eve, Kim Johnston Ulrich - Dr. Eleanor Visyak, Demore Barnes – Raphael, Laura Mennell – Brigitta, David Paetkau - Mark Campbell, Sonya Salomaa – Rachel, Lanette Ware – Raphael, Steven Williams - Rufus Turner, Rick Worthy - Alpha Vampire, Amber Benson – Lenore, Samantha Ferris - Ellen Harvelle, Fredric Lehne – Azazel, Lindsey McKeon – Tessa, Rachel Miner - Meg Masters, Kim Rhodes - Sheriff Jody Mills, Julian Richings – Death, Samantha Smith - Eve

Credits: Directors – Phil Sgriccia, John F. Showalter, Robert Singer, Jensen Ackles, Rod Hardy, Jan Eliasberg, Guy Bee, Mike Rohl, David Barrett, Jeannot Szwarc, Charles Beeson, Ben Edlund; Created by – Eric Kripke; Executive Producers – Robert Singer, Sera Gamble, Eric Kripke, Phil Sgriccia, Ben Edlund, McG

For a year following the thwarting of the Apocalypse, Dean Winchester tries to live a normal family life with Lisa and Ben. When his brother Sam suddenly turns up freed from Lucifer's cage in Hell, Dean teams up with him and becomes a hunter again but soon discovers there is something different and more ruthless about Sam. The two become entangled in a quest for souls that ties in with Crowley's scheming and Castiel's struggles with Free Will and determination to win the civil war raging in Heaven.

Home Viewing publication. DVD. Dual Layer Format. Region 2. 6 Discs. 876 minutes (approximate). 16:9 Full Frame. Colour. Dolby Digital. Language: English. Optional languages: Castilian, Spanish, French, Hearing Impaired English. Optional subtitle languages: Castilian, Spanish, Danish, Dutch, Finnish, French, Norwegian, Portuguese, Swedish.

Contains:	Exile on Main Street Two and a half Men The Third Man Weekend at Bobby's Live Free or Twihard You Can't Handle the Truth Family Matters All Dogs Go to Heaven Clap Your Hands if You Believe Caged Heat Appointment in Samarra Like a Virgin Unforgiven Mannequin 3: the Reckoning The French Mistake ...And Then There Were None My Heart Will Go On Frontierland Mommy Dearest The Man Who Would Be King Let It Bleed The Man Who Knew Too Much Special Features: Jensen Ackles: a director's Journey Supernatural and the Quest for the Soul Executive Producers Commentary on 2 Episodes The French Mistake Alternate Takes and Outtakes Gag Reel

Supernatural. Let it Bleed Record number: 6789
Let it Bleed
Season 6. Episode 21
USA, 2011. First Broadcast: 2011-05-20, Friday, 21:00 – 22:00, USA, The CW.

Fiction, Horror, Fantasy
Angels, Demons, Kidnapping, Possession, Betrayal, Relationships, Trust, Purgatory

Production companies – Kripke Enterprises Scrap Metal & Entertainment, Wonderland Sound and Vision

Cast: Jared Padelecki, Jensen Ackles, Misha Collins, Jim Beaver, Mark A. Sheppard, Sebastian Roché, Kim Johnston Ulrich, Cindy Sampson, Nicholas Elia; co-starring – Adam Greydon Reid, Antony Holland, Panou, Peter Ciuffa, Ian Butcher

Credits: Directed by – John F. Showalter; Written by – Sera Gamble; Created by – Eric Kripke; Producer - Todd Aronauer; Co-producers – Jerry Wanek, Serge Ladouceur; Executive Producers – McG, Ben Edlund, Robert Singer, Sera Gamble, Eric Kripke; Co-executive Producers – Jim Michaels, Adam Glass, Peter Johnson; Associate Producer – Kristin Cronin; Story Editors – Eric Charmelo, Nicole Snyder; Executive Story Editors – Andrew Dabb, Daniel Loflin, Brett Matthews; Director of Photography – Serge Ladouceur; Editor – Nicole Baer; Production Designer – John Marcynuk; Production Manager – Craig Matheson; Music – Jay Gruska; Music Supervisor- Alexandra Patsavas; Music Editorial by – Dino Moriana; First Assistant Director – Kevin Parks; Second Assistant Director – Debra Herst; Casting by – Robert J. Ulrich, Eric Dawson, Carol Kritzer, Alex Newman; Original casting by – Patrick J. Rush; Costume Designer – Diane Widas; Set Decorator – George Neuman; Property Master – Chris Cooper; Key Makeup Artist – Sarah Graham; Key Hair Stylist – Jeannie Chow; Script Supervisor – Pam Lawrence; Stunt Co-ordinator – Lou Bollo; Special Effects Supervisor – Randy Shymkiev; Special Effects Makeup – The Schminken Collective Group Inc.; Sound Mixer – Donald Painchaud; Re-recording Mixers – Dennis Kirk, Todd Orr; Supervising Sound Editor – Charlie Crutcher; Visual Effects Supervisor – Ivan Hayden; Visual Effects Producer – Grant Lindsay; Transportation Co-ordinator – Mark Gould

Sam, Dean, and Bobby investigate a possible breakthrough to the secret of opening Purgatory, linked to events at a dinner party hosted by horror author H.P.Lovecraft back in 1937. However, King of Hell Crowley kidnaps Lisa and Ben to try and distract the brothers from their investigations and interfering with his and Castiel's plans. Castiel unsuccessfully tries to persuade Dean to trust in him and what he is doing and the brothers summon the angel Balthazar for help. During a rescue attempt Lisa is critically injured.

Home Viewing publication. DVD. Region 2. Dual Layer Format. Viewing copy. Disc 6. 42 minutes 16 seconds. 16:9 HD. Colour. Dolby Digital. Language: English. Optional languages: Castilian, Spanish, French, Hearing Impaired English. Optional subtitle languages: Castilian, Spanish, Danish, Dutch, Finnish, French, Norwegian, Portuguese, Swedish

Contained in: Supernatural. The Complete Sixth Season (Record Number: 12345).

Appendix J, Bibliography

A/V Artifact Atlas [online]. Last modified on 26 October 2015 [viewed 2016-04-04]. Available from: http://avaa.bavc.org/artifactatlas/index.php/A/V_Artifact_Atlas

ALA-LC Romanization Tables [online]. Last Updated: 02/24/2016 [viewed 2016-04-04]. Available from: http://www.loc.gov/catdir/cpso/roman.html

Anglo-American cataloguing rules. 2nd ed., 2002 revision, 2005 update. Ottawa: Canadian Library Association; Chicago: American Library Association; London: Chartered Institute of Library and Information Professionals, 2002-2005. 1 volume (loose-leaf). ISBN 978-0-8389-3555-2.

Also available from: http://www.rdatoolkit.org/

Archival moving image materials: a cataloging manual. 2nd ed. AMIM Revision Committee. Motion Picture, Broadcasting, and Recorded Sound Division. Washington: Library of Congress, Cataloging Distribution Service, 2000. 1 v. (loose-leaf). ISBN 0-8444-1008-X.

Also available from: http://www.itsmarc.com/crs/mergedProjects/archmov/archmov/Contents.htm

COPYRIGHT BOARD OF CANADA. *Unlocatable copyright owners: brochure* [online]. [Viewed 2016-04-04]. Available from: http://www.cb-cda.gc.ca/unlocatable-introuvables/brochure1-e.html

Copyright Law of the United States of America and Related Laws Contained in Title 17 of the United States Code [online]. Washington: U.S. Copyright Office [viewed 2016-04-04]. Available from: http://www.copyright.gov/title17/92chap1.html

Describing archives: a content standard. Chicago: Society of American Archivists, 2004. xxii, 269 p. ISBN 1-931666-08-3.

EBUVideoCompressionCode [online]. Version Date: 03.08.2010 [viewed 2016-04-04]. Available from: https://www.ebu.ch/metadata/cs/web/ebu_VideoCompressionCodeCS_p.xml.htm

EN 15744:2009, *Film identification – Minimum set of metadata for cinematographic works*.

EN 15907:2010, *Film identification – Enhancing interoperability of metadata – Element sets and structures*.

ENTERTAINMENT ID REGISTRY ASSOCIATION. *EIDR: Entertainment identifier registry* [online]. Entertainment ID Registry Association (EIDR), c2016 [viewed 2016-04-04]. Available from: http://eidr.org/

EUROPEAN UNION INTELLECTUAL PROPERTY OFFICE. *Orphan works database* [online].

European Union Intellectual Property Office, c2013-2016 [viewed 2016-04-04]. Available from: https://euipo.europa.eu/orphanworks/

EUROPEAN UNION INTELLECTUAL PROPERTY OFFICE. *What are orphan works?* [online]. European Union Intellectual Property Office, c2013-2016 [viewed 2016-04-04]. Available from: https://euipo.europa.eu/ohimportal/en/web/observatory/orphan-works-database

FÉDÉRATION INTERNATIONALE DES ARCHIVES DU FILM (FIAF). *The FIAF cataloguing rules for film archives*. Compiled and edited by Harriet W. Harrison for the FIAF Cataloguing Commission. München; London; New York; Paris: K. G. Saur, 1991. xvi, 239 p. Film, television, sound archive series; vol. 1. ISBN 3-598-22590-3.

Also available in PDF from: http://www.fiafnet.org/images/tinyUpload/E-Resources/Commission-And-PIP-Resources/CDC-resources/FIAF_Cat_Rules.pdf

Part 1 http://www.fiafnet.org/~fiafnet/pdf/uk/FIAF_Cat_Rules_-_1.pdf

Part 2 http://www.fiafnet.org/~fiafnet/pdf/uk/FIAF_Cat_Rules_-_2.pdf

Part 3 http://www.fiafnet.org/~fiafnet/pdf/uk/FIAF_Cat_Rules_-_3.pdf

FIAF. *Glossary of filmographic terms* [online]. [Viewed 2016-04-04]. Available from: http://www.fiafnet.org/pages/E-Resources/Glossary.html

FIAF. *Glossary of technical terms* [online]. [Viewed 2016-04-04]. Available from: http://www.fiafnet.org/pages/E-Resources/Technical-Terms.html

Final report of the Working group on Aggregates [online]. September 12, 2011 [viewed 2016-04-04]. 20 p. Available in PDF from: http://www.ifla.org/files/assets/cataloguing/frbrrg/AggregatesFinalReport.pdf

Frequently Asked Questions about Library of Congress Genre/Form Terms for Library and Archival Materials (LCGFT) [online]. Revised June 6, 2011 [viewed 2016-04-04]. 20 p. Available from: http://www.loc.gov/catdir/cpso/genre_form_faq.pdf

GETTY RESEARCH INSTITUTE. *Getty thesaurus of geographic names online* [online]. The J. Paul Getty Trust, c2015 [viewed 2016-04-04]. Available from: http://www.getty.edu/research/tools/vocabularies/tgn/index.html

GETTY RESEARCH INSTITUTE. *Union list of artist names online* [online]. The J. Paul Getty Trust, c2015 [viewed 2016-04-04]. Available from: http://www.getty.edu/research/tools/vocabularies/ulan/

HIRTLE, Peter B. *Copyright term and the public domain in the United States* [online]. Cornell Copyright Information Center, Last updated 3 January, 2016 [viewed 2016-04-04]. Available from: http://copyright.cornell.edu/resources/publicdomain.cfm

IFLA STUDY GROUP ON THE FUNCTIONAL REQUIREMENTS FOR BIBLIOGRAPHIC RECORDS. *Functional requirements for bibliographic records: final report*. München: Saur, 1998.

viii, 136 p. UBCIM publications ; new series, vol. 19. ISBN 3-598-11382-X.

Also available in PDF from: http://www.ifla.org/files/assets/cataloguing/frbr/frbr.pdf

Also available in PDF from [Current text (including amendments and corrections to date)]: http://www.ifla.org/files/assets/cataloguing/frbr/frbr_2008.pdf

IFLA WORKING GROUP ON FUNCTIONAL REQUIREMENTS AND NUMBERING OF AUTHORITY RECORDS (FRANAR). *Functional requirements for authority data: a conceptual model*. Ed. by Glenn Patton. München: Saur, 2009. 101 p. IFLA series on bibliographic control; vol. 34. ISBN 978-3-598-24282-3.

Also available in PDF from [FRAD 2009 as amended and corrected through July 2013]: http://www.ifla.org/files/assets/cataloguing/frad/frad_2013.pdf

IFLA WORKING GROUP ON THE FUNCTIONAL REQUIREMENTS FOR SUBJECT AUTHORITY RECORDS (FRSAR). *Functional requirements for subject authority data (FRSAD): a conceptual model*. Editors: Marcia Lei Zeng, Maja Žumer, Athena Salaba. Berlin; New York: De Gruyter Saur, 2011. vi, 74 p. IFLA series on bibliographic control; vol. 43. ISBN 978-3-11-025323-8.

Also available in PDF from: http://www.ifla.org/files/assets/classification-and-indexing/functional-requirements-for-subject-authority-data/frsad-final-report.pdf

INTELLECTUAL PROPERTY OFFICE. *Exceptions to copyright: Libraries, archives and museums* [online]. ntellectual Property Office, October 2014 [viewed 2016-04-04]. 10 p. Available in PDF from: https://www.gov.uk/government/uploads/system/uploads/attachment_data/file/375956/Libraries_Archives_and_Museums.pdf

INTELLECTUAL PROPERTY OFFICE. *Orphan works diligent search guidance for applicants* [online]. [Viewed 2016-04-04]. Available from: https://www.gov.uk/government/publications/orphan-works-diligent-search-guidance-for-applicants

INTELLECTUAL PROPERTY OFFICE. *Orphan works guidance* [online]. [Viewed 2016-04-04]. Available from: https://www.gov.uk/government/collections/orphan-works-guidance

INTERNATIONAL DOI FOUNDATION. *The DOI System* [online]. Updated April 4, 2016 [viewed 2016-04-04]. Available from: http://www.doi.org/

ISAAR(CPF): International standard archival authority record for corporate bodies, persons and families [online]. 2nd ed. International Council on Archives (ICA), 2004 [viewed 2016-04-04]. 70 p. ISBN 2-9521932-2-3. Available in PDF from: http://www.ica.org/sites/default/files/CBPS_Guidelines_ISAAR_Second-edition_EN.pdf

ISAD(G): General international standard archival description [online]. 2nd ed. Ottawa: International Council on Archives (ICA), 2000 [viewed 2016-04-04]. 91 p. ISBN 0-9696035-5-X. Available in PDF from: http://www.ica.org/sites/default/files/CBPS_2000_Guidelines_ISAD(G)_Second-edition_EN.pdf

ISAN INTERNATIONAL AGENCY. *ISAN: International Standard Audiovisual Number* [online]. Geneva: ISAN International Agency, c2013 [viewed 2016-04-04]. Available from: http://www.isan.org/

ISAN INTERNATIONAL AGENCY. *ISAN Glossary of terms* [online]. Geneva: ISAN International Agency, c2013 [viewed 2016-04-04]. Available from: http://www.isan.org/resources/glossary.html

ISAN INTERNATIONAL AGENCY. *ISAN user guide* [online]. Version 2.2.2. Geneva: ISAN International Agency, February 2012 [viewed 2016-04-04]. 49 p. Available in PDF from: http://www.isan.org/docs/isan_user_guide.pdf

ISBD (NBM): International standard bibliographic description for non-book materials. Rev. edition. München: K.G. Saur, 1987. vii, 74 p. Also available in PDF from: http://www.ifla.org/files/assets/cataloguing/isbd/isbd-nbm_1987.pdf

ISBD REVIEW GROUP. *ISBD: International standard bibliographic description.* Consolidated ed. Berlin; Boston: De Gruyter Saur, 2011. xvii, 284 p. IFLA series on bibliographic control; vol. 44. ISBN 978-3-11-026379-4.

Also available in PDF from: http://www.ifla.org/files/assets/cataloguing/isbd/isbd-cons_20110321.pdf

ISNI INTERNATIONAL AGENCY. *ISNI Search* [online]. [Viewed 2016-04-04]. Available from: http://www.isni.org/search

ISO 9:1995, *Information and documentation – Transliteration of Cyrillic characters into Latin characters – Slavic and non-Slavic languages.*

ISO 639-1:2002, *Codes for the representation of names of languages – Part 1: Alpha-2 code.*

ISO 639-2:1998, *Codes for the representation of names of languages – Part 2: Alpha-3 code.*

ISO 639-3:2007, *Codes for the representation of names of languages – Part 3: Alpha-3 code for comprehensive coverage of languages.*

ISO 639-4:2010, *Codes for the representation of names of languages – Part 4: General principles of coding of the representation of names of languages and related entities, and application guidelines.*

ISO 639-5:2008, *Codes for the representation of names of languages – Part 5: Alpha-3 code for language families and groups.*

ISO 3166-1:2013, *Codes for the representation of names of countries and their subdivisions – Part 1: Country codes.*

ISO 3166-2:2013, *Codes for the representation of names of countries and their subdivisions – Part 2: Country subdivision code.*

ISO 3166-3:2013, *Codes for the representation of names of countries and their subdivisions – Part 3: Code for formerly used names of countries.*

ISO 4217:2015, *Codes for the representation of currencies.*

ISO 8601:2004, *Data elements and interchange formats – Information interchange – Representation of dates and times.*

ISO 15706-1:2002, *Information and documentation – International Standard Audiovisual Number (ISAN) – Part 1: Audiovisual work identifier.*

ISO 15706-2:2007, *Information and documentation – International Standard Audiovisual Number (ISAN) – Part 2: Version identifier.*

ISO 15836:2009, *Information and documentation – The Dublin Core metadata element set.*

ISO 26324:2012, *Information and documentation – Digital object identifier system.*

ISO 27729:2012, *Information and documentation – International standard name identifier (ISNI).*

Library of Congress Genre/Form Terms [online]. 2011-04-26: modified [viewed 2016-04-04]. Available from: http://id.loc.gov/authorities/genreForms.html

Library of Congress Names [online]. 2011-04-26: modified [viewed 2016-04-04]. Available from: http://id.loc.gov/authorities/names.html

Library of Congress Subject Headings [online]. 2011-04-26: modified [viewed 2016-04-04]. Available from: http://id.loc.gov/authorities/subjects.html

LIBRARY OF CONGRESS. Network Development and MARC Standards Office. *Extended Date/Time Format (EDTF)* [online]. September 16, 2015 [viewed 2016-04-04]. Available from: http://www.loc.gov/standards/datetime/

LIBRARY OF CONGRESS. Network Development and MARC Standards Office. *ISO 639-2* [online]. October 18, 2010 [viewed 2016-04-04]. Available from: http://www.loc.gov/standards/iso639-2/

LIBRARY OF CONGRESS. Network Development and MARC Standards Office. *ISO 639-5* [online]. February 18, 2009 [viewed 2016-04-04]. Available from: http://www.loc.gov/standards/iso639-5/

Media Types [online]. Last Updated 2016-04-18 [viewed 2016-04-18]. Available from: http://www.iana.org/assignments/media-types/media-types.xhtml

NATIONAL FILM AND SOUND ARCHIVE OF AUSTRALIA. *Technical glossary* [online]. [Viewed 2016-04-04]. Available from: http://www.nfsa.gov.au/preservation/glossary/

OLAC CAPC. Moving Image Work-Level Records Task Force. *Final report and recommendations. Part IIIa: Operational definitions: a thought experiment* [online]. August

21, 2009 [viewed 2016-04-04]. 39 p. Available in PDF from: http://olacinc.org/drupal/capc_files/MIW_3a.pdf

OLAC CAPC. Moving Image Work-Level Records Task Force. *Report and recommendations. Part I: Moving image work definition and boundaries. Part II: Core attributes and relationships* [online]. January 5, 2009 [viewed 2016-04-04]. 21 p. Available in PDF from: http://olacinc.org/drupal/capc_files/MIW_1-2.pdf

Open Metadata Registry [online]. [Viewed 2016-04-04]. Available from: http://metadataregistry.org/

PALLANTE, Maria A. *Priorities and special projects of the United States Copyright Office: October 2011 – October 2013* [online]. United States Copyright Office, October 25, 2011 [viewed 2016-04-04]. 16 p. Available in PDF from: http://copyright.gov/docs/priorities.pdf

PBCore: Public broadcasting metadata dictionary project [online]. [Viewed 2016-04-04]. Available from: http://pbcore.org/

PBCore essenceTrackAspectRatio. In: *Open Metadata Registry* [online]. [Viewed 2016-04-04]. Available from: http://metadataregistry.org/vocabulary/show/id/129.html

PBCore essenceTrackEncoding. In: *Open Metadata Registry* [online]. [Viewed 2016-04-04]. Available from: http://metadataregistry.org/vocabulary/show/id/156.html

PBCore instantiationPhysical. In: *Open Metadata Registry* [online]. [Viewed 2016-04-04]. Available from: http://metadataregistry.org/vocabulary/show/id/145.html

RDA STEERING COMMITTEE. *RDA: Resource description and access* [online]. American Library Association; Canadian Library Association; Facet Publishing, the publishing arm of CILIP: the Chartered Institute of Library and Information Professionals, c2010 [viewed 2016-04-04]. Available from: http://www.rdatoolkit.org/

ROSENBAUM, Jonathan – THOMAS, François. Dossier Mr. Arkadin. In: Cineteca del Comune di Bologna. *Il cinema ritrovato 2006.: 20. edizione: sabato 1 luglio-sabato 8 luglio*. Bologna: Cineteca del Comune di Bologna, 2006, p. 154. Also available from: http://www.cinetecadibologna.it/files/festival/CinemaRitrovato/archivio/catalogo2006.pdf

ROSS, Thelma – BALZER, Detlev – MCCONNACHIE, Stephen. The EN 15907 moving image metadata schema standard and its role in a DAM infrastructure. In: *Journal of Digital Media Management*. ISSN 2047-1300, 2013, vol. 2, no. 3, pp. 251-262.

TECH 3293. EBUCore metadata set (EBUCore) [online]. Specification v. 1.6. Geneva: EBU, June 2015 [viewed 2016-04-04]. 40 p. Available in PDF from: https://tech.ebu.ch/docs/tech/tech3293.pdf

UCLA FILM & TELEVISION ARCHIVE. *UCLA Film & Television Archive Cataloging Procedure Manual--Voyager* [online]. Last modified: March 6, 2007 [viewed 2016-04-04]. Available from: http://old.cinema.ucla.edu/CPM%20Voyager/

UNITED STATES COPYRIGHT OFFICE. *Revising section 108: Copyright exceptions for libraries and archives* [online]. Washington: U.S. Copyright Office, Revised: 20-Feb-2013 [viewed 2016-04-04]. Available from: http://www.copyright.gov/docs/section108/

VIAF: Virtual international authority file [online]. OCLC, cop. 2010-2016 [viewed 2016-04-04]. Available from: https://viaf.org/

YEE, Martha M. *Cataloging rules* [online]. June 15, 2008 draft, rev. [viewed 2016-04-04]. 139 p. Available in PDF from: http://myee.bol.ucla.edu/catrul.pdf

Also available from: http://myee.bol.ucla.edu/catrul.htm

YEE, Martha M. *Moving image cataloging: how to create and how to use a moving image catalog*. Westport; London: Libraries Unlimited, 2007. 273 p. Third millennium cataloguing. ISBN 978-1-59158-438-4.

YEE, Martha M. The concept of *work* for moving image materials. In: *Cataloging & Classification Quarterly*. ISSN 0163-9374, 1993, vol. 18, no. 2, pp. 33-40.

Also available from: http://escholarship.org/uc/item/6hk8h9vp

ZENG, Marcia Lei, ŽUMER, Maja, and SALABA, Athena. Functional Requirements for Subject Authority Data (FRSAD): A Conceptual Model. Berlin: De Gruyter Saur, 2011.

Appendix K. List of Elements

WORK Section	WORK: Element Name	MANIFEST. Section	MANIFESTATION: Element name	ITEM Section	ITEM: Item Name
1.2.1	Work/Variant Description Type				
1.2.2	Variant Type	2.2.1	Manifestation Type		
1.3.1	Identifier	2.3.1	Identifier	3.1.1	Identifier
1.3.1.1	Identifier Type	2.3.1.1	Identifier Type	3.1.1.1	Identifier Type
1.3.2	Title	2.3.2	Title	3.1.2	Title
1.3.2.1	Title Type	2.3.2.1	Title Type	3.1.2.1	Title Type
1.4.1	Agent	2.4.1	Agent(s)	3.3.1	Agent(s)
1.4.1.1	Agent Activity	2.4.1.1	Agent Activity	3.3.1.1	Agent Activity
1.3.3	Country of Reference				
1.3.5	Language(s)	2.3.3	Language		
1.3.5.1	Language Term	2.3.3.1	Language Terms		
1.3.5.2	Usage Type	2.3.3.2	Usage Type		
1.3.4	Year/Date of Reference				
1.3.4.1	Date Type				
1.3.4.2	Date Precision				
1.4.3	Subject/Genre/Form Terms				
1.3.6	Content Description				
1.3.6.1	Content Description Type				
1.3.7	Notes	2.3.6	Notes	3.1.7	Notes
1.3.8	History				
1.3.8.1	Custodial History				
1.3.8.2	Censorship History				
1.3.8.3	Other Work/Variant History				
1.4	Relationships	2.4	Relationships	3.3	Relationships
1.4.2	Events	2.4.2	Events	3.3.2	Events
1.4.4	Other Relationships	2.4.3	Other Relationships	3.3.3	Other Relationships
		2.4.4	Items		
				3.1.3	Holding Institution
				3.1.4	Element Type
		2.3.4	Format	3.1.5	Item Physical-Digital Description
		2.3.4.1	Carrier Type	3.1.5.1	Carrier Type
		2.3.4.1.1	Carrier Type: General	3.1.5.1.1	Carrier Type: General
		2.3.4.1.2	Carrier Type: Specific	3.1.5.1.2	Carrier Type: Specific
		2.3.4.3	Sound Characteristics	3.1.5.3	Sound
		2.3.4.3.1	Sound systems	3.1.5.5	Sound System
		2.3.4.3.2	Sound Channel Configuration	3.1.5.4	Sound Channel Configuration
		2.3.4.4	Colour Characteristics	3.1.5.6	Colour
				3.1.5.7	Unit Number
		2.3.5	Extent		
		2.3.5.1	Logical Extent		
		2.3.5.2	Physical Extent	3.1.5.8	Extent
		2.3.4.2	Projection Characteristic	3.1.5.9	Projection Characteristics
				3.1.5.10	Broadcast Standard
		2.3.5.3	Duration	3.1.5.11	Duration
		2.3.5.3.4	Duration Precision	3.1.5.11.1	Duration Precision
		2.3.5.3.5	Duration Type		
				3.1.5.12	Frame Rate
				3.1.5.13	Base
				3.1.5.14	Stock
				3.1.5.15	Stock batch
				3.1.5.16	Video Codec
				3.1.5.17	Audio Codec
				3.1.5.18	Resolution
				3.1.5.19	Line Standard
				3.1.5.20	Bit Depth
				3.1.5.2	Item Status
				3.1.6.1	Item Condition
				3.1.6.2	Item Location
				3.1.5.21	Source Device
				3.1.5.22	Source Software
				3.1.5.23	Transfer Speed